Ⓢ 2663327

D0558510

Deaf Subjects

CULTURAL FRONT
General Editor: Michael Bérubé

PIERCE COLLEGE LIBRARY
PUYALLUP WA 98374
LAKEWOOD WA 98498

Deaf Subjects

Between Identities and Places

Brenda Jo Brueggemann

NEW YORK UNIVERSITY PRESS

New York and London

NEW YORK UNIVERSITY PRESS
New York and London
www.nyupress.org

© 2009 by New York University
All rights reserved

Library of Congress Cataloging-in-Publication Data

Brueggemann, Brenda Jo.
Deaf subjects : between identities and places /
Brenda Jo Brueggemann.
p. ; cm. — (Cultural front)
Includes bibliographical references and index.
ISBN-13: 978–0–8147–9966–6 (cl : alk. paper)
ISBN-10: 0–8147–9966–3 (cl : alk. paper)
ISBN-13: 978–0–8147–9967–3 (pb : alk. paper)
ISBN-10: 0–8147–9967–1 (pb : alk. paper)
1. Deaf. 2. Deafness. I. Title. II. Series: Cultural front (Series)
[DNLM: 1. Deafness—Essays. 2. Culture—Essays. 3. Deafness—
history—Essays. 4. Hearing Impaired Persons—Essays. 5. History,
19th Century—Essays. 6. History, 20th Century—Essays. 7. Sign
Language—Essays. HV 2390 B846d 2009]
HV2390.B74   2009
305.9′082—dc22   2008051610

New York University Press books are printed on acid-free paper, and
their binding materials are chosen for strength and durability. We
strive to use environmentally responsible suppliers and materials to
the greatest extent possible in publishing our books.

Manufactured in the United States of America
c   10 9 8 7 6 5 4 3 2 1
p   10 9 8 7 6 5 4 3 2 1

Contents

Acknowledgments

First, always, I nod to Jim Fredal, who not only read drafts of every chapter but listened for long hours as my ideas took, shifted, bent, and shipped in and out of shape. My children, Karl and Esther, also patiently endured—and even sometimes claimed interest in—some of my subjects and strategies, particularly when images and the Internet were involved.

The College of Humanities at Ohio State University afforded me two different research leaves and a subvention grant for the project—support that gave me time and funding free from administrative and teaching du ties to complete the work and important assistance in finalizing elements of the manuscript. The Colleges of the Arts and Sciences (ASC) at Ohio State also aided the work in its earliest stages with a research grant in recognition of exemplary ASC service; that recognition essentially seeded the research that became this book. In conjunction with Ohio State University, the Battelle Foundation offered significant support to parts of this manuscript through its funding of the American Sign Language and Literature Digital Media Project (the ASL-DMP) with the Battelle Endowment for Technology and Human Affairs (BETHA) grant in 2004–05.

Throughout the development of the manuscript, several graduate student colleagues (at that time) provided research—along with collegial interest and even, at times, invaluable advice—that moved the material in meaningful ways: Marian Lupo, who provided inspiration for the chapter on the T-4 program; Kristina Torres, who helped in locating many of the images for conference presentations and visiting lectures that I first conducted on the T-4 program material and the "betweenity" argument overall; Rebecca Dingo, who always asked questions about my work, lent an honest, collegial ear, and aided me in my other duties so that I had more time and mental space to begin mapping out this manuscript; Sarah Smith, who provided similar duty-free assistance over the course of these past four years and, most recently, sanity-saving last-minute searches to finalize sources and permissions for the use of certain images.

I have friends, who are also colleagues, in all the right places. Their impressions are left all over these pages. Comrades in disability studies whose ideas have intersected with, enveloped, or developed my central concept of betweenity these past five years include Susan Burch, Michael Davidson, Lennard Davis, Jim Ferris, Georgina Kleege, Catherine Kudlick, Steve Kuusisto, Robert McRuer, Sue Schweik, Katherine Sherwood, Tobin Siebers, and Rosemarie Garland Thomson. To Steve Kuusisto and Georgina Kleege, most especially, I owe modeling, as well as inspiration for the craft, care, and keeping of good prose. Susan Burch's sisterhood throughout the entire project—her direct interpretive and intellectual influence in the Allen Sisters and Mabel Hubbard Bell material and her literal and figurative hand-holding during the last hard year of making this all happen—can't really even be measured. No bucket is big enough.

Comrades in Deaf Studies have also influenced my subject, even as they have been a part of my own (ever-between) identity and place in the complex sphere of Deaf-world. Again, Susan Burch, Michael Davidson, and Lennard Davis matter here. Additionally, the creativity and critical camaraderie offered by others in this field run like a current—electric, illuminating, and sometimes even hot and a bit jolting—through my own words: I am thinking of Dirksen Bauman, Kristin Harmon, Christopher Krentz, Jennifer Nelson, John (Vic) VanCleve, and the dynamic duo of Flying Words Project, Peter Cook and Kenny Lerner. Likewise, important friends and figures from my time on the Gallaudet University Board of Trustees whose support of my authorial and intellectual life was especially keen, deserve mutual recognition: Jane Fernandes, Bill Graham, and I. King Jordan.

Some colleagues at large, whose work intersects my own in domains outside (but alongside) Disability Studies and Deaf Studies have also had a hand in making these pages: Bobbi Bedinghaus, for her superb service in building the American Sign Language program at Ohio State with me in its earliest years and, in particular, for standing with me on the American Sign Language and Literature Digital Media Project (ASL-DMP); Suzanne Flynt, for her introduction to, and companionship over, the Allen Sisters project; Susan Williams, for her similar engagement with the Allen Sisters material and for her reading of earlier drafts of that work; Wendy Hesford, for her spirited sisterhood in critical, rhetorical readings of visual material; Debra Moddelmog, for her many years of mentorship and for modeling a meaningful way to conduct ethical, engaged, intersected identity studies; and Ivey Pittle Wallace, managing editor at Gallaudet University Press, for her steady support of my work overall in and through the development of the "Deaf Lives" series.

The three reviewers who helped shepherd and shape this book once New York University Press had it in hand deserve a deep bow: Rosemarie Garland Thomson, Robert McRuer, and one anonymous and careful reader. Eric Zinner, editor in chief at NYU Press, really made the book happen when he insisted that I send him a proposal—even though I did not yet really know what cracks my thoughts lay on, in, or between. Ciara McLaughlin, assistant editor at NYU Press, has provided exemplary clarity and care through the final stages of preparing the manuscript.

And, last, yet again, Jim Fredal—who helped me to navigate, both emotionally and intellectually, some of the hardest between spaces of the project throughout its various phases. His presence is between each line.

Introduction

The Deaf Subject Places Herself

> When a thing ceases to be a subject of controversy, it ceases to be
> a subject of interest.
>   —William Hazlitt, *The Spirit of Controversy*

The deaf subject, the subject of "deafness," is of interest—without cease and with considerable controversy of late. Lately, the deaf subject is also anxious. She is anxious about her identity, anxious about her place, anxious too about her anxiety. Attempting to cope with her anxiety, she tries to remember what some philosophers and great authors have told her about her subjectivity, her anxiety, and the placing and questioning of her very identity. Wittgenstein whispers to her (and she reads his lips) that "the subject does not belong to the world; rather, it is a limit of the world" (70, 5.632). Anxiously, then, she wonders a lot these days about the limits of her subject, the limits of her world. She wonders, for example, about such subject matters as how to define "deaf"; whether "Deaf" (capitalized) is useful anymore;[1] whether deaf people are an "endangered species;"[2] what her relationship is with other subjects of difference and/ or disability;[3] how much, if at all, her languages, signed or written, belong to her own hands; who writes her history, and why; what her role and place is in the academy; how technologies—of both communication and biomedicine—are changing the shape of her mouth, her mind, her morphology; and how, as the American deaf subject (particularly as a white American subject), she represents the world of deaf subjects even though she is more unlike the rest of the deaf world than perhaps ever before.

1

She finds herself placed, then, *between* on many matters of her identity, and she wonders how she feels about this. She notes how that between space is one of longing, yet also one of belonging, and one, too, of limits. She paces in this anxious between space.

In addressing her anxiety over these and other subjects, Freud seems to want to help her. Freud assures her that her anxiety is okay, perhaps even necessary, though nevertheless potentially neurotic, as well. Anxiety, he signifies to her, is "the defensive behavior of the ego transfigured in a rational light" (166). Defensively, however, she sometimes distrusts the "rational light" as one shined on her subject by hearing behaviors that, it seems, more often than not seek to transfigure her. What she does understand, on both hands, from Freud is how "anxiety is . . . on the one hand an expectation of a trauma, and on the other a repetition of it in a mitigated form" (166–67). The very subject of her deafness has almost always been read—socially, educationally, linguistically, culturally, philosophically—as a trauma, both expected and repeated, both mitigated and amplified in the history of "reason." As a modern deaf subject in an age of considerable controversy and interest over her identity and subjectivity, she has also begun not only to understand but also to make use of Freud's analysis that "anxiety is the original reaction to helplessness in the trauma and is reproduced later in the danger-situation as a signal for help" (167).

These days, she signals more for help, actively engaging her (former) helplessness and meeting a "danger-situation" more head, and hands, on. Given the menaces she has found herself faced with lately, she is coming now to understand James Baldwin's engagement with identity (and its politics) as she often dons her own chosen identity:

> An identity is questioned only when it is menaced, as when the mighty begin to fall, or when the wretched begin to rise, or when the stranger enters the gates, never, thereafter, to be a stranger. . . . Identity would seem to be the garment with which one covers the nakedness of the self: in which case, it is best that the garment be loose, a little like the robes of the desert, through which one's nakedness can always be felt, and sometimes, discerned. This trust in one's nakedness is all that gives one the power to change one's robes. ("The Devil Finds Work," 606–7)

To be sure, she gathers the robes of identity perhaps a little too tightly at the moment, cinching her own waist pseudo-slim, as when the media refrain of "not deaf enough" binds her (both to and against others) in the

2006 protests at Gallaudet University over the selection of a new president. But she is learning more these days about not just her nakedness but also what robes she looks best in, what places she should wear which garment, when and how to change the outfit. She reads more of James Baldwin and nods, knowingly, when he tells her that "an identity would seem to be arrived at by the way in which the person faces and uses his experience" ("No Name in the Street"). She's facing, and placing, her experience these days, anxiously and defensively shaping her identity, transfiguring her own rational light.

But still: she is not always sure who her audience is. She often feels caught between potential and real audiences—deaf, hard-of-hearing, and hearing alike. And this too is a considerable source of anxiety, since it is hard to shape one's subject and self without some sense of one's audience. On the one hand, she knows that what her hand offers, what she writes, will be read by other deaf subjects. She addresses them, then, calls them forth as subjects too. Yet, because her subject—that of deaf identity, anxiety, and place—is also a subject of language, community, "reason," voice, experience, resistance, otherness, power, and more, she also understands that she will invariably invoke other audiences. Perhaps at times defensively but always carefully and rhetorically, she seeks, then, to actively engage and directly address (not just invoke) more than (and less than) other deaf subjects. She wants, yes, to be heard. Yet, she realizes that she will also have to teach them how to listen.

Deaf but deftly then, she'll need to change the subject some; she'll need new metaphors.

A Commonplace Book of the Deaf Subject

These essays constitute my commonplace book on "the deaf subject," particularly the modern deaf subject since the turn of the 19th century— the subject that has more often than not found itself *between*. In Greek rhetoric and education, the *topoi* were the "topics of invention" that later became, in Roman education, the *locus communis* ("commonplaces") for discovering the best means for one's argument. The *topoi* were templates and heuristics for inventing what one might say about a subject. Later, around the 15th century and primarily in England, commonplace books (also known as "commonplaces") were used by readers, writers, students—both famous and common—as collections, much like a modern scrapbook, for remembering pithy sayings or aphorisms, key concepts, facts, or events that one had learned, read, encountered. The practice of commonplace books dates back to the 5th century b.c.e. and the Sophist Protagoras (Anderson). Francis Bacon kept one, Thomas Jefferson kept two (one legal and one literary), John Locke wrote a book about how to keep a commonplace book, and Virginia Woolf references them in her own "Hours in a Library":

> [L]et us take down one of those old notebooks which we have all, at one time or another, had a passion for beginning. Most of the pages are blank, it is true; but at the beginning we shall find a certain number very beautifully covered with a strikingly legible hand-writing. Here we have written down the names of great writers in their order of merit; here we have copied out fine passages from the classics; here are lists of books to be read; and here, most interesting of all, lists of books that have actually been read, as the reader testifies with some youthful vanity by a dash of red ink. (25)

Like any commonplace collection, mine is not complete. There is surely some telling vanity in dashes of my own (metaphoric) red ink. There are also surely blank pages—places where I've left off or let go or still don't know what to write or just grew weary, even wary, of my subject. I only gesture toward cochlear implants in passing over other matters of technology and anxiety, for example. This is not because I believe that cochlear implants are undeserving of a place in my book or that they are not connected to, or manifested from, the betweenness issues of identity, anxiety, and place that concern my deaf subject everywhere. They are. But implanting rhetoric—the rhetoric of the cochlear implant—is perhaps a topic worthy of its own commonplace book. What's more, the big smoke of the cochlear implant often obscures many smaller fires long burning or newly lit around the deaf subject and her technology. I also do not take on, directly, the subject of the 2006 protests at Gallaudet University regarding the selection of Gallaudet's ninth president, even though I had a place, an identity, and considerable anxiety, too, in those events. The aftermath of those protests is still not sufficiently "after," and lava flows hot in the cracks that produced those volcanic events. It is still too hot to get in between those cracks.

I open this volume with an essay that cracks a common place for my own deaf identity while also offering a larger theory of "betweenity" applied to the modern deaf subject. In five movements, this chapter offers a rhetorical analysis of four significant commonplaces for deaf people's identities and the field of "Deaf Studies" at the turn of the new century. First, I interrogate anxious efforts to separate and distinguish "deaf" and "disabled" and to uncouple the fraternal twins "deaf" and "Deaf." Second, I meet up with the new deaf cyborg, equipped with cochlear implants, digital hearing aids, and multiple forms of technologically savvy communication options such as video relay systems, e-mail, the Internet, and text-capable pagers. Third, I examine the radically changing nature of American Sign Language as it undergoes both shift and standardization, goes ever more global, and also comes significantly into the hands of (mostly hearing) students here in America who are eager to learn it as a "foreign" language. And, in my fourth commonplace, I trace Derrida to consider the relationship between writing (and) deafness. I end this chapter in a fifth movement, marking out a new epistemological and ontological between space, positing a place I call the "think-eye" space.

The second chapter illustrates the betweenity power and potential of American Sign Language (ASL) in the academy, wedged as it is between traditional letter-bound views of language and literature and a wave of 21st-century students who now actively engage in—and seek out—visual ways of learning. In this chapter, my use of the powerful little "I think I can" blue engine story helps place modern "deafness" in the institutional framework of larger academic language learning. I map the intricate and considerable—but also exciting—challenges and arguments that face the development of American Sign Language programs in the contemporary academy.

The third chapter also places modern deaf identity and language in the institutional framework of the production and reception of "literature." In 1910, George Veditz, then president of the National Association of the Deaf, capitalized on the technology of film to produce the "Sign Masters Series" featuring ten nationally known "master signers" in an effort to "preserve and advance" the tradition of American Sign Language, which he claimed we must "possess and jealously guard." Almost one hundred years later, supported by a grant from the Battelle Endowment for Technology and Human Affairs (BETHA) at Ohio State University, we used new digital media technologies to re-enact the "Sign Master Series"—to digitally remaster the potential that exists in the creation, production, publication, and reception of sign language "literature." Based largely on issues, elements, and challenges for the creative production and critical reception of ASL literature that were discussed during a historic three-hour forum with seven ASL author-performers and seven ASL literature critics, this chapter argues for a rhetorical approach and a digital future for American Sign Language literature.

In the fourth chapter, I offer a critical summary of the purpose, events, and key points of a three-day international conference sponsored by the Gallaudet University Press Institute and held November 2004 at Gallaudet University. I also discuss the "Deaf Lives" series I edit for Gallaudet University Press. The centerpiece of this essay pivots around "writing" (as a technology) and all that it has meant and does and can mean for narrating deaf lives. I also imagine how digital media, video, film documentary are all technologies that can increasingly be used to convey deaf life stories. These technologies now, more often than not, move deaf lives into the mainstream (where they are "heard" by more hearing people) while also helping convey deaf lives to other deaf lives; thus, these technologies are, in effect, the between space. Thematically, I also attend to the new commonplaces of deaf subjects in late-20th- and early-21st-century life narratives: diversity within the identity known as "deaf"; further representation of the complex relationship between deaf and hearing people; illustrations of the intertwined, and sometimes knotted, nature of individual and collective identities within "Deaf culture" or "the deaf community"; and anxiety over identity and place in the "deaf world" and as a deaf subject.

From here, I turn back. I also turn increasingly visual as the final three essays step back in time but also look forward in the way they combine visual material with my own words. In the fifth essay, I circle back to the earlier moments of "modern deaf identity," the turn of the last century. In this chapter, I also focus on the intersections of gender and deafness (where so little work has yet been done), as I examine the work of Mary and Frances Allen, two sisters who were first teachers but then went deaf in their early twenties and became fairly famous pictorial photographers. The Allen Sisters and their photography are contextualized in five interwoven commonplaces: their own brief biographies; the Deerfield, Massachusetts, arts and crafts community to which they belonged; women and photography at the turn of the 20th century; visual-rhetorical categorizations of the body of their photographic work; and their deafness in relation to their own lives and their location in time, gender, and geographical space.

Other famous deaf women at the turn of the 20th century have also caught my eye. In my sixth chapter, I offer a work of creative nonfiction that explores the world of Mabel Hubbard Bell, Alexander Graham Bell's deaf wife. Because Mabel Bell (the original "Ma Bell") was a voluminous letter writer herself, I engage her as a deaf subject by writing postcards to her. Each postcard comes with an image from the Bell family papers that sets up the subject of my post; each post includes lines from Mabel's own letters. The postcards are both biographical and autobiographical (for I write myself alongside Mabel), critical yet friendly, fictional yet framed everywhere with facts. Although she herself deliberately chose not to associate with other deaf people in her lifetime, Mabel Bell may well be my classic case study, the quintessential "between" subject of modern deaf identity.

Rubbing against the era of Mabel Bell and the Allen Sisters, I end in a very hard between space. In my final essay, I also return to the concept of the commonplace. I come again to the topics of invention for an argument—anxious and awful—about identity. Here deafness is not always easy to see. But it is there in the cracks, gesturing from the shadows, of a dark moment in history. A colleague in Deaf Studies recently told me that my work with subjects like the Allen Sisters, Mabel Hubbard Bell, and the Nazi T-4 program (as it concerned "disability" more largely) might not really be "Deaf Studies" because technically it was work on "oral deaf people" and that he would "put that on the borders of Deaf Studies." I appreciated his efforts to clarify how he defined the field, yet I admit—even argue—and submit here that these borders are precisely the place of "happening" when it comes to deaf identity, Deaf Studies, Deaf culture. We do not know and cannot know what is *inside* Deaf culture or deaf identity unless we also know what its borders and boundaries are. What is *between* matters. The Nazis' collapsing of so many boundaries with regard to disability and difference (and deafness was included here) makes for a difficult and uncommon, yet necessary, boundary place in which to leave my deaf subject.

1

Between
A Commonplace Book for the
Modern Deaf Subject

Perspective, as its inventor remarked, is a beautiful thing.
—George Eliot [Mary Ann Evans], *Daniel Deronda*, 1876

For some time now, I have been imagining a theory of "be-tweenity," especially as it exists in Deaf culture, identity, and language. And because I teach a great deal in the larger umbrella of "Disability Studies" these days, I've also been thinking about the expansion of that deaf-betweenity to "disability" in a larger sense.[1] (Of course, I've also been thinking about the way that deafness itself occupies an interesting "be-tweenity" in relationship to disability identity.) In any case—whether deaf, disabled, or between—I'm finding that I'm generally more interested in the hot dog than the bun, the cream filling in the Oreo (which, if you've noticed, has been changing a lot lately) than just the twinned chocolate sandwich cookies on the outside. Give me a hyphen any day. To be sure, the words on either side of the hyphen are interesting, too, but what is happening in that hyphen—the moment of magic artistry there in that half-dash—is what really catches my eye.

Between "Deaf" and "deaf" (or, the Names We Call Ourselves)

In disability culture and studies, as well as in Deaf culture and Studies, we often get back to—or maybe, yes, we also get forward to—discussions about what we do and don't want to be called. Deaf culture, in particular, has been around the block with this discussion for a long, long time. I of-fer three exhibits for consideration:

Exhibit A (from the University of Brighton, United Kingdom; http://staff-central.brighton.ac.uk/clt/disability/Deaf.html):

> Note on terminology:
> The term "Deaf" (with a capital D) is the preferred usage of some people who are either born profoundly deaf or who become deaf at a very early age and who regard themselves as belonging to the Deaf community. Like people in many communities, those within the Deaf community are bound together by a feeling of identifying with other Deaf people. People in the Deaf community share, amongst other things, a sense of Deaf pride, traditions, values, lifestyles, humour, folklore, art, theatre, as well as a rich common language.

Exhibit B (from a copyedited essay on interpreters that I received back from the university press editors):

> I do not understand the distinctions between use of upper and lower-case D for deafness? Please clarify for my own knowledge and for the general scope of this book.

Exhibit C (from Gina Oliva, author of *Alone in the Mainstream: A Deaf Woman Remembers Public Schools*, the first book in the new "Deaf Lives" series of autobiography, biography, and documentary at Gallaudet University Press that I edit. This is a memo Gina sent to me after the copyeditors asked her to doublecheck and "clarify" her use of Deaf/deaf in the manuscript):

> Subject: deaf vs. Deaf
> To: brueggemann.1@osu.edu
> Hi Brenda . . . I took a look at Padden and Humphries and decided it made sense to use Deaf when referring to adults in the Deaf community. If they are oral deaf, I will call them deaf. As for children, I would stick with deaf and hard of hearing children (lower case). This means that the "big D" will appear much in my book, as I say "Deaf adults this" and "Deaf adults that" a lot. I also say "deaf and hard of hearing children" a lot.
>
> Then I looked at "Journey into the Deaf-World" (Lane, Hoffmeister, Bahan) and see that they advocate using Deaf for any child who is deaf and couldn't access info without assistance.

Hmmmmm. . . .Do you have any opinion about this???? I checked some other books. . . . Wrigley uses Deaf predominantly. Preston does not. I have others I can check . . . but my guess is there is little consensus about this.

As these three exhibits illustrate, where we draw the line in relationships between "deaf" and "Deaf" is a question of common placement.

In Deaf Studies we can explore, and perhaps even expand upon, the definitions of the terms of d/Deaf operations—subtracting, adding, dividing, and multiplying the possibilities—for the key naming terms like "deaf," "Deaf," "hard-of-hearing," "late deafened," "hearing-impaired," "has hearing loss," "think-hearing," and, my mother's personal favorite for me, "has selective hearing." But we can also move further out in the concentric circles by studying, for example, the mapping and meaning of mental proficiency labels alongside audiometric ones and noting their in-common categorizations—"moderate," "severe," "profound." Interestingly enough, these IQ labels parallel those assigned to hearing loss by medical practitioners—and both sets of terms came onto the diagnostic screen in our culture at about the same time. Moreover, if you simply rotate the axes of the two bell curves created by either the IQ or the audiometric charts as they plot out "normal," "moderate," "severe," and "profound" you would find them folding neatly right on top of each other. Is this parallel only circumstance, or do the angles between these two medical charts make more meaning in their overlay and intersections?

As but one example of a way to further explore this curious commonplace, we might consider that in the Nazis' national socialist regime during the early 1940s, people with disabilities in psychiatric institutions throughout the German Reich became subject to "euthanasia" at the hands of their own doctors and nurses. (I explore this subject in depth in my final chapter.) My point in telling these troubling facts is that at this time, as well as in other times both past and present, people who were deaf in Germany (*taubstumme*—deaf and dumb) were often as not collapsed into diagnoses of other mental disabilities as well. I have looked at remaining records from one of these killing centers (which is still, eerily enough, a fully functioning psychiatric institution even today), as well as some records from the T-4 program housed in the German federal archives (*Bundesarchiv*), and I have, for myself, seen this conflation written on the records of several patients.[2]

My point is that, in the commonplace book of "deafness," things are not always clearly or singularly defined, designated, determined as "just" or "pure" or "only" deafness. And, however much some deaf people may want to resist being labeled "disabled," the fact remains that they *are* often labeled as such and that these labels—in all cases—are not always accurate, though they may be, as it were, with consequences. Certainly, deaf people should want to resist the easy conflation of their "condition" with others that coexist in degrees of "moderate," "severe," and "profound"—realizing the violence that can be (and has been) done with such an overlay. Yet, just as certainly, I suggest that to resist and distance one's self-identity and group identity from those whose condition has been deemed (for better or worse, for right or wrong) affiliated with hearing loss would also be, in essence, to do further violence to those others with whom "authorities" have placed us (deaf people) in categorical similarity. Who—or what—are deaf people so afraid of when they resist placement in the commonplace of "disability"?

The relationship between "deaf" and "disabled," between "deafness" and "disability," between "Deaf culture" and "Disability culture," between Deaf Studies and Disability Studies has been the subject of several major conference sessions in recent years. The 2006 Society for Disability Studies conference featured several sessions devoted to these questions of relationship and difference, and a plenary session at a February 2007 symposium held at George Washington University on the development of Disability Studies focused on the dance between Deaf and Disability Studies.

As but one specific example of the current tensions between "deaf" and "disabled," in March 2007, news in central Ohio (and all throughout the American deaf community) that the Ohio School for the Deaf (OSD) would soon be merging campuses and resources with the Ohio State School for the Blind shocked and troubled many. A March 2007 news story in the *Columbus Dispatch* featured virulent remarks by Richard Heuber, the president of the Ohio State School for the Deaf's alumni association. Heubner claimed that "We [deaf alumni of OSD] will start a petition. Rally and protest," and "We'll fight this to the bitter end to keep them separate" because "Forcing the students to interact will destroy the deaf school's culture." Heubner concluded to the reporter that "I don't feel I have a disability. Many deaf people don't," and "If you add another handicap (at the school) . . . they'll have no identity, no self-esteem" (Sebastian, 2007). By September 2007, the state of Ohio had retracted its plans to merge the two schools.

My colleague, the author (and blogger) Steve Kuusisto—who happens to be blind—took up the subject of the "no identity, no self-esteem" concerns raised by the OSD alumni in a reply on his own "Planet of the Blind" blog as he attempted to "stir the slum gullion with a stick." Among his stirrings were these that pointed out the swirling stew bits of difference and definition in this issue around the merger of the two state schools and the OSD deaf alumni's response to it:

> The problem isn't that some deaf activists want to be thought of as a cultural group, a collection of people who have their own language, who are not at all disabled. The problem is that by wanting to disassociate themselves from a historical relationship with disabilities these deafness advocates are overtly contemptuous of other people who would quite likely love to declare themselves no longer disabled but who find themselves genuinely struggling with serious physical and social obstacles. I would love to say that blindness isn't a disability but currently it is certainly a profound employment obstacle and the issues that are associated with this are both economically determined and are additionally rooted in historical attitudes that Mrs. Gandhi would likely recognize.
>
> Contempt for the blind emerges in this instance with the force of a geyser. The reasoning works like this: deaf people are not disabled; to put them into a facility where they would have to share space with people who really are disabled would be demeaning to deaf students. (March 20, 2007; http://kuusisto.typepad.com/planet_of_the_blind/2007/03/in_our_own_back.html)

This same string of reasoning and the often unnamed fear of how deafness and deaf people are labeled also have us (and them) working (hard, very hard) to contrast "deaf" and "Deaf." The originary location of the Deaf/deaf divide dates to around 1972, purportedly from coined usage in a seminal Deaf Studies essay by James Woodward, *How You Gonna Get to Heaven If You Can't Talk to Jesus? On Depathologizing Deafness.* Thus, the definitional divide has been around for more than thirty years. Yet, aside from its usage in presses and publications long familiar with the commonplaces of "deafness," it must commonly still be footnoted in an academic text in order to explain, yet again, what the distinctions between Big D "Deafness" and little d "deafness" are. Even when the distinctions are used, they are most often used, interestingly enough, in direct relation to each other; one is just as likely to see "d/Deaf" or "D/deaf" written as one is to see just "Deaf" or even "deaf" standing alone in a text that has set up this distinction. Thus, the divisional/definitional terms of "Deaf" and (or versus) "deaf" more often than not come in tandem as d/Deaf. As such, they are twinned, they are doppelgangers. *Mirror mirror on the wall* . . . they whisper and sign back and forth to each other.

The twinning of d/Deaf is perhaps safer that way, since often, when one is pressed, it is hard to determine at any one moment in a text whether the Big D cultural/linguistic arena is where we are or whether we are just in the small d audiological/medical space. And what if we are in both places at the same time? The long-standing and footnoting practice of establishing some kind of border patrol between these terms tries to define and differentiate—apples here, oranges there—but, more often than not, the aliens still wind up looking very much like the natives. And perhaps it is really an avocado that is wanted, anyway? In most cases, for example, deaf students can't enroll in a state residential institution—long deemed the center of American deaf culture and the sanctuary for American Sign Language (ASL) and thus a common place for Big "D" cultural/linguistic Deafness—without offering an audiogram and first being able to claim their little "d" deafness. Until as recently as 2002 and the establishment of Gallaudet University's new HUGS program (Hearing UnderGraduates), you could not get into the world's only liberal arts college for deaf and hard-of-hearing students without proof of a (flawed) audiogram: as an undergraduate, you had to be *deaf* in order to go there and engage in the particular Gallaudet cultural practices that might also then mark you as *Deaf*. The irony (and anxiety) of placement and identity at Gallaudet is perhaps further magnified by the fact that many, even the majority (58 percent), of Gallaudet's graduate and professional students are hearing students working on degrees in the fields surrounding the curious state of "deafness."

Yet, when the question is posed about the differences between "deaf" and "Deaf"—as it was by a recent editor I worked with (see Exhibit B) and, really, by almost every editor I've ever had in twenty years of writing about, in, from, around deafness[3]—most often the answer given is either "language—the use of ASL" or, even more simple (yet, paradoxically, complex), "attitude." And suddenly, there you are again, in another dark and thick forest without a working compass: "What kind of attitude?" you have to wonder. And then: "Attitude? You want attitude? I'll give you attitude!"

And what does it mean, anyway, to locate the choice position within the capital D? Is this not also an attitude of assault and an oppression—a dominance of one way of thinking (epistemology) and being (ontology) over another? This think-between space between "deaf" and "Deaf" is a rock and a hard place for Deaf Studies. I wonder what happens, then, if we work to squeeze (more) in there? What if we don't "draw the line" on, around, through, or under where someone is (and isn't) "culturally deaf" or not? What if we stop footnoting and explaining and educating *them*—meaning largely hearing people—again and again and again? For almost thirty years now, we've learned to chant, from almost rote memorization, when we explain the "difference" between little d and big D deafness. But they never seem to hear a word of any of this, and so we go on footnoting and explaining and educating about the distinctions between "Deaf" and "deaf." If a (deaf) tree falls in the (hearing) forest, does anyone then really "hear" it?

Can we create a new geometry, a new space for "deaf" (and, thus, "Deaf," as well) to be in and for those trees to fall in? To answer such questions might be to enter more into questions of perspective. How, for example, might we follow both the dynamic flow and the static stance of terms like "deaf" while, along the way, working also to understand our culture's long-standing cure-based obsessions with definitive causes and effects where deafness matters? What were—and are—the circumstances that create "deaf" or "Deaf" to begin with (and in continuance)? Whose testimony counts—and when and where and why and how—when it comes to authorizing d/Deaf identity or the "condition" of "deafness"?

What I am suggesting with these questions is that we might begin in Deaf Studies to push beyond the mere recitation of the "d/Deaf" pledge in our footnotes and to explore instead all the rhetorical situations that arise from the d/D distinctions, that bring the distinctions to bear, and that, most important, keep shifting them like an identity kaleidoscope in our own hands.

The (Deaf) Cyborg Space

Within the deaf kaleidoscope is the fragmented but also contained— and beautiful—image of the ever-shifting deaf cyborg. The seamed and seeming boundaries between "cure" and "control" in constructing the deaf cyborg body is a potent commonplace, especially for late-20th- and early-21st-century Deaf Studies. Obviously, this seamed space might be illustrated in the controversy over cochlear implants and the deaf cyborg who, borrowing on the cultural critic Donna Haraway's terms, becomes the "hybrid of machine and organism," the creation of "a creature of social reality as well as a creature of fiction" that has already "change[d] what counts as [deaf people's] experience in the late twentieth century" (149).

What Haraway's cyborg myth foretells is that deaf people and the deaf-world won't likely disappear, implanted as alien others. This is, instead, likely to be a tale of "transgressed boundaries, potent fusions," as Haraway's cyborg myth suggests: the boundaries might change, cracks may well appear, life will likely occur in the between spaces, and yet the fusion will likely remain potent. At Gallaudet University, for example, officials have begun counting the number of their students who arrive now with cochlear implants, and, for each of the past years that they have been counting, the number has virtually doubled itself each year. In effect, the cochlear implant seems to be squaring itself as the technology advances and the next generation of young deaf and hard-of-hearing people comes of counting age. Even at Kendall School, the demonstration elementary school on the Gallaudet campus, education about the implant (for those who have them as well as for those who don't) takes the form of several children's books and a Barbie-like doll, "C.I. Joe" (who also happens to be African American). And at hearing-dominated state universities like my own (Ohio State University), the cochlear implant makes headlines as one of the major Friday feature stories in the campus newspaper—and this at a university that records only two students with cochlear implants (among the 54,000 enrolled here). Likewise, memoirs by authors with new cochlear implants have also now begun to crop up, like the new season of dandelions on the lawn of deafness (Chorost; Swiller; Thompson).

In Deaf Studies we might begin to rethink the potent fusions in the between spaces created by cochlear implants—between then (the past) and now (the present), as well as between now (the present) and then (the future). Tough, opportunistic, interesting, and sometimes even beautiful things grow in the cracks of structures seemingly well established and impenetrable; the cochlear implant cyborg might just be such a crack-dweller. It will take far more than an implant to make deaf identity (whatever it might be) go away. Like dandelions on the hearing lawn, deaf people greet the cultivated green with sunny color and tenacious bearing season after season, generation upon generation. Hearing aids have never pulled the rug entirely out from under deafness; eugenicists couldn't, either (although they are tugging very hard again); and oral-focused educators mostly just continue to sweep things under the rug so that the house looks very tidy on the surface.

This is not to suggest that we should not worry. We should. We need only glance over our shoulders at the specter of those doctors during the Nazi era who had themselves (and important others) convinced that living a life with a disability was a life simply not worth living. Under such a conviction, these doctors killed more than 240,000 of those lives deemed "unworthy" in gas chambers (as well as through nurse-administered drug overdoses or even through "simple" starvation) in a program they termed "euthanasia." Deaf people were one of the eight categories of people targeted for these "mercy deaths" in the T-4 program of 1941–42, as well as being common victims of the sterilizations that occurred for a decade before the T-4 "euthanasia" program. Those Nazi doctors also thought they were "improving" the lives of their patients, and they developed chilling technologies (the gas chambers) to efficiently carry out those "improvements." The smoke rising in thick, acrimonious billows day and night from the psychiatric institute set up on the hill over the sleepy little village of Hadamar, Germany, during 1941–42 (as but one example captured with disturbing clarity in several photos of the time) makes at least one thing very clear: where there is smoke, there is fire.

Still: while we look for the fire, we should also be critically careful not to let cochlear implants create a smokescreen that hides other strong magic at work. Even the technology in hearing aids, FM systems, real-time captioning, video conferencing, instant messaging, the Internet, and e-mail matters in the cyborg mix here. If you had been to Gallaudet University lately, you would likely have noticed how electronic pagers (instant e-mail) have radically changed "the Deaf gaze." These days, when you walk across the campus of the world's only liberal arts university for deaf and hard-of-hearing students, you are just as likely—perhaps even more likely—to see only the crowns of heads as you walk past deaf students and faculty with their heads bent and thumbs flying at their pagers as you are to see the older scene of two students signing with hands high above their heads, "shouting" at each other from across Kendall Green, the oval grassy area at the center of Gallaudet's campus.

Do these pagers and other devices of instant communication really connect—or disconnect—deaf people? What distortions and/or enhancements are aided by "the electronic eye" extension of the Deaf gaze in these instances? What might be the form of the "see" sign for extended pager gazing? And why are such devices, when used to aid the deafened ear, commonly referred to as "assistive" or "adaptive" technologies when, after all, technology/ies are—by the very nature of the definition of the term—assistive and adaptive to begin with? Why is it, for example, that a Black-Berry in the hands of a hearing person suddenly sheds its adaptive or assistive skin and becomes instead just another device to fill up one's airport or driving time or to conduct one's business incessantly?

With questions like these, as well as attempts and critical discussions about them, Deaf Studies would be attending to the rhetorical relationships between our technologies and our identity. In essence, we would be investigating the shape and substance of purpose, intention, motivation, and communication that such small but strong technology has in refiguring "the Deaf gaze," in changing deaf people's status as "people of the eyes" (McKee). We would be considering the dynamic or static perspectives that these technologies—as "adaptive technologies" or "assistive technologies"— play not just in our (deaf) lives but in hearing lives, too, as well as the relationships and lives between those spaces. Deaf Studies would do well to gaze here.

Lingering in the (Un)Common Space of Language

Deaf people and their uses of signed (or even/additionally/predominately oral) languages offer a rich commonplace site for the study of how language inherently oppresses, standardizes, and yet also resists—all at the same time—whatever it comes in contact with and even, too, whatever it makes for and of itself. Language duplicates, replicates, reinforces itself (so that, as George Bernard Shaw wrote in "Maxims for Revolutionists," "no man fully capable of his own language ever masters another" [254]); yet, language also resists its own pure replication and dominance. This is not to signify that deaf people have no respect for their sign language (or their multiple other forms of language) but only to suggest that language is always refiguring its own space, just as it makes that space operate much like a kaleidoscope—where elements and perspectives may often shift but the whole and its contents really remain the same. Thus, to aim for some sort of standardization of (a/the) language is only, in effect, to ensure that it is awfully (and awesomely) darn slippery to begin with; sooner or later, something or someone comes along and bumps the kaleidoscope—a little or a lot—and a new image (still with the same basic contents) appears. Perspectives shift.

Such shifting also happens to represent the slippery business of rhetoric, where the communication triangle and its emphasized angles are always in changing relationships to each other. Aristotle's entire second book of the *Rhetoric* emphasizes this contextually dependent shifting as he attempts to categorize and consider all the kinds of audience a rhetor might need to deal with and how those audiences might react to given kinds of subjects presented in certain kinds of ways. "Discovering all the available means of persuasion," which was how Aristotle defined the art of rhetoric, becomes much like the number of combinations one can view in the elements contained in a kaleidoscope.

In this space of ever-unfolding possibilities, Deaf Studies (which is, often as not, associated with the study and teaching of sign languages) could consider the way that sign languages are themselves reaching for, lurching toward, grasping at, and pushing against standardization. And this is not uncommon. Language is only a tool—and an often inadequate one—for trying to get at or toward or even around "the truth."

Dictionaries and attempts to "capture" or standardize any language also operate under such perspective-oriented prevailing paradigms. Yet, dictionaries are definitely needed—if for no other reason than to record the revolutionary and rhetorical shifts that language can make. "Hold still, we're going to do your portrait," writes the French feminist theorist Hélène Cixous about the rhetorical act of representation, "so that you can begin looking like it right away" (1244). In Deaf Studies, we should be focusing on the portrait-doing involved in developing and publishing any kind of sign language. No scholar has yet, for example, to undertake a serious study of even the earliest representations of hand alphabets or sign systems published. To be sure, these early printed representations can often be found in history/ies written about deaf people and their use of sign languages. But they are more often than not simply gestured toward and not ever (yet) analyzed in terms of what their shifting representations might mean and say at large for language systems or even in comparison with each other as commonplace sign systems.

We might also then look backward (yet still forward) to the commonplaces of a sign language's (near) disappearance or considerable reconfiguration. For an example of its reconfiguration, there are sites such as the 17th-century English educator and rhetorician John Bulwer's adaptation of signs, gestures, body configurations, and facial expressions in his classical and seminal rhetorical-elocutionary treatises, *Chirologia* and *Chironomia*. Bulwer is credited with founding the "elocutionary movement" in the history of rhetoric with his elaborately detailed descriptions (and prescriptions) of what the hands, body, and face could do in the act and art of persuasion in his two treatises on "the art of the hand." We now also know that he was one of the earliest English deaf educators and, even more significant, we now also know that he had a deaf daughter whose name happened to be *Chirolea* (Nelson). Yet, Bulwer himself never credits any "language of gestures" he might have acquired from these two deaf sites in his life that, most likely, had a significant influence on his ability to create these two rhetorical treatises to begin with.

We could also contemplate, for example, the changing shape of sign language in places like rural Nebraska now that the state residential institution for deaf students has been closed. How does the lack of such an important site for developing and sharing language among deaf and hard-of-hearing children, who are more often than not isolated and singular in their deafness, change the face of American Sign Language overall? Or, too, we might explore more deeply how deaf people negotiated sign language in Germany during the Nazi regime when they were not only targets of forced sterilization but also the potential victims of the T-4 "euthanasia" program of 1941–42. How did deaf people sign when their lives likely depended on not marking themselves as deaf in any way? And, after World War II, what happened to deaf ways—their schools, clubs, workplaces, and shared language—in East and West Germany? Further, how have (or haven't) German signs "reunified" since the wall fell, in 1989? We would also want to look forward to the development of "new" sign languages in developing countries (such as Kenya) or in places like reunified Germany or even, say, across the city of Berlin, where not so long ago four nations occupied the city limits. What can we learn about standardization and the values of language—any language—from these developments?

And, finally, we would also do well to look across the plains of the present, to squint our eyes in the startling sunlight of American Sign Language's immense popularity on high school and college campuses, where it is now taught (usually to fulfill a "foreign" language requirement). While the deaf world frets over the loss of Deaf culture and identity at the hands of geneticists, cochlear implant surgeons, and hearing parents (to name but a few of the largest threats), the truth of another matter is that, on campuses where it is offered, no language except Spanish enrolls better than ASL right now. In summer 2003, the Modern Language Association's new report on college foreign-language offerings marked ASL courses in higher education as up a remarkable 432 percent in the past five years (Welles). (The next closest increase figure was 94 percent, for Arabic.) This put ASL officially in fifth place seat for "most commonly taught language in college." Yet, if we were also to factor in that the other four languages ahead of ASL in this survey are likely taught at each and every college where foreign language is offered and that ASL is still very much a lesser-taught language that is, in fact, still rarely taught at most colleges, the popularity of ASL probably outstrips that of the four languages that place ahead of it. In fact, demand almost never matches supply in the case of ASL instruction, since qualified ASL instructors at the high school and university certification level are almost as rare as, say, waterfront property in Kansas.

How is this massively popular instruction changing the face—and shape—of ASL?[4] And what should be the "perspective" of Deaf Studies on these issues when, ironically, more and more deaf and hard-of-hearing children are "mainstreamed" and implanted and often kept away from sign language even as their hearing peers flock to ASL classes? What interesting rhetoric is at work on the two sides of this single language-learning coin? Who profits from such a great increase in ASL instruction? The wise owl of Deaf Studies should be forming this "who?" on its own lips and hands.

Writing (and) Deafness

The wise owl should also ponder writing. As a form of expression typically (and too often) considered oppositional for modern deaf people, what, in fact, might writing have in common with signing? How might writing extend signing—and how, too, might signing extend writing? Jacques Derrida has raised this question "at hand":

> When we say that writing *extends* the field and the powers of locutionary or gestural communication, are we not presupposing a kind of *homogeneous* space of communication? The range of the voice or of gesture appears to encounter a factual limit here, an empirical boundary of space and of time; and writing, within the same time, within the same space, managed to loosen the limits, to open the *same field* to a much greater range. (311)

In Deaf Studies, I think we have some remarkable and rich work still left to do, philosophically and practically, in the space between writing and signing. Not only can we perhaps de-Derrida Derrida himself in expanding the philosophical space between writing and signing, but we can, just as important, work to find better ways to translate and transliterate what happens in the space between English and ASL. This multiperspective orientation would be especially important for both deaf and hearing students who are struggling to enter that between space.

It will be most fruitful to do this practical and philosophical "perspectival" work not from the center of English studies (where it has already been tried and yet never true) but rather from the center (and margins) of Deaf Studies. When Deaf Studies starts thinking about how to translate, transliterate, and teach in the space between English and ASL, for example, we are likely to become all the more "capable of relaxing those limits and of opening the *same field* to a very much larger scope," as Derrida has suggested. Why leave it up to English departments and deaf education and (socio)linguistics? These three sites, in particular, have long skewed the center and arranged themselves as the triangle of matters associated with "deaf language and literacy instruction."[5] Why keep the location of locution always already there? Certainly, English Studies and Deaf Education and scientific linguistic study have things to offer the study of signed languages—and they should continue to do so. But how much longer must we continue to look for the keys to the uses and power of signed languages for deaf people under the brighter lamps of these more dominant (and better-funded) areas of the academy just because the light is there when, in fact, we know the keys are in a less well-lighted place a few steps back or around the next corner?

Let Deaf Studies take up the questions often left to the long legacy of Western philosophy—from Plato to Derrida and back again: What difference does writing make? Do feminist theories about "writing the body" (Cixous, for example) apply to and invigorate, or further erase, deaf people and their way of performing literacy? If writing is a performance (as the latest theoretical rage proclaims)—and sign language is also performative—do these two have even more in common than we have yet begun to explore? Is deafness the hiccup—the errant locution in the location—of the all-too-standardized connections between reading and writing that are chanted in our educational history? Deaf Studies might attend to asking and exploring a question that one professor of philosophy at my own university recently used to title his own campus lecture (even though he did not have sign languages in mind)—"how can language change your hearing?"

Let us begin, now even more than ever, to answer that question from within Deaf Studies. Not only should we begin, for example, to critically engage the construction of "deaf lives" from these other fields, but we should also (and this is very important) be encouraging the creation, production, and reception of deaf lives through such channels as biography, autobiography, and documentary. As I revised an earlier version of this essay in a café in Berlin, Germany, I was reminded, you see, that I am deaf in any and all languages and culture; the German language does not, in essence, seem to change my hearing.

"How can language change your hearing?" Indeed, that is no small question. It is also not an unfamiliar question, since "deaf education" has been around the block with it at least several times over. What if we also began to ask more about how it is that "deaf-ways" can actually be used as a method and means of changing even dominant Western classroom and pedagogical practices? And what if we just stopped rehearsing the already well-articulated history of deaf education in the United States? What if, instead, we asked, for example, what this history (of "deaf education") shows us about *all* of Western education? As Margret Winzer has challenged us in her excellent history of special education, we might think more about how deaf education ripples in the larger pond:

> The way that children are trained and schooled is a crucial demonstration of the way that they are perceived and treated in a given society. . . . Discovering who was taught, and when and how, is related far more to the social, political, legislative, economic, and religious forces at work in a society than it is to the unique social and educational needs of disabled persons. At the same time, this history mirrors our progress toward appreciating the basic humanity of all people. (xi)

Deaf education did not—and does not—occur in a socioeconomic-historical vacuum. We can get so hung up on A.G. Bell and his legacy, for example, that we forget to answer the other incoming calls about the interplay of speech, education, and "normalcy" as this tangled braid brought us into the twentieth century.

Think-Eye

Where I fit in and can answer the calls I've proposed myself for Deaf Studies is also about all the calls I probably can not answer but still yearn to engage in or make. Some days I am so energized by all the possibilities of Deaf Studies that I am exploding. Other days, I am so daunted by all the possibilities that I am imploding.

I come to Deaf Studies as a "hard-of-hearing" (the only term my family could use) girl from an extremely rural region of western Kansas; there are still fewer than twenty-five people per square mile in Greeley County, Kansas. I come as someone who didn't even know what sign language or, say, Gallaudet University was (let alone a single sign or the idea of "deaf education") until the age of twenty-nine. I come as the granddaughter of a deaf woman (although she was called hard-of-hearing, too) and the inheritor and carrier and engenderer of a complicated string of hearing loss and kidney "abnormalities" in my family. I come with two children (one has the kidney abnormalities) who perhaps understand my "deafness" in ways that my own parents didn't and in ways, too, that I myself still don't. They are perhaps more "deaf" than me, as I've written elsewhere ("Are You Deaf or Hearing?").

I come always wanting to fit in. Yet I also come always wanting to ask questions and not fit in. I arrive doubly hyphenated (hard-of-hearing), with a lot going on in those multiple hyphenated between spaces. I come, I suppose, thinking between—thinking in another kind of between space between think-deaf and think-hearing: think-eye. For the deaf space is a visual space, an "eye" space. It is also, I submit, an I-space. We still have a lot to learn from each "I" and from each "eye." Perspective (the "eye") really matters; the personal (the "I") experience really matters, as well. This little between eye/I space can be, in fact, rather expansive. It is a space of potent possibilities, contained and yet kaleidoscopic in its perspectives. As the late-19th-century English novelist George Eliot (Mary Ann Evans) knew, as she was writing a novel named for a male protagonist and using a male pseudonym herself—perspective is a beautiful thing.

There are so many ways to bump and see the same pieces again, but now all arranged differently. In keeping our eyes out for deaf commonplaces while also admiring the ever-shifting capabilities of perspectives (in both our "eyes" and our "I's") and attending to the value of being *between* worlds, words, languages, cultures even as we can be contained in either one, the sites and sights of Deaf Studies promise us ever-enchanted explorations.

2

American Sign Language and the Academy

The Little Language That Could

Once upon a time, and not so very long ago, American Sign Language (ASL) was barely known to the Modern Language Association (MLA), an organization of more than 300,000 members in one hundred countries whose "members have worked to strengthen the study and teaching of language and literature."[1] Until 1997, in fact, ASL was listed in only the definitive *MLA International Bibliography* under "invented" languages—followed directly by the Klingon language of *Star Trek* fame. In 1997, the MLA formed the Committee on Disability Issues in the Profession (CDI). Spurred on by some members of the MLA's newly formed CDI and grounded in remarkable linguistic scholarship over the previous three decades that has documented the unique but also common language features of ASL (Klima and Bellugi; Stokoe, Casterline, and Croneberg), a formal request was made to the MLA that ASL be included among the "natural" languages, alongside Spanish, German, French, and the like. The MLA bibliographers, staff, and executive director, then Phyllis Franklin, listened intently to our argument. We gathered a substantial record of linguistic scholarship not only about ASL but also about sign languages around the globe, demonstrating the foundational nature of sign languages *as languages* and illustrating their unique contributions to both the study and the expression of language as we had come to know it in oral/aural and print-dominated cultures.

Yet, some forty years after William Stokoe's groundbreaking dictionary on ASL and despite considerable linguistic research pouring in from all around the globe that could easily prove that ASL is indeed a natural language, a real language, even a wondrous language (as indeed all languages are), we are still trying to "invent" ASL as an entity within such key academic organizations as the MLA and within the academy gener-ally.[2] Scholars of ASL literature, literacy, and linguistics continue to strug-gle to find a comfortable place within the MLA—especially deaf scholars, whose access is still limited at the MLA conferences, and ASL teachers, who might belong to the national American Sign Language Teachers As-sociation (ASLTA) but who generally do not hold terminal degrees and often teach only part time, at most, in colleges and universities around the country.[3]

It is time to move on. It is time to move away from the defensive out-sider and approval-seeking positions that ASL has typically occupied in the academy, especially in relation to other foreign and modern languages. It is time to move our discussions, perspectives, and placements of ASL into a position of potential, promise, and linguistic-cultural power.

In the spirit of that move, I will ground all the points I make in this chapter by invoking ASL as the little language that could: the little lan-guage that could in fact turn out to be anything but little for those stu-dents who get the chance to learn it during their college years; the little language that could make us think hard about what language *is* and *can do*, challenging and yet also affirming our ideas and beliefs about lan-guages and culture; and the little language that could rumble and steam right through the established stations of language and literature programs in the academy, potentially overtaking some of the bigger trains.

The use of the "little engine that could" narrative is not incidental. As a moralistic children's story with a decidedly (American) nationalistic slant in the 1930s, authored by a pseudonymous "Watty Piper" and featuring the little blue engine as female against her stronger, tougher male counter-parts, the metaphor/narrative reconstructs much of the Deaf community's considerable efforts to assimilate and paint its (deaf) faces as American in the first half of the 20th century in particular (Buchanan; Burch, 2002).

An Academic Home for ASL?

Take but one brief and bold example of the challenges offered by the little language that could: ASL offered to American college students and con-firmed as credits on their transcripts as a *foreign* language. In the United States, how can an *American* language also be a *foreign* language? What nation declares its own language to be foreign?[4] Perhaps, then, what ASL helps illuminate is the very (odd) nature of terms like "foreign" (as opposed to "modern") used in describing languages during an era of fluid and frequent global interactions. With American Sign Language, the poles and grounds for "national" versus/and "foreign" more or less dissolve.

Just as ASL questions the place of adjectives like "foreign" and its own place within a construct of "foreign," it also articulates—and complicates—questions of disciplinary and departmental boundaries in the academy. We might think of ASL as the engine with no house—a gypsy language, as it were. Sheryl Cooper's 1997 dissertation on the academic status of sign language programs in institutions of higher education in the United States demonstrates ASL's wanderlust. Although 36.8 percent of the programs and administrators that Cooper surveyed recommended placing ASL among the modern or foreign languages, this percentage obviously did not constitute a majority, let alone a strong one. Interestingly enough, 12.6 percent recommended that sign language be a department of its own, a situation that does not commonly exists for any language. Meanwhile, 10.5 percent placed it in speech pathology/audiology departments, and a nearly equal number suggested that it be placed in any one of five different places: Deaf Education, Deaf Studies, Interpreting, Linguistics, or Special Education.[5]

Such variation in views regarding ASL's academic affiliation highlights the challenge of administrative structure for ASL in the academy. And this challenge, I argue, illustrates how much ASL has gathered steam in challenging the university overall and our ideas about language departments, more specifically. Consider for a moment what it means when a language can stand on par with other modern languages in the university structure—even occupy a space all its own—but can also be placed in domains alongside the professional instruction of those who "help" or "service" deaf and hard-of-hearing people. Imagine for a moment if we taught so-called developing-world languages only within departments that might send professionals to relevant developing countries to "help" their people or if religion (through missionary work) or medicine (through general health care or even AIDS research or care programs) became the predominant home for such languages. What a "foreign" idea that would be![6]

At my own institution, Ohio State University, we have built an ASL program that gives students general-education credit (GEC) in a "foreign" language, in a unique answer to the "placement" question posed by Cooper's dissertation.[7] The program is now in its sixth year. Our ASL program for undergraduate foreign-language credits has spanned and involved three different colleges. Initially, the two introductory courses, ASL I and II, were taught in the College of Humanities, under the wing of the English department. And, while "under the wing" does have significant metaphorical potential, both positive and negative, we argued that we could place part of the ASL program in that position because at Ohio State we have nothing like an American Studies program. English Studies, where American language and literature is typically taught at Ohio State University, is the closest fit. We could also argue that ASL would best be housed in the English department because the department is widely familiar and has a long track record of running a significant number of the university's required general-education and basic-level courses—courses like the first- and second-year required writing courses and Introduction to Fiction, Introduction to Poetry, and so forth. The English department knew well how to handle the business of all those students in introductory, skills-based courses. (And this argument has, I would add, proved to be all the more important as we have worked to iron out policies and procedures for hiring qualified teachers, for continuing the professional development of our teachers, and for addressing students' concerns and complaints.)

Students who have completed ASL II can then move to the third- and fourth-level courses in the sequence (four courses in a language are required for the completion of the general-education foreign-language requirements at Ohio State). These last two courses can be taken either in the College of Education and Human Ecology (in the Department of Teaching and Learning) or in the College of Social and Behavioral Sciences (in the Speech and Hearing department). What we have tried to set in motion, then, is a triangulated program in which students get at least two (and possibly even three) different disciplinary entries into, and intersections with, the language. The content of each course—the actual skills to be learned—is supposed to remain the same for each level of the course, no matter where that course is taught. The teachers and coordinators have worked out a kind of standard curriculum and syllabus for each course; while variation is allowed in an individual teacher's approaches and activities, the key objectives and elements for the courses remains the same, no matter where it is being taught. In theory, at least.

We are still not sure how all this is playing out in practice. The ASL program is currently undergoing an extensive "outcomes" assessment, as well as engaging in its own study of itself via focus-group discussions of students, teachers, and program administrators across the three colleges/

units, ASL at Ohio State is new, and we are in fact still driving it without a dashboard of standardized assessment measures in place. In some ways, this reminds me of how I learned to drive growing up in western Kansas: my parents and grandparents turned me loose behind the wheel of grandpa's old blue Ford pickup in the big, open cow pasture behind their farm house, gave me some basic instructions on gears, clutches, brakes, accelerator—and then let me go. It was exhilarating to get the feel of the thing, bumping along over gopher holes with dried cow patties flying behind me, creating a little dust cloud to mark the path I had taken, and not worrying about which way I should turn or go next. And I learned well the basics of the machine and its movement by driving this way. But soon I wanted more: a road to travel, a radio that actually worked, a destination and goal, a more finely tuned knowledge of navigation involving blinkers, lights, different driving conditions, and—most important of all—the ability to travel and negotiate with others also on the road.

In thinking about ASL's attempts and abilities to navigate and negotiate with other languages currently on the road, let me dwell for a moment on our own enrollment numbers and issues at Ohio State. With approximately 300 new students enrolled each quarter in our ASL I classes and also up to three hundred students on the waiting lists for that first-level course every quarter (some students wait up to four quarters), ASL is obviously a language that is very popular with our students these days. And that popularity on my own campus has been borne out by a recent survey completed by the Association of Departments of Foreign Language (ADFL) and published in the *ADFL Bulletin* in 2004.[8] Whatever the reasons for ASL's considerable popularity—and we do have some sense of those various reasons from our survey of students in the ASL I course—the evidence does seem to indicate that ASL has the potential to threaten other languages being offered on college campuses.[9]

I use that verb "threaten" quite deliberately. For, in a university fiscal environment where budgets are now built on enrollments generated—the "butts in seats" budget, as I have heard it called at my own university—ASL constitutes a potential "cash cow." When one adds to its revenue-generating status the fact that foreign and modern language enrollments on college campuses overall have been noticeably lower over the past decade or so (although they are now showing a slight increase again), the threat of one language "stealing" seats from another becomes very real. At Ohio State University, in fact, our Foreign Language Center (FLC)—which houses virtually all the other languages taught at our huge university—would not initially touch ASL with the proverbial ten-foot pole when we began trying to build the program six years ago.

After six successful years with the ASL program located across three colleges (but not as part of the FLC)—from 2002 through 2008—we have just recently reconfigured the program again so that it is now squared (as opposed to triangulated in three areas), and the FLC does, in fact, house the key administrative coordinator who will help right the angles better among the other three original units invested in the program. In the original construction of the ASL program, however, it was explained to me, while the FLC faculty were not at all "philosophically opposed" to the language, they also did not want to take on the sizable faculty resistance that would likely be encountered from colleagues who taught German, Italian, French, and so forth, who feared that ASL might begin to siphon off their already dwindling enrollments. Only enrollment in Spanish-language classes, it seems, remains unaffected by ASL enrollments. Yet, our own survey at Ohio State has shown us that ASL does not really seem to be threatening enrollment in (other) languages, since many of the ASL students already have another language enrollments on their record or are declaring their interest in ASL as a result of direct family or other personal or professional interests.

Moreover, when our FLC proposed and received significant funds from the SBC-Ameritech communications company some years ago in order to establish research and innovation in instruction using various technologies as part of its presence in Ohio State's new World Media and Culture Center, ASL was not included in that funding proposal. On this matter, I could not help pondering the irony of Alexander Graham Bell's legacy in relationship to deafness and deaf people: his early role as an oral-focused teacher of the deaf (including his future wife); his place as the son and husband of deaf women; his niche in the American eugenics movement, carved out predominantly because of his work on charting and graphing the "marriages and progeny" of deaf people in order to prove that when deaf people married deaf people, they tended to produce deaf children and that therefore their marriage should be discouraged and even forbidden; and his invention of the telephone, which resulted from his search to find an oral/aural mechanism to help teach his method of oral instruction, called "Visible Speech," to deaf students. Thus, when SBC-Ameritech, the offshoot of the once-powerful Bell phone company, provides significant funding for the study of foreign languages at my university that conveniently does not include ASL, Bell's legacy seems to continue to haunt us.

The Association of Departments of Foreign Language (ADFL) Survey

But perhaps we should not look backward, yet again, to Bell's toll on ASL and the American Deaf community. Perhaps we should instead cast our gaze forward to the 2002 ADFL survey and study the face that ASL is showing us, at present and for the future. The report, published in the Winter–Spring 2004 issue of the *ADFL Bulletin* and written by Elizabeth B. Welles, presents not one but many interesting faces for ASL. What I want to do here is outline a few of the faces that I find most interesting and prominent. Let me confess before I go any further that, much like a witness profile, my sketch will be, at its best, probably only sketchy. I also want to clarify that the ADFL survey covers foreign-language enrollments up to 2002 in institutions of higher education. This is important even to me because the program at Ohio State, as but one significant example, has been built *since* 2002.

Among undergraduates and graduates at four-year (or plus) colleges, ASL ranked fifth in language course enrollments, with Spanish, French, German, and Italian placing ahead of it. This constitutes a shocking 432 percent increase in ASL enrollments at four-year colleges since 1998. When the ADFL began its survey, in 1986, ASL did not even exist in numbers on the survey. This ADFL report also tells us that ASL has been recorded in the ADFL survey of foreign-language enrollments only since 1990 and that it "has shown a tremendous increase for each survey since then as more institutions begin to report it." As the report tries to analyze this trend, however, my own analysis finds the report's analysis considerably lacking. That is, I want to suggest that there is much left unidentified as to the impact and place of ASL within the ADFL and its official surveying. As Welles begins to work through the massive data now piling up for college enrollments in ASL, she indicates: "The comparison of the 1998 and 2002 institutional figures is particularly useful for explaining the enormous growth of ASL [because] the bulk of the increase occurred through the reporting of institutions that had not responded previously."[10]

But why, we should ask, did these institutions previously not respond? Were they perhaps not asked the right questions to begin with? If the right kinds of questions weren't being asked in order to elicit responses about ASL offerings and enrollments in the past, would it be surprising that the ADFL was not really receiving any responses? We know that ASL was not even listed in the *MLA International Bibliography* as a "natural" language until 1998; this is the place and point at which I began this chapter. It would probably be hard for an institution's response regarding its ASL offerings even to be "heard" if the language itself had not yet been placed in the *MLA International Bibliography*.

It seems possible that at this point even the ADFL and MLA do not yet know exactly what questions they could, should, or would ask regarding ASL's entrance and growth in colleges and universities across the United States. It is only through some solid affiliation with such organizations as the American Sign Language Teachers Association (ASLTA) or with the full participation of ASL and Deaf Studies scholars in the MLA and the ADFL that we are likely to get the right questions—followed by some meaningful answers—about ASL in the academy.

I do not presume to have all the questions (much less the answers) that should be offered, since, as I suggest, framing them would require the collective knowledge of a body of ASL and deaf scholars and teachers. However, I might quickly outline a few key questions:

- Are there patterns in the kinds of colleges offering ASL?
- Where is ASL located within the structures of these colleges in relation to the other languages offered there?
- Is it included among the modern languages or located elsewhere in the college's disciplinary structure?
- What are the reasons students give for their interest in taking ASL classes?
- What do students say they gain from taking ASL as a language?
- How do overall enrollment patterns (entry level, retention, completion of a sequence of courses) in ASL classes compare to those for other languages taught in U.S. colleges?
- How does the teaching pool (faculty, part-time, graduate student) in ASL offerings on college campuses compare to the teaching pools in the other languages offered?
- How many "native" users of ASL teach it in comparison to the percentage of "native" users who teach other languages?
- How does the professional development and research base in ASL linguistics, teaching, and literature compare to that in other languages?

The 2002 survey report published by Welles in 2004 does in fact suggest some food for further thought, while leaving a lot unchewed. In puzzling over the formidable increase in ASL enrollments, Welles offers the following explanation:

Besides student interest, the increase recorded in 2002 also has to do with a change in the nature of our survey. For over thirty years we have elicited enrollment data on less commonly taught languages by requesting information about "other languages" rather than listing them individually on the survey form. Through the 1998 survey, ASL was in this category, but with the enrollments reported in that survey it joined the list of the more commonly taught languages, then numbering fifteen. As a result, in 2002 ASL was among the fifteen languages about which we explicitly requested information. Many institutions that had not reported their existing ASL programs in 1998 did so in this survey. If these institutions had previously reported their existing ASL enrollments, the remarkable growth in ASL in the current survey might have been more evenly spread out across the three surveys from the 1990s. But it is also notable that 187 new programs were created between 1998 and 2002 to meet growing demand.[11]

There are several things I find interesting in this explanation for the skyrocketing increases in ASL enrollments between 1998 and 2002. First, it is almost as if institutions are being scolded for not reporting their ASL enrollments and for somehow creating a false sense of "remarkable growth." Shame on *us* for hiding our ASL programs! But we might look at the explanation another way—in 1998 the re-placement of ASL in the MLA bibliography was only just under way. How, then, would one report and register a language not yet even sanctioned as a language by the very authorities conducting the survey? (I think here of the way that the 2000 U.S. Census finally allowed citizens to check more than one identity box—and people did so in astonishing numbers.)

Why, then, was there no mention in this report of the exclusion of ASL as a recognized "body" within the politics of the ADFL and the MLA in the years before 1998? Why is there not a more careful and thorough attempt to explain the growth in study of a language that enrolled students in numbers somewhere between those for students studying Ancient Greek and Biblical Hebrew in 1998 but then rose 432 percent in its numbers to take fifth place behind Spanish, French, German, and Italian (all languages that did not increase enrollments by more than 30 percent in those same years)? Why is this remarkable increase brushed off in a single paragraph that ends really before it even begins any real discussion or consideration, simply saying that "it is also notable that 187 new programs were created between 1998 and 2002 to meet growing demand." Notable, indeed. Yet, somehow, even the more phenomenal weight of ASL offerings in two-year colleges—where it now places second in numbers, behind only Spanish, and has seen a 457 percent growth in the past six years—goes utterly unnoted in this report. What are we to make of these omissions?

I do not have the answers to this seemingly rhetorical question, and I realize that an organization such as the ADFL may not often focus exclusively on one language. I intend not to point fingers only at the ADFL or MLA but, in fact, to beckon us all to the table to discuss this together. That is, I believe that the question of ASL's clear presence in current college language offerings but its absence in overall discussions about language (and culture) learning within higher education is a question that we—meaning not only academic organizations such as the MLA and the ADFL but also scholars of Deaf Studies and ASL (and organizations such as the ASLTA)—ought to be taking up. And taking up together.

Pointing: Toward Politics, Power, and Philosophy

Let me first turn back to my subtitle, "The Little Language That Could," and gesture toward at least some of the important and interesting things we can learn through the study and use of ASL and contact with it. I want to point to what I hope is a significant amount of promise and potential for the future of ASL in universities like my own and then take us back to what I believe are some of the biggest challenges and potential crises we still have ahead of us for ASL instruction in higher education.

First, the potential. The unique nature of ASL—its performance and passage as a nonprint, nonwritten, visual, and embodied language—is, of course, one of the most significant things that students of the language learn about, through, and with ASL. Consider, for example, the role of new technologies in relation to ASL. What happens to a language like ASL in the wake of digital and video technologies that can now enable sign-language literature to be "published" and shared across distance, time, and space? These are the kinds of questions students and future scholars and teachers of ASL can explore about the little language that could. At my own university, for example, we had some of our ASL students consider these very questions as they participated in a project funded by Battelle Foundation awards for "technology and human affairs."[12]

"The ASL Literature and Digital Media Project," further funded by a local central Ohio organization called the DEAFund, involved three groups of people: local, national, and international sign-language storytellers and poets; a troupe of digital media people, including students learning about digital media technologies alongside people who use these technologies as part of their daily work in various studios around our large campus; and students in contact with ASL from at least three groups: deaf and hard-of-hearing students in central Ohio, grades 9–12, who participate in CHIPS, the Columbus Hearing Impaired Program; students in grades 7–12 at the Ohio School for the Deaf, in Columbus; and college students (mostly hearing) enrolled in ASL courses at Ohio State. These three groups met for three primary events over the course of two days in May 2005: a three-hour dialogue between scholars and critics who had written about ASL literature and some of the ASL authors and performers who had created that literature; a public evening performance of ASL literature; and all-day workshops where participants learned some of the fundamentals and techniques for creating their own ASL literature. All of these events were recorded with multiple video cameras (in order to capture the language itself in more of its 3-D dimensions). The summer of 2005 was then spent editing and creating a master DVD of the three events for further public distribution.[13]

To date, ASL poetry and storytelling exist in limited degree and quantity on videotape and DVD/CD-ROM. But the movement of ASL literature into the digital realm—on-line and thus potentially shared globally and free anywhere a person can get to a networked computer—is a fairly new phenomenon. And the potential is vast for the further development of sign-language literatures.

Yet we also still have some advances to achieve in the teaching and learning of ASL. And, while I am buoyed by the potential of endeavors and events like the ASL Digital Media Project, I am also admittedly a bit deflated by the daily teacher shortage we face as we ride on the crest of that 432 percent enrollment increase wave. We have a crisis already near at hand in the adequate instruction of ASL in both higher and public education: we simply do not have enough qualified teachers to meet the demand for these courses. Sometimes we have very qualified interpreters who love the language and also like the idea of teaching ASL; sometimes we have native signers from the deaf community who have taught community-service courses in ASL; and sometimes we actually do have a few truly skilled and qualified language instructors. But it is not easy at this point in the history of ASL instruction, particularly at the college level, to find someone who knows the language well; who knows how to teach a skills-based and skills-level language-program course at the college level where a student's ability to attain skills at one level can seriously affect that student's ability to succeed at the next level; who knows what it means to teach the average college student, someone between eighteen and twenty-two years old; who knows what it means to teach in a freshman-sopho-more-level general-education required course; and who is willing to only teach part time (and with no real benefits) at our university while also trying to earn a living elsewhere.

As I keep having to remind administrator after administrator in meetings too numerous to remember, just because someone is able to "speak" and "use" the English language, or even write it, does not necessarily mean that he or she is equipped to teach those skills to young college students. The same principle applies to ASL use and to ASL instruction, specifically to college-level instruction of ASL. We simply do not yet have the programs to train the needed teachers or even to establish the qualifications we would want those teachers to have. The American Sign Language Teachers Association (ASLTA) has been working on the training, qualification, professional development, and ethical issues for ASL teachers for almost two decades now, although, by its own admission, it is still an organization largely focused on secondary (9–12) instruction of ASL.[14]

In addition to the valuable work of the ASLTA, we also need the MLA and its ADFL—and they need us. We need to work together, in affiliation, to establish teacher hiring, professional development, promotion standards for ASL teachers, and the programs that train such teachers in a way that will allow ASL to continue as a unique language among the others so often offered at our colleges and high schools, while also permitting ASL to function equally on the language-learning playing field. American Sign Language—its scholarly research, its literature, and its pedagogical theories and practices—needs a place at the ADFL executive committee table and also in the MLA delegate assembly. From our place at the MLA and ADFL tables, we can watch and learn, among other things, how to negotiate for standards and employment with benefits, dignity, decent pay, and advancement for all those ASL teachers now joining the academic ranks, largely without a Ph.D. in hand and with only part-time employment.

And, as we find our place at those existing tables of language power, we will also need to borrow and adapt knowledge from them to inform the ways we create our own new responses to and knowledge about issues that are important and unique to ASL. There are at least four major considerations we need to hold before us when we place ASL within the academy. First, we need to consider how a college ASL program can help provide access and equity at that institution to deaf and hard-of-hearing members in the community it serves and surrounds. Second, we need to ensure that we develop ASL responsibly—with caution and careful deliberation—in the academy so that we maintain its linguistic and cultural integrity in the face of the cash-cow role it potentially plays. Third, we need to consider how an ASL program within higher education can best work to "give back" to the deaf community, finding ways to invite, involve, and invest in the skills and presence of local deaf people. Finally, we cannot ignore the fact that it surely means something for the shape and change of ASL when so many hearing students in American higher education are eager to learn it, while deaf or hard-of-hearing kids all across the country are still all too often kept away from learning ASL.

These are four of the most significant issues we will need to continue to address as ASL grows in the academy. I want to end by emphasizing as strongly as I can our need to organize our political and intellectual forces to advance the promise of ASL literature and language instruction with dignity and grace, with quality and care, and with all the *could* that we can muster.

3

Approaching American Sign Language Literature
Rhetorically and Digitally

Let me start with a bold claim: currently, one of the most significant problems we have when we try to study American Sign Language (ASL) literature is linguistics. The study of ASL has, especially in the past two decades, been all but consumed by and with linguistics, sociolinguistics, and the cognitive-scientific measures of American and other sign language systems. A quick search through the *MLA International Bibliography* reveals 696 pieces of research on American Sign Language recorded there.[1] But, of these 696, only 20 also cross-reference with the subject/search term "literature." Only twenty articles on ASL *literature*, I repeat, are currently in the entire MLA bibliography—and six of these are essays from the same collection published in 2006, *Signing the Body Poetic: Essays on American Sign Language Literature.*

I have directly experienced the heavy hand of ASL linguistic studies in my teaching, as well. When I teach an Arts and Sciences senior capstone course at my own university on "Deaf-World: Global, National, and Local Perspectives" my students become quickly and deeply frustrated with the significant amount of linguistic material they have to wade through just to understand "Deaf-world." The brush strokes of linguistics and sociolinguistics cover much of the canvas of late-20th- and early-21st-century publications on deaf culture, community, and language.

The first time I taught this course (in Spring 2004), I tried, for example, to make use of the new groundbreaking text from Gallaudet University Press, *Many Ways to Be Deaf*; it seemed ideal for a senior capstone course on global, national, and local deaf communities, particularly because of its global coverage. It was new, the cover was interesting, and the promotional material in Gallaudet University Press's catalogue made it sound like the perfect match, calling it:

an unmatched collection of in-depth articles about linguistic diversity in Deaf communities on five continents. Twenty-four international scholars have contributed their findings from studying Deaf communities in Japan, Thailand, Viet Nam, Taiwan, Russia, Sweden, Austria, Switzerland, Great Britain, Ireland, Nigeria, South Africa, Brazil, Nicaragua, and the United States.

But my students—all graduating seniors, most of whom were heading into various graduate and professional programs—could not often make the proverbial heads or tails out of most of those twenty-four essays without a great deal of handholding and concept unpacking. They grew increasingly surly at what one student claimed was just "linguists talking to other linguists."

Now, it is not that I have anything against linguists, especially those who study sign languages in general or American Sign Language in particular. Some of my best friends are linguists. And, to be sure, the linguistic study of ASL has done much to advance national and global Deaf pride and awareness in the last two decades—a claim I make and discuss at some length in my 1999 book, *Lend Me Your Ear*. But, still, I think we must face the problem: the linguistic study of ASL often overtakes other ways to study and obscures other frames and lenses for looking at the richness of language, community, culture, tradition, history, and *literature* related to sign language. It's like we sometimes can't see the forest of ASL literature out there for all the linguistic trees.

What I want to argue for here is an alternative critical frame for studying and thinking about ASL literature in particular—a rhetorical approach. And, in advancing this rhetorical approach, I will also suggest the potential (and some perils) for advancing the production and creation of ASL literature, along with the critical reception and interpretation of it, via digital technologies. There are at least three major values inherent in using a rhetorical approach to ASL literature. First, such an approach would focus on the persuasive, meaning-making, community-creating potential of ASL literature. Second, such an approach would also force us to pay more attention to the role of *audience* in the process and production of ASL literature. We would need to move beyond looking at just the trees of specific linguistic functions and forms in ASL and instead explore the entire interactive system—the rhetorical forest of *subject* in relation to *author* and also in relation to *audience* and situation. And, third, a rhetorical approach to ASL literature places us in a solid—although also complex and contested—philosophical and poetic tradition at the center of Western history and culture. For the long-standing tradition of rhetoric, in both theory and practice, has always been tied up with performance, poetics, and philosophy, as well. Both Plato and Aristotle articulate, and trouble over, these ties (Brueggemann, "Delivering"; *Lend*).

In the remainder of this essay, I map some applications of a rhetorical and digital approach to ASL literature in three major sections. I begin by exploring, rhetorically, classifiers in ASL literary forms. I use a well-known ASL poem that is available digitally as my sample text—"Eye Music," by Ella Mae Lentz. In the middle of this chapter, I then broaden my analysis by identifying and outlining a number of the major critical and creative challenges that face ASL literature at the turn of the 21st century. This outline arose largely from a three-hour discussion that took place on the Ohio State University campus in May 2005 among seven ASL authors/performers and seven scholars who often study and write about ASL literature. At every turn during this historic conversation, the challenges and potential for ASL literature were framed rhetorically and digitally. Finally, in the third section of this chapter, I gesture toward the need for the development of an ASL literature "anthology," done digitally.

Rhetorical Classifiers, ABC and 123

Anyone who studies or uses ASL for very long comes to know that classifiers make up one of the most unique and complex aspects of sign languages. Yet, classifiers, for all their complexity, are also stunningly simple because their foundation lies largely in the basic hand shapes of the signed language. Moreover, they uniquely employ both noun and verb functions together; they are used in American Sign Language to indicate and show movement, location, and appearance. After a signer indicates a certain person or thing, a classifier can then be used in its place (much like a pronoun) to show where and how it moves, what it looks like, and where it is located. In this way, the "1" classifier, for example, can represent a thing—a single person—but it can also illustrate that person in some movement or action, verb-ing along.[2]

English, of course, can't do this: we have nouns; we have verbs. They typically keep to themselves and their separate functions. To be sure, we can and sometimes do turn an English noun into a verb form. And the results, I might add, are typically awkward and awfully academic; for example, we take a *problem* and we *problematize* it, or we start with an intellect and intellectualize it.

The ABC and 123 classifiers—and their use in the creation and performance of ABC and 123 stories and poems in ASL—employ both simple complexity and complex simplicity. As such, classifiers mark a between space in American Sign Language and its literature. An ABC or 123 narrative or a poem-performance in ASL is built, cleverly but simply, on hand shapes from the most fundamental concepts in human literacy—alphabet letters and numbers. Linguistically, of course, this construction may not actually be unique or innovative; plenty of languages, after all, create literature from their alphabets.

But, rhetorically, I believe it is substantially more important and interesting than that. For ASL actually borrows an alphabet and makes its own innovative use of these borrowed characters. As Susan Rutherford has explained in her *Study of American Deaf Folklore,* an ABC story is one that makes use of the "interplay between the community's two languages, ASL and English." ABC storytellers "consciously manipulate the phonetic system of one language with the phonological system of the other" so that the storyteller may, in effect, be using ASL while also employing the "external structure of the English alphabet [to determine] the handshapes used for the story" (28). In this borrowing, ASL uses its alphabetic or numeric classifiers in a quite subversive way. For to create an ABC story in ASL is, in effect, to take a written, print-based alphabet from one linguistic tradition and transform it onto the body and then to place it in the deaf hands of the ASL author. An ABC story, built upon alphabetic principles from print languages (English, in this case) but rendered in a visual-spatial, embodied, and nonprint language, narrates a between space for ASL-English.

We move and merge, then, from one linguistic modality (print, writing, script) into another (visual, spatial, embodied.) Both forms, of course, are "written" with "the hand" and often aided or enhanced by various technologies. But one master tradition—the Roman alphabet, for example—is now subverted into the service of another. Such service and subversion makes for powerful rhetoric—the kind of political yet artistic move that can help create and sustain communities. As the Internet columnist Jamie Berke explains on about.com's site for deafness, ABC stories "are used as entertainment, and as an educational tool to develop deaf children's language. Deaf Studies classes frequently include ABC stories."[3] The genre also seems to have a considerable history in the American deaf community, possibly existing even at the turn of the 20th century at the Ohio School for the Deaf, as reported by Ben Bahan in his important essay on ASL literature, "Face-to-Face Tradition in the American Deaf Community" (37–41); Bahan also notes some problematic and promising issues surrounding ABC stories, such as the flexibility often allowed in modifying hand shapes and the limited number of signs available in certain hand shapes (similar to the limited number of rhyming words for certain words in English, such as *purple*).

And ABC and 123 stories and poems in ASL are rhetorical in precisely this community-building way to begin with. For it is actually quite common practice for someone who is acquiring or learning ASL to engage in the creation of an ABC or 123 story. The production of an ABC or 123 narrative is something akin to a rhetorical rite of passage in this linguistic community. Much as hearing grade-school children learn how to create their own "once upon a time" and "happily ever after" stories or how to write a friendly letter, deaf children often learn to create or tell an ABC or 123 story, building a narrative on the basis of the numbers 1 up to 5, 5 down to 1, 1 through 10, 1 through 20, and so on—all classified in dominant hand shape representations throughout the story. The use of the form is so popular that examples of ABC or 123 stories created in response to the 2006 protests at Gallaudet University can now be found all over YouTube.com.

These alphabetic (ABC) or numeric (123) classifiers become, then, a multifaceted, triangulated rhetorical act that merges subject, "speaker," and audience (or teller, tale, and audience, as Bahan would have it). First, these narratives bond ASL-using audiences that recognize their deployment in the story or poem. The audience comes to find both comfort and interest in the signer's run through the signed alphabet, knowing in part that the next sign or part of the story will feature some aspect of the hand shape for letter *a, b,* or *c, x, y,* or *z*. The attraction gained through such familiarity functions the same with hearing audiences who might bond and be engaged through a speaker's use of a certain local reference (as when almost all public figures, whether politicians or rock stars, end up saying something about Buckeye football when they visit Columbus, Ohio) or other formal patterns. Creating and performing an ABC or 123 story is thus rhetorically based in large part on recitation and *imitation*. That is, the storyteller must reproduce the form (proceeding forward or backward through the alphabet or number signs), but then he or she must also employ *invention* (the first canon of rhetoric) in order to offer some innovation on the imitated form, to create variance in *arrangement, style,* or *delivery* (the second, third, and fifth canons of rhetoric) so that the audience's *memory* (rhetoric's fourth canon) of the ABC/123 form is satisfied while it also, it is hoped, creates a new memory of this fresh, yet familiar, story. In this way, the seemingly simple act of signing one's way through the signed alphabet or a series of numbers becomes a complex rhetorical act.

In the second angle of this rhetorical act, ABC and 123 stories serve as a familiar narrative structure—functioning much like the "once upon a time," "and then, and then, and then," and "happily ever after" structure that English-speaking children often learn. Imitation of the structure and form guides the story at its most basic level, while new styles and arrangements of the form delight, entertain, engage, and persuade the audience. Like the *progymnasmata* (preliminary exercises) of classical and Renaissance rhetorical pedagogy, the telling of an ABC or 123 story in sign language is an "exercise in providing a preliminary training for the future orator" (Bonner 260); in fact, an ABC-123 story might be analogous to the second standard lesson of the original *progymnasmata*, the *diegema,* or narrative. As Gideon Burton, developer of the Forest of Rhetoric (*silva rhetoricae*), Brigham Young University's project, explains *diegema:*

> Telling narratives was one of the first exercises in a rhetorical education according to Quintilian, and included students retelling a story from the end to the beginning, or from the middle backwards or forwards. From providing students an initial experience in expression, narrative exercises became the building blocks for the progymnasmata exercises that followed it (which required summaries, digressions, or narrations of various sorts). (http://rhetoric.byu.edu/Pedagogy/Progymnasmata/Narration.htm)

In performing the narrative exercise of an ABC or 123 story, the deaf "orator" typically builds upon an already existing myth, much as the boys in their ancient Roman education did when they performed *diegema* (Bonner 260). Ben Bahan, a linguist and both an ASL literature author-performer and a critic, explains the mythic grounding of the deaf version of *diegema* in ABC stories in terms of the "possible themes" used by this genre; "one common theme is the haunted house story," he claims (37)—and then he goes on to illustrate with an ABC "haunted house" story of his own—and, too, he suggests that "ABC stories have several classical opening motifs" (40).

Building classically, then, upon the block of seemingly simple narration, in a third rhetorical angle, ABC and 123 stories might also be said to re-employ the kind of "muscular" and "closed-fist" nonverbal rhetoric that Edward P. J. Corbett once famously discussed (borrowing Zeno's analogies) as signifying "the kind of persuasive activity that seeks to carry its point by non-rationale, non-sequential, often non-verbal, frequently provocative means" (288). In the hands now of the signing rhetor and poet, the so-called closed-fist, nonverbal, and frequently provocative rendering of an ABC or 123 story is also, however, rational and sequential. Yet, furthermore, and paradoxically, following on Zeno's original discussion, the "open-hand" rhetoric (of an ASL storyteller) is also symbolic of "the relaxed, expansive, ingratiating discourse of the orator (*sic*)" that Corbett assigned to "open-hand" rhetoric in his 1969 discussion of these two rhetorical forms (288). "Closed-fist" and "open-hand" rhetoric work together in sign-language ABC or 123 "oratory." Whether open or closed, the hands, face, and body of the signing ABC-123 storyteller set up the entire grammar of the story, poem, or performance. The classifier of the "A" or "5" hand shape, for example, comes to represent the characters and objects in the prose or poem, as well as supplying the actions, adverbs, and adjectives around that character or agent that propels the plot.

In the particular case of 123 stories or poems performed in ASL, math also provocatively merges and morphs into performance and artistic "utterance." This kind of merging does not happen often—or successfully—in Western literary traditions. As a young modernist poet who described himself as an "Objectivist," George Oppen attempted, in an early volume of his poetry, *Discrete Series*, "to construct a meaning by empirical statements, by imagist statements . . . I had in mind specifically the meaning to the mathematician—a series of empirically true terms" (Dembo 161). That was in 1934, at the start of his poetic career. Later in his life, however, even Oppen himself had to reject his earlier attempts to make math and poetry objectively merge. His Pulitzer Prize–winning volume published in 1968, titled *Of Being Numerous*, is, in many ways, an argument against his own poetics of the 1930s, which he had come to see as obscure and unsuccessful. Yet, in ASL literature, numbers and poetry can be quite successful together, powerfully merged to make meaning.

As one example of this successful merger, I offer Ella Mae Lentz's "Eye Music" (Lentz, 1995). This is a profound little poem, I think, where memory (or nostalgia), narrative, music, and the clever use of technology and film technique are all carried out largely on the little linguistic shoulders of 123 classifiers. In my 1999 book, *Lend Me Your Ear*, I offer a critical reading of Lentz's "Eye Music" (along with four other ASL poems), and, in order to present this reading in printed English to an audience that likely is largely hearing, I (somewhat reluctantly) also offer an English gloss of the poem as follows:

> This poem stylistically features a common technique used in sign folk-lore—to create a story using letter (*a, b, c*) or number (*1, 2, 3*) signs. Here the numbers used are 1, 2, 3, 4, and 5. They are mostly signed on the horizontal plane (with the poet's palms flat to the ground) rather than vertically with palms out and away from the body, as numbers are typically signed in ASL. "Eye Music" begins with a brief explanatory opening in which Lentz tells of how she used to lie in her mother's lap, while traveling in a car, and watch the telephone wires whiz by. This is, she states, an experience common to many children (especially of her generation). The wires, punctuated with telephone poles, reminded her of sheets of music, and she came to think of this experience as her "eye music."
>
> Lentz performs the videotaped poem in black and white with some sepia tones, so the audience seems to be viewing a photograph from the past. The camera shifts slightly (though not abruptly) from viewing her almost top down (from her head down) to straight on, at eye level. Remarkably, you seem to *move* while viewing the poem, as if you yourself are in the car and in the young girl's place on her mother's lap. This effect is created both through the camera and video technology and through Lentz's fast, smooth, flowing movements from one sign to the next. The poem takes but a minute to complete.
>
> Lentz also creates an impression, fittingly, of herself as the conductor of an orchestra as she creates a lyric that is far more sensual than in any way linguistic.
>
> The poem runs at a fast tempo, with feelings of excitement, wonder, and mesmerism. She changes tempos (one might even say that she changes tone, pitch, and volume) and intensity as the telephone wires change speeds and directions—undulating, sometimes flutelike (she signs this instrument), punctuated by the drums of telephone poles (again this instrument is signed). All this is indicated with merely the signs for numbers 1 to 5.
>
> The upbeat tone throughout the poem indicates the child's peace and joy in this experience. At the end, the pace slows a bit, and she ends by questioning where all the lines have gone? Poked in tubes? Her face puckering. A questioning. Slight frustration. Eyes squinted, searching. "Where?" (204–5)

Because of digital technologies, the poem has now been "anthologized" in several ways, and, I would argue, this canonizing has, of course, increased its rhetorical appeal—for both hearing and deaf audiences that can now gain easy access to it. Featured as one of the sample poems in *Slope* magazine's online journal and in its special issue in 2003 on ASL poetry, Lentz's poem is characterized by the issue editors as

> a frequently "anthologized" ASL poem, described and contextualized in Carol Padden's and Tom Humphries' significant study of Deaf culture, *Deaf in America* and critically analyzed in Brenda Jo Brueggemann's sharp, eclectic *Lend Me Your Ear*. . . . In this poem, number signs (1–5) reinforce the sense of visual rhythm created by the telephone wires and telephone poles as the narrator rides by in a car. "Eye Music" shows the rhythm and meter of visual experience. (http://slope.org/asl/)

To view the short poem in its entirety, one need only access the active online "ASL Poetry" issue of *Slope* magazine.

What we need in ASL literature is a way to talk about all the things going on in this marvelous little poem. Linguistics alone won't get us there. But digital technologies will, with the digital ability to parse and prod the poem in a close "reading," and a rhetorical frame can further aid an understanding of the dynamics of the embodied delivery in "eye music." While we might linguistically recognize Lentz's use of number classifiers, particularly the numbers 1–5, to convey this "music" of her childhood eye, we also need a way to consider how the author's perspective and "stance" are represented through an apparently simplified and perhaps childlike use of number classifiers to convey the gist of the poem; how the camera angle puts the audience in an "adult" frame above her; how the 1–5 number classifiers almost always occur paired and thus in rhythm and "rhyme" with each other; how the visual tone of the poem is set by the nostalgic sepia hues and the rhetorical impact of memory laced with imagination created from that nonverbal, provocative element; how, almost in ironic synesthesia, an aural art such as music is represented in her (deaf) hands (and how classifiers help convey this).

To be sure, a rhetorical approach might not give us all the angles we want, either. But, combined with digital technology that makes the poem accessible and "anthologized" for a wider range of "readers," it allows us to consider more layers of ASL literature as we explore, in rhetorical triangulation, how the poet's use of the number classifiers engages a certain kind of *audience,* how she conveys a *subject* in complex and yet simple terms, and also how her own *authorial* perspective and presence in the poem matters.

Critical, Creative, and Rhetorical Challenges to ASL Literature in a Digital Age

On May 19, 2005, seven ASL authors (performers, storytellers, poets) met in a videotaped three-hour conversation with seven critics/scholars of ASL literature.[4] The "ASL Literature Author and Critic Forum" was part of a two-day event held on the Ohio State University campus in May 2005. The entire event, "The ASL Literature and Digital Media Project" (ASL-DMP), was funded by a Battelle Endowment for Technology and Human Affairs (BETHA) grant. The fourteen participants discussed the past, present, and future possibilities and difficulties regarding the creation, production, and reception of literature in American Sign Language. Starting questions for the conversation included the following:

1. In 1910, George Veditz, then president of the National Associaton of the Deaf (NAD), used the new technology of film to produce the "Sign Masters" series of ten nationally known skilled masters of American Sign Language. Since Vedtiz's use of film and the screening of ten nationally known "sign masters," how have (or haven't) things changed for the creation, production, and shared reception of ASL literature with new digital media technologies?
2. How should we define "ASL literature"?
3. Where, and how, do you imagine the differences between the genres of "sign-language storytelling" and "sign-language poetry?"
4. Where, and how, does dramatic performance—either solo performance or staged group theater performances—impact and intersect with sign-language storytelling and poetry?
5. Whom do you reference and acknowledge as the current national and international leaders in these sign-language literary forms (storytelling and poetry)?
6. What do you believe the role of national organizations—academic or public—should (or could) be in the continued creation, production, and reception of sign-language literature? (Consider public organizations such as the National Association of the Deaf or the World Federation of the Deaf, as well as academic-affiliated organizations such as the American Sign Language Teachers Association, the Modern Language Association, or the Associated Departments of Foreign Language.)

7. What are some of the strongest barriers and issues at the turn of the 21st century for the creation and production of ASL literature? Have you seen digital and electronic technologies make any difference in these barriers and issues, or can you see this happening in the future?

8. What are some of the strongest barriers and issues at the turn of the 21st century for the critical and public reception of, and response to, ASL literature? Have you seen digital and electronic technologies make any difference in these barriers and issues, or can you see this happening in the future?

9. What signs have you seen of further growth, potential, or innovation in the creation, production, and reception of sign-language literatures?

10. What do you imagine the relationship should be between American Sign Language (ASL) and other sign languages around the world in advancing and exploring the global network of sign-language literature?

11. How can—or should—sign-language "authors" and sign-language literary critics and scholars work together fruitfully on these issues, barriers, and promises for sign-language literature and digital media production?

Whither ASL Literature?

Near the end of the three-hour discussion, the author-performer[5] Mindy Moore circled back to some of the opening remarks and also captured much of the essence of the forum: "Where is ASL literature?" she asked. She summarized well then some of the key elements and issues we had covered so far that morning:

> ASL doesn't have a written form. It's not in print. . . . ASL is a visual language, and the oral history, we try to capture that in film, but then we have the technical barriers and the funding barriers. . . . How are we going to capture it and document it? Just as black people have organizations that preserve their culture and their literature, and just like with Russian culture, they have organizations and funding to preserve their literature and culture, but where are those entities for the Deaf community?

Capturing and documenting; history, print, and preservation; funding barriers and technical barriers—these were indeed the pulse points of our forum.

Our morning had opened, in fact, with some wondering about "the library" for ASL literature—a place where the literature and history of the literature and language could be archived and accessed. The author-performer Cinnie Macdougall had posited a possible comparison with "other foreign languages [that] have a literary form and a literature that's been preserved through videotape and audiotape" that might offer "the same concept for ASL, because there is something other than just [print] text." The critic Michael Davidson responded that, yes, we would call that place "the library" and that it could indeed "include videotapes, CD-ROMS, as well as codex books, journals . . . a body of video material and representations, in other words, of ASL performances."

The critic Dirksen Bauman had tied the archive issue (the library of and for ASL) to what he determined was "the basic question . . . how can you explain ASL literature?" He anchored his question about the challenge of defining ASL literature in the very etymology of the word *literature*: "Typically literature has been in print. The word itself, *literature*, means, in Latin, 'in letter.'" Without a lettered (printed) form, ASL literature would "challenge the basic foundation of literary work itself."

Yet, beyond or, perhaps, before, the question of literature's tether to letters, ASL literature presents another challenge to the current construction of letter-bound literature in that it uncannily takes us back to the earliest forms of literature, which, as Bauman pointed out, "had its influence from the oral," which we can "link back to the body." In fact, the "poetic foot" of iambic pentameter is, Bauman continued, "actually based upon the Greek dancing with the poetry." The (human) body was always there in the body of literature. Print, and the letter-bound tradition of literature, he offered, "has its influence from oral and visual sources." And such sourcing perhaps makes ASL literature not so much off the map, anyway. The oral-body anchor of ASL literature places it at the (oral) ocean bottom of literature writ large; the two really are not oil and water, after all. Perhaps the only real problem we have in defining or imagining "ASL literature," quipped the poet/performer Peter Cook, is imagining how to put the grammar of ASL (which is always said to be cemented in and on the face) in the poetic foot of literature: how, that is, to put the foot on one's face.

In the introduction to the only critical anthology on American Sign Language literature, *Signing the Body Poetic*, Bauman's collaborative introduction with his co-editors, Jennifer Nelson and Heidi Rose, argues for the redefining potential of "sign literature" in questioning "the assumption that human language is exclusively spoken or written" and challenging "such fundamental notions as textuality, genre, performance and body as they have been constructed within a decidedly hearing model" (3). As illustrations for the "redesigning of the literary landscape" offered by ASL literature, they cite at least three instances. First, they offer the (ironic) "oral tradition" embedded in all sign-language discourse, so that "sign poetry not only resembles ancient literary forms [in its orality] but also engages the current literary practices of oral, performed poetry" (6). Second, they point to the way that sign poetry naturally engages a merging with the "visual arts" that has been attempted elsewhere in "pattern poetry" and "the formidable output of ekphrastic poetry, the accumulation of illustrated books over the centuries, and modernist and postmodernist poetic forms—Futurism, Dadaism, concrete poetry, L = A = N = G = U = A = G = E poetry, and multimedia cyberpoetry" (7).

And, third, they tell again the creation myth surrounding the invention of a new ASL sign for "poetry" that changed it from the English-based construct of the handshape "P" indexing the sign for music or song to a new form based on the sign for expression, where "one closed hand [rests] at the chest" and then moves outward and opens up (4). This new sign, derived from the hands of deaf poets themselves at the 1989 international Deaf Way Conference, "suggests that poems emerge directly out of the body as offerings from the chest, heart, and lungs, unmediated by speech or writing" (4). Sebastian Knowles, a colleague of mine who teaches 20th-century literature and who is a Joyce and Eliot scholar, once observed a class I was teaching on the day we were discussing ASL literature (especially performance-poetry). Largely unfamiliar with ASL, he still described the newer ASL sign for poetry quite well as "a hand opening from the heart, held covered and then opening out towards the viewer, as one would present a flower or a visiting card." As a flower or as a visiting card, ASL literature is indeed an offering: natural, appreciative, and invitational.

Preserving the Flowers of Signed Languages

Yet other issues related to the archives for ASL literature exist beyond situating its nature in relation to the larger history of "letters," and some of these issues do seem to make it unnatural and unappreciated. Preservation has been a particular concern for sign-language scholars and authors in the modern era, particularly since the turn of the 20th century. The earliest manual (hand/signed) alphabet we know of was based on the Greek alphabet and was described by a Benedectine monk, Bede, in 710 A.D. Yet, an illustration to mark or match that description did not appear until 1140.

Indeed, literally hundreds of medieval and Renaissance paintings contain manual alphabet gestures in them, such as Fernando Gallego's retablo panels, from 1480–1488, in Ciudad Rodrigo. Yet, illustration and painting could never capture this embodied literature; the visual archiving needed to properly store a sign language, let alone its literature, really could not happen until the advent of photography and film. And film is, of course, a better means of archiving a visual, spatial, embodied, moving language than is the single-image photograph.

In their Appendix, "Time Line of ASL Literature Development" (241–52), Bauman, Nelson, and Rose set the dawn of ASL Literature at 1813–17, when Thomas Hopkins Gallaudet, a Connecticut minister, inspired by his teaching of a young deaf girl, Alice Cogswell, traveled to Europe to learn about methods of deaf education. In London, he met the famous Abbé Sicard and the teachers Jean Massieu and Laurent Clerc—all Frenchmen—who invited him to visit the deaf school in Paris, where the manual (signed) method of instruction was in use. Gallaudet went to Paris, saw the manual method of instruction, and promptly invited Clerc back to America with him in hopes of raising money for and founding the first school for the deaf, what became the American School for the Deaf (ASD) in 1817. Bauman, Nelson, and Rose go on to outline the next two periods of ASL Literature's development through the theme of deaf education—"1817–80: The 'Golden Age' of American Deaf Education" and "1880–1957: The 'Dark Age' of Deaf Education." They note that during these times, "the concept of deaf *literature* could be defined only as deaf people writing and publishing in English" because, "while creative forms of sign language thrived, they could not possibly have been equated with literature because ASL was not considered a 'real' language," even though "its utility in the classroom and Deaf community was certainly acknowledged" (242). It is only when they come to the fourth major period of ASL Literature's development that "education" takes a back seat and actual "literature" comes forward, as is evident in the title given to this period: "1960–Present: Video Period of ASL Literature" (244).

What also comes forward and seems to bring literature (and not education) into the picture in the 1960s is *video*—the camera, the cinema—what the critic Christopher Krentz (in both the ASL-DMP forum and in the *Signing the Body Poetic* volume) calls "the printing press" that has "influenced ASL Literature" (2006: 51). According to Krentz, film not only influenced ASL literature but has played a role in helping to standardize the language, making Deaf/ASL culture accessible (to both hearing and deaf audiences) and, significantly, both promoting *and* preserving ASL/Deaf culture and identity (51–70). During our forum discussion, the author-performer Mindy Moore connected the importance of preservation through video especially when working with young deaf children, as she does at the Texas School for the Deaf: "ASL literature . . . is videotapes, the ABC stories, the number stories and we really don't have a lot to choose from in those media . . . we need that history preserved on videotape. . . . As I teach children, we need to have ASL stories captured on video—that's important."

The author-performer Cinnie MacDougall, who also often works with deaf children, was perhaps the first to evoke the issue of control in the important preservation work of ASL literature during the forum. In support of her positive view of ways to have and take control of ASL literature in an audience-removed video setting, she used the example of her friend Ella Mae Lentz's work on the now-famous "videobook" *The Treasure*:

> Seeing ASL live on stage, seeing ASL performances like you said, having that is more meaningful than just being able to have it filmed and having the cameras and the editing. The other thing we need to take into consideration then is the control—having that control and changing the camera views. There's a beautiful work by Ella Mae Lentz, the video series of her poetry, *The Treasure*. That work she does here is beautiful. It's just so fascinating, so intriguing. And the camera views, and the angles and the way she rotates with the sign itself, even though it's not live, the way it's being captured on film, is almost as good as live. There was a lot of control with the way her work was captured on that film. And I think we need to talk about those controls, and how we can make capturing it on film almost like it is live.

Yet film, even if it is "almost like it is live," also has what Krentz notes is a potential "paradoxical" effect on ASL literature in the way it can forfeit control as it puts ASL and its literature into broader public consumption—out of the eyes and hands of only the deaf community meeting and sharing its language and creativity in deaf clubs and schools. Thus, while "almost-live" film productions of ASL literature offer some authorial control of the the text or material itself, such productions also forfeit some of the ASL author's direct control or interface with her audience, since a video or film production separates a dynamic performer from his or her (plural) audience and places the literature or performance in the arena of often solitary video viewing. "Deaf Americans," writes Krentz, "may be losing some control over their language and literature" (2006: 68).

Control is a consistent concern for the modern Deaf community, as is its identity, and the prominence of that concern is reflected in its literature, as well; this point was made time and again throughout the ASL-DMP forum. The control offered in NAD president George Veditz's 1913 "Sign Masters" film project—to "possess and jealously guard a language different and apart from any other in common use" and to "fix and give [the Deaf community a] distinct literature of its own by means of the moving picture film" (NAD)—the issue of that control still haunts and invigorates ASL literature today. The technological ability now to collect, archive, analyze, contextualize, and historicize ASL literature through film, video, and digital media—and the power of "literary criticism" then made possible, as well—launches ASL literature into a new age.

Yet, it is also an age of authorial anxiety, an age when the work of the ASL author can now easily slip from the author's own hands as virtually everyone and anyone—the young deaf student, the hearing college student learning ASL, a gathering of the Deaf community, a curious public, literary scholars, anthropologists, linguists, and the like—can pop in a VHS, CD-ROM, or DVD or turn to his or her browser and eyeball it. And when you perform the liturgy and publish "the word" no longer in unfamiliar Latin but in the language of the people—when you make it accessible to the wide and unwieldy "public"—you lose, as we know, some control over your text. Thus, the preservation that ensures greater accessibility can also fan the flames of interpretation. And we wait anxiously; no one quite knows whether the flames will consume the texts and even burn the library buildings down—or just offer a good light and a warm place to "read" them by.[6]

Who Signs? Who Sees? Access, Audience, and Translation of ASL Literature

Who "reads" ASL literature, and why? Who can and can't get access to it, and why? Should it be translated? And who would carry out that translation, and how? These are all questions of *audience*. They are also questions very much on the mind of both ASL author-performers and critics today.

In an appendix to *Signing the Body Poetic*, co-editors Bauman, Nelson, and Rose offer a list of "ASL Video References"; the list contains 21 items, with the most recent listing dating from 1997, now more than a decade ago. Clearly, the thinness (and datedness) of the "library" is, in and of itself, no small issue. In fact, there are two video references listed from 1997, and, while one of those is entirely unobtainable through any of the numerous comprehensive library systems I can access from my own university library,[7] the other is one I own and show in my senior capstone course on "Deaf-World" at Ohio State University. This "accessible" one is actually the remastering of George Veditz's 1913 "Sign Masters" series.[8] "The NAD Films," as they are now commonly called, feature "master signers" and deaf leaders from the early 20th century performing—deliberately for this special "preservation" film recording (and not before a live audience)—material that generally followed what the historian and ASL literature critic Susan Burch (2002) calls "one of three themes: American patriotism, Deaf history, or religious faith" (58). The significance of these films is not only for preservation, but also for the American deaf community to access its own culture, identity and language. As Burch claims:

> The NAD films not only feature a successful attempt to document sign language for future generations; they also signify the outward expression of many Deaf cultural values. What made the participants master signers was not solely their ability to express ideas articulately in manual communication. Of equal importance was their identity as Deaf citizens. (57)

In this historic video collection are stories such as "The Irishman and the Flea" (also called "The Irishman's Flea" in some listings of the films) and "The Lady and the Cake" by Robert McGregor, the first NAD president and a former student and then principal of the Ohio School for the Deaf, whose uncaptioned (untranslated to English) performance is said to be "eminently comprehensible" to all viewers (Burch 59). In this particular film, the story of the flea is particularly chock-full of cross-cultural humor and is aimed at a wide audience as McGregor "emphasized commonalities between Deaf and hearing people" (Burch 59) and "turned witty and iconic as he told of his search for a deaf person anywhere who suited the oralist ideal of someone who could speak without strain or effort" (Padden & Humphries 2005: 60). Crossing cultures and potentially appealing to both deaf and hearing audiences, these signers also perform classic American songs such as "Yankee Doodle," by Winfield E. Marshall, and a Longfellow poem, "The Death of Minnehaha," done in complete Indian dress, by Mary Williamson Erd.

There are also, in bulk, ceremonial and rhetorical addresses; these moments of more classic "oratory" typically fork two ways. First, some recapture key American events and discourse, thereby cementing deaf identity as also an essentially *American* identity and illustrating, as Burch documents, "in concept and application the goals of elite Deaf people to prove their commonality with hearing Americans and their loyalty as American citizens" (59): "The Gettysburg Address" by T. F. Fox; "Discovery of Chloroform," by George Dougherty; "Address at the Tomb of Garfield," by William Hubbard; "Glimpses of the Battlefield," by the Reverend Bryant; and Gallaudet's first president (a hearing man), Edward Miner Gallaudet, signing his version of the tale of "Lorna Doone." If nothing else, these "sign masters" classics demonstrate the nationalism of early-20th-century Deaf identity. But, on a second prong of the fork, other films in this series seem aimed more at illustrating the shared history of the American Deaf community itself, while also demonstrating the sheer intelligence, benevolence, morality, and rhetorical finesse of deaf people and their language. Here the nationalism is more about outstanding citizenship in "Deaf nation" than perhaps it is about being a good *American* citizen; yet, either way, the nationalist tone remains. Thus, these particular "sign masters" films display the American deaf version of Quintilian's *vir bonus*, the "good man speaking [*sic*] well": "The Signing of the Charter of Gallaudet College," by Amos Draper; "Plea for a Statue of de l'Epee in America," by the Reverend Cloud and the Reverend McCarthy; and even the opening argument for the creation of the films themselves, "The Preservation of Sign Language," by George Veditz, then president of NAD.

Everywhere in this historic film collection is evidence of an anxiety about audience and access. Working consciously to "possess and jealously guard a language different and apart from any other in common use" and "striving to fix and give [that language] a distinct literature of its own," Veditz (who became deaf at the age of nine from scarlet fever) and the others he filmed here sign originally, without caption or voiceover; yet there is also evidence of an appeal to the broader American hearing culture.[9] This double audience appeal still occupies the body of contemporary ASL literature, with its soul perhaps troubled anew by all the capabilities of new media technologies. As the critic Chris Krentz (who also participated in the ASL-DMP forum) outlines, in his essay "The Camera as Printing Press," film and media technologies can arguably distance live ASL performers from their audiences (56–59), stopping still a vital and vibrant part of the "agonistic" (Ong and face-to-face nature of sign-language discourse. Captured on film, ASL literature can, in a sense, risk alienating its audience. Yet, ironically, it can also increase its audience, reaching wider to the thing known as the "mass audience" and effectively "increasing [its] output" (Krentz 59–60). It also has the potential to expose largely unknown individual ASL author-performers (like American Idol contestants performing week after week on national network TV) and even train audiences of ASL literature to become more analytical (63–65), while encouraging the author-performers ("artists," as Krentz calls them) to become more "self-conscious" and "experimental" (61–62).

Audience is indeed a good thing in ASL literature (an audience is a good thing for any literature). ASL authors (and critics too) may still, however, be a bit unsure about the shape-shifting nature of audience here in the dawn of the digital age, where we not only watch TV and movies but can now make them in the mere blink of a videocamera lens and a little iMovie editing, where everyone's chance to perform his Warhol-ish fifteen minutes of fame on YouTube.com has obviously arrived. To be sure, the power of YouTube.com-published videos and vlogs in the 2006 protests at Gallaudet University made it very clear that the camera had indeed become a "printing press" for the public and a rhetorical sphere of community and dissent in Deaf-world.

The critics and author-performers at the ASL-DMP forum mulled heavily the nature of audience in ASL literature for the past, present, and future. The literary scholar Chris Krentz directly acknowledged early in the two-hour conversation how "ASL literature started at the deaf club, that's where it had its original roots" and noted that in those roots "ASL literature always had a live audience," so that "when you try to capture it in a digital format or film, something is lost there. That's very dangerous, and it's a risk." Later, near the end of our time, the historian Susan Burch came back to this same issue but framed it squarely in terms of audience. Responding to comments from the author-performer Werner Zorn (from South Africa) about the role of audience in his own performances, Burch wondered about:

> the audience [because] in the live performance, you have the interaction, and how that experience affects the ASL performance itself. Now, if they click on the Internet, or it's produced virtually, how would you feel about that, and the shift from a live performance with the interaction, where you can get eye contact . . . compared to the simple streaming through the Internet and disseminating it that way? . . . Here we are in a physical location, face to face, in a live setting, and would performances produced through the Internet and streamed . . . what would be their effect?

The author-performer Cinnie MacDougall replied to Burch's concern about the effect of audience and seemed open and flexible regarding both live stage performance with audience present and the more controlled audience distance possible with edited video. Sounding less anxious about audience, in fact, than many of the critics, Macdougal suggested that it might not be all that different from "hearing people that would look at a hearing performer" and "go back and forth" between viewing a live stage performance and a "movie or DVD on their TV" of that performer or a certain performance. "Which would we choose?" she asked herself and all others at the forum, "or would we do both at the same time?" Following her less-anxious lead, the critic Michael Davidson (who is also a poet in written English but not in ASL) made an analogy to the tape recorder and poetry readings: "did the tape recorder eliminate poetry readings? Well, in fact, the tape recorder allowed poetry readings to get much wider circulation and certainly enhanced live poetry readings, in a way that no other technology did before." Furthermore, Davidson suggested, we might not have to imagine "this technology [digital media, video, the Internet] as being the primary place where the performance would happen but it would be strictly a matter of storage and recording performances that could be live or not live."

Another place where technology seems to interact heavily with issues of audience and "live or not live" performances of ASL literature is in the business of translation. Twice during the forum—near the beginning and near the end—the critic Kristin Harmon (who has written about ASL literature and who uses ASL as her primary language today but who authors scholarship and creative work—largely fiction—in English) brought us all around to the always thick and thorny topic of translation. "To analyze it and to write it is a translation," she argued. She then asked how "do we translate a visual language into sound?" The challenge of translation between visual-spatial, embodied ASL—a language still, oddly, perhaps as "American" as the American use of English—and the disembodied print of an English-based literary journal still carries rhetorical force. Harmon characterized that force:

> One of the challenges for deaf poetry and for us who analyze it into English print and then go back to the [ASL] performance [is] how it all is translated into one another. Does that mean [ASL literature critics] borrow words from the theoretical parts of English? How do we do that? How do we translate it so the words [in English] and the content [in ASL] match up with one another?

Where—and how—should the interpreter (another embodied figure) and the interpretation (the act) go? Surely more than a transparent fiberoptic conduit, the body and the act of translation and interpretation are a body of matter, a body that matters.

Several of the author-performers take up the double-edged sword of tyranny and empowerment that can be present in the translation and interpretation of ASL literature. The author Theron Parker, one-half of the Mindy and Theron collaboration, recounted how his long experience in (signed, ASL) theater has shown him that the interpretive zone between author and audience in an ASL performance (when some of the audience members are hearing and not skilled ASL users) is often cluttered and even, at times, a space of considerable control and contest:

> Finding interpreters for the performance is challenging. The interpreters want to be prepared, they want me to prepare them, they want to be ready for the performance. And I give them my script, which is in a printed form and I tell them, no matter what you see me doing, just go off the printed script. I've already interpreted my performance and here it is—ready for you.

What happens of course is that the interpreters do not always, if ever, follow the script of the author's preprovided translation. Audiences, alas, are like that—they bring to the theater (or text) their own stage, as well.

The other collaborative team present at the forum, Flying Words Project (Peter Cook and Kenny Lerner), is well known in ASL literary circles for many things, and one of those is their unique style of translation. When they perform, the process all seems seamless, of course. But Kenny Lerner, the hearing member of the creative duo, confessed that "we've really had a difficult time" and then went on to briefly outline the interface between sign and speech that the duo attempts to animate as they work to incorporate the (voice) translation into the body of the performance itself. In this way, a Flying Words Project performance (text) may sometimes be signed with a voiced English translation, while another may be a more seamless, merged sign-voice performance. But, whatever the final product, Kenny Lerner's description of the basic process makes it evident that the *image* Peter first performs is "the literature":

> We've come up with some work, we sign it . . . it would probably take a year, maybe to create a poem, and then how are we going to voice that? Peter and I work so diligently at trying to figure out the words that the audience will

see, we want them to identify the words that they're going to hear and what they see so they can actually put those together. So Peter's our visual image, and he's very clear. The frustration is how do we express that auditorially so that the hearing people will have the same visualization? And then, we'll have to do it again. We'll voice something and then we don't do it. We're like, yes that's what we want to capture visually, but is the hearing audience going to have the same visual image? Peter is the literature, his body, his image is the literature. Hearing people, how can we get them to understand Peter, and that's the goal. When we're trying to translate his work, that is our goal: How is the hearing audience going to understand him?[10]

Interestingly enough, the critic Dirksen Bauman (who has known Flying Words Project for at least a dozen years and who has written often on their work), had suggested early in the forum that use of digital media could actually *improve* control over translation, especially with regard to the ASL author's original "text" making its way to the eyes of a (hearing) audience. He articulated this idea with an example from a recent film festival at the National Technical Institute for the Deaf (NTID), part of the Rochester Institute of Technology (RIT):

We had a poet from Holland, and we had different cameras. At the opening of his show we had written words, so you could actually capture his own hand, his handwriting of his own poetry [in the printed language form]. We were able to capture that in film and then he signed it. And it was beautiful. We were able to show the printed text, through digital media and then it was put into a visual form alongside his actual visual and signed performance. . . . That was a very creative way to have control over it.

Early in the forum conversation, the author-performer Mindy Moore (of Mindy and Theron) had also advocated the use of a similar kind of digitally enhanced translation of ASL literature that would "put English and ASL on videotape" together. So, for example, she suggested, "you'll have one out of five handshapes [being used in the ASL text/performance] and you'll have a printed formation of that projected or put onto the digital media, so you'd be able to see both of those perspectives." This was important, she insisted, because "I think that's very important to include that English." Later, near the end of the forum, when translation came again to the front of our conversations, an audience member (yes, an audience was there, live!) asked the panelists directly, "Would you just prefer not to even have the English format of that?" And it was Mindy Moore again who quickly answered that she believed it was "critical for hearing people to work with deaf people and vice versa," and so, she argued, "we have to have it in a written format."

The critic of ASL literature, who often as not writes about ASL literature in printed English, also creatively exercises some control in the work of translation and interpretation of course—a point raised both early and late in the forum by Kristen Harmon. Interestingly enough, in another arena of translation, even the ASL authors were not entirely clear on what "the job" of the critics was, and so, at this forum, some of the critics found themselves interpreting what it is that they do. Late in the session, the author Cinnie MacDougall finally asked, "I'd just like to know—is it your job [as critics] over there to translate our work or to analyze our work?"[11] Several of us on the critic side of the fence immediately responded, almost in chorus, "Oh no, we analyze!" Yet such analysis is, of course, a form of and includes interpretation. And it was obvious in the room that several ASL authors (including a few local ones who were in the audience) were having trouble understanding the difference between interpretation that is (language) translation and interpretation that is (literary) analysis. The critic Michael Davidson went on then to clarify how criticism was different than interpretation as translation and how he saw his interpretive, analytical role:

> And if that [translating] were the definition of what I do as a literary critic, then I wouldn't be interested in writing criticism. I'm interested in how that work [of literature] responds to a much larger question—to issues about deafness, issues about culture, issues about gender and so forth. So in many cases, a reading [analysis] of a work will be in conversation with a much larger argument of which it is just a kind of small component. . . . My reading of an ASL piece of literature is always in dialogue with the big picture of the essay or the book it is placed in.

But even as Davidson explained the interpretive act of analysis and criticism, it seemed the whole room now was grappling with wonder and doubt. Perhaps the rhetorical effect of living in a culture and using a language that is, and always has been, in direct contest with English and subject to the anxieties of translation for even the smallest of daily communicative interactions is just too significant to get us truly past translation and into analysis. Perhaps the time—the *kairos*—for that kind of critical move in relation to ASL literature has not yet (quite) arrived.

Yet, there were also critical signs of movement and understanding at this forum when both critics and authors found themselves asking each other, as Cinnie Macdougal had done, what we do and what the challenges are in that doing.[12] Just as the ASL authors had articulated their attempts, both positive and negative, to work through and with translation and technology and just as they (and the critics along with them) had thoroughly considered the place of audience in ASL literature, the critics were also now asked to articulate, as Peter Cook had put it, what our "battles" are:

> We, the poets, the storytellers, the creators, the authors over here, you take what we create and in your academic world, you have your discussions. . . . What are the barriers that you are experiencing? You find something that we did, you talk about it, you present it to someone and say, "this is ASL literature." We're unaware, we just put our work out. So, in your world—what are the issues that are there? . . . I'm trying to figure out what are the frustrations and barriers that you are experiencing from your academic world?

In answering these critical questions, we found ourselves facing audience, yet again, in another way.

Explaining Ourselves: The Politics of the Product

The distance between a dominant (and typically English-based) critical reading of ASL literature and the culture, language, ways, and experiences it represents was indeed almost a motif for the forum. The barriers highlighted by the critics (which were also, of course, barriers for the authors) were those of the politics of publishing and funding for the advancement, dissemination, and archiving of ASL literature. Like Horton who hears the Whos and then must convince others that they exist, sign-language scholars have to keep convincing language and literature scholars again and again that ASL (including its literature and culture) exists. The critic and historian Susan Burch conveyed the rhetorical situation of "who hears who" quite persuasively:

> I don't think it's necessary that we have to convince individuals that English has a culture, a history. French has its history, its culture, its language. We don't need to convince those people—it's there. I believe that the deaf

situation is different, and the sign community is different. When I went into my Ph.D. program [at Georgetown University], I informed them that I actually plan to study the Russian deaf culture and history. I do believe that deaf individuals have a history, they have a community, a culture, an identity. I wanted to study Russian deaf culture, and I was turned down. And I actually had said that American Sign Language and Russian sign language are both true languages, and they believed that it was like a monkey sign language—yeah, a monkey language. It took a long time for me to get them to allow it; I actually had to go into a linguistic program to study ASL, so we are unable to convince people that the sign community is alive. . . . We don't have to prove that America has a culture, that America has a language. But we still have to prove today that the deaf have their language.

Likewise, Dirksen Bauman, a critic and scholar in the ASL and Deaf Studies program at Gallaudet University, insisted that "we've been telling and we've been telling and we've been telling them all about the ASL literature and they're just not getting that point. So we have to show them. And I think that's the purpose of why we're here today." Indeed, as Bauman said, the very purpose of the entire ASL Literature and Digital Media Project was to *show*—at a large "research one" public (hearing) university and with funding from a major "global science and technology enterprise" (the Battelle Institute)—that ASL literature was a literature, perhaps like those Whos on Horton's dust speck, "no matter how small."

Yet how to get around, over, under, and through the significant barriers still in place for the funding and "publishing" of ASL literature? Do we really need an elephant with extraordinary "hearing" to help us out? Following on Dirksen Bauman's "telling and telling and telling" about ASL literature, Susan Burch also called out the various factors that might be contributing to the "resistance" many of us believed ASL (as a language and a literature) keeps encountering:

> If we keep explaining it, and we have a definition of ASL, and we feel it has a literature, what's happening that people are still having this fight and struggle at all in having the academy see it as a literature? Is it political factors, economic factors, social factors that are causing this resistance? . . . Different languages have different words describing friendship, for example, but they also don't entirely always mean the same thing—and so we have to be flexible about translation and understanding across those languages. Perhaps the people in the academy need to be a little bit

more flexible about ASL? Sometimes maybe we need to be more flexible about what the deaf community and culture has to offer? Maybe mainstream society needs to be a bit more flexible so we have some place to meet in the middle?

Once Burch pointed out the need for this between space where the academy itself might come to be "a bit more flexible" in bending in the direction of ASL (instead of requiring that ASL do all the bending), Michael Davidson, who has been involved some in the politics surrounding the development of an ASL program at his own public university (UC-San Diego), dove right into that space, as well:

> I think what Susan is saying when she talks about the economic problems of adding ASL to a curriculum, is very important, I mean language departments in the humanities are feeling increasingly marginalized, as students increasingly become monolingual English, and so language programs are to some extent hostile to the idea of adding ASL, which in my university is the largest language program studied outside of Spanish. The increase according to the Modern Language Association, recently, for two years is something like 400 percent ASL, dominating all other languages. So this is an economic and political threat to universities, so that helps to explain why there might be some resistance to admitting it as a literature. Using the term literature as the red herring to avoid confronting the kind of institutional threat that ASL may represent.

At my own university, the "red herring" place of ASL as a potential economic and political threat is indeed felt.[13]

And, given the potential economic and political threat ASL poses in the academy, added to its distance from print culture and its odd, unsettling performance on the body (a performance the academy rarely seems comfortable with unless it is bracketed off as "art"), it is little surprise that the funding for historical, cultural, artistic, and literary projects related to American Sign Language—anything outside the trees of that linguistic forest—is scant and dismal. To be sure, some projects do thrive at Gallaudet University, the cultural-intellectual center of the U.S. deaf community and perhaps even the global deaf community. The March 2006 conference at Gallaudet University, "Revolutions in Sign Language Studies: Linguistics, Literature, Literacy," is one example of a successful, well-funded event, and the National Science Foundation's recent seed award of $3.5 million over two years to establish the Science of Learning Center on Visual Language and Visual Learning (VL2) on Gallaudet's campus is yet another. But even the projects and products from Gallaudet University often don't make it much outside their gates and into the wider academic arena. For example, the second most recent entry (from 1997) in Bauman, Nelson, and Rose's appendix on "ASL Video References," *Telling Tales in ASL: From Literature to Literacy*, produced by the Gallaudet University Distance Education Program, has not yet made it into my statewide library consortium of 86 colleges and universities, as well as the State Library, of Ohio. Students and scholars cannot see and study what libraries do not purchase and make available.

Other telling stories about the politics of "publishing" and funding for ASL literature projects were also shared (and shown) at the ASL-DMP forum. Susan Burch, for example, addressed the significant need to "get a grant involved in sign language preservation" (related to old films in the Gallaudet archives), after she recounted an experience "years ago . . . watching several films, and it looked like there was a fire on the screen. The film just started to burn . . . we almost destroyed the film and so we couldn't continue to show it. Now, it no longer can be viewed and the money, again, it's a financial issue around trying to preserve it." She went on to lament the efforts she had already been involved in, as yet unfunded, to preserve these old films:

> One of the problems is how do you define the old deaf films? You could get a grant involved in language preservation but the criteria for language preservation do not often fit with ASL, with American Sign Language films. And then you could apply for an art preservation grant, but there are arguments against that too. [The funding agencies] could likely say, oh well, these are just showing so many community activities, is that really considered art? So it's a complicated issue. Some people don't understand the reason for preserving those videos. But we want to make sure that people have access to the ASL, so we do need to preserve them.

The need to find the right kind of rhetoric, to open the particular persuasive door that would facilitate the further development of ASL literature, seemed important to both critics and authors at this forum. Dirksen Bauman discussed the academic focus on "phonetic" and "phonocentrism" (which he equated with "voice") and how that has "had a great influence on the mechanics of production, printing, and all on one format—a print-based book." Addressing his own experience as the editor to the recent (and groundbreaking) volume *Signing the Body Poetic: Essays on American Sign Language Literature* (which comes with a CD-ROM containing many signed illustration of concepts discussed and literature analyzed in the print-bound version of the book), Bauman outlined an amusing, but sad, history of frustrations with "publishing" ASL literature:

> So here comes a visual language, and it really doesn't fit into the system of the mechanics of publication and production we have in the academy. . . . In 1986 [for example] there was an idea to collect articles and journals and to have them in sign, and at that time VHS was a popular medium, so we thought we'd have VHS tapes with books and we would put them out there. But that kept getting put off. Because we were frustrated with how we would put the VHS with the books. And then while we were waiting to solve that, CDs came around and we are all happy about the CDs. But the one company would produce a CD and then another company would produce the book and they weren't compatible. And that was all we had out there for the market. The marketing departments would want it only in printed form, and we were like, "No, we can't do that; how are we going to do this then?" And we would struggle some more and finally, we would just have to sell them separately. . . . And then along came DVDs, and now that we have DVDs we have that [the visual version] but we haven't had anything else. The DVDs have already been produced [of ASL literature] but the books haven't been produced to go along with the DVDs. . . . We need to reinvent publishing and distribution obviously because having the voice [and print] first isn't working for us. It needs to be visual, it needs to be with the body. Now with digital media, having that medium, we can stream video . . . it's on the verge of happening, it's going to be a big catalyst for us, having digital media.

Yet, even digital media will still present some problems in the face of modern thinking about literary products and publication. There are also "legal and technical questions we still have yet to answer," indicated the critic Peter Novak. Novak's ASL Shakespeare Project, which grew out of his 1999 dissertation project at Yale University's School of Drama, is one of the most successfully funded projects we have to date in ASL literature.[14] Novak was also excited about the potential of "burgeoning technology that can distribute some sort of standard [for and in ASL literature]," and he hoped that such technology would also advance "the need to develop more standards of what ASL literature will look like technically even." But he was also cautious about the costs of "material production" as they collided with access for the intended audiences on the basis of his experience with the ASL Shakespeare Project:

> When we did *Twelfth Night* in sign language, for example, we wanted to videotape the production to make it available for deaf students. But the Actor's Equity Association refused to give us permission to video tape because we wanted to make it accessible to people. But that production was the only translation we had because it was the only way to fix it in time and space, like a book, on videotape. So we videotaped the production, and they said they would fine us $10,000 and never allow the theater company to produce an Equity contract again, unless we gave them the videotapes. So, I sent them the video tapes. . . . Anyway, we're now making this available on DVD, and will soon be able to do that, but we still have to pay the actors and everyone who was involved. And that cost will probably be $15,000 and so trying to get the unions to understand what sign language literature is, trying to legally make definitions that say this translation should be able to be available to anybody who the authors want it to be available to . . . but we don't have the rights over that, because the individual bodies of the people who performed it belong to a different union. So, it brings up a whole host of questions about material production and how material production is involved in the process of making ASL literature.

Issues of material production and access for an audience that has typically not been anywhere near the top of the mainstream intellectual or socioeconomic ladder (deaf audiences) are also folded up in the wrinkles surrounding what film, video, and digital media can do with a three-dimensional act like ASL literature in a flat two-dimensional format.

Technology, particularly film technologies, argued some of the authors, was as much a problem as it might be a solution for ASL literature. Peter Cook (of Flying Words Project) explained his "love-hate" relationship with cameras in particular:

> Kenny and I have tons of experience with technology, and a lot of it's been bad, and the reason is that when you have the camera, it's still a 2-D form. It's flat. In our work, Kenny and I, we are really creative. We use movie techniques. We see something in the film and movies, and we do that shot in reverse, we use that technology if you had one person capturing it on film and then you do the editing, maybe there were two

cameras, but we're only editing from one camera, because we are doing two characters, back and forth at a very fast pace. So it doesn't work. And technology doesn't allow us to use that technique. It actually limits us. When we look at our work, we're not very pleased with it. So, we tell the camera person to stay in one place, but they want to move and be artistic and move the camera, and we really have constant arguments with the camera technicians because they don't want to stay in one place. We've been really frustrated.

Peter Novak went on to give a specific example of the obsession with editing in filmed versions of ASL performances, and he did so using a scene from the *Twelfth Night* production (for the ASL Shakespeare Project) that Peter Cook was involved in:

I saw Peter doing this one or two-minute song, performing it, and between the different camera angles and editing, there were 72 different edits, in two minutes. Seventy-two edits of Peter going back and forth, back and forth, from one shot to the next shot, from camera to different camera angle, and it just makes, you know, ASL artists, look complicated.

"Yes, it does [make ASL literature look more complicated]," added Kenny Lerner (of Flying Words Project). But he also concluded, in reference to the extensively edited video-poem, that, "You know this was a very exciting poem [performed live] that instantly became very boring."

Kenny Lerner also explained how Flying Words Project has actually remastered certain film techniques into its ASL performances so that a certain performance will conceivably play better on film. In this way, the artists have already begun to adapt their art for the medium. What is really needed, however, quipped several members of the forum, is not so much the ASL Digital Media Project but the ASL Hologram Project.

The Archives and the Anthology: Creating a Digital Collection of ASL Literature

Whether one is working in digital media or hologram form, collaboration is needed to construct an anthology of ASL literature. As the authors and critics at the ASL-DMP forum made clear, American Sign Language (ASL), like all other sign languages around the world, does not have a written form. Nor does it desire one. The camera is as close as we might get to the capturing of a codex for ASL literature. In fact, a unique and ironic core feature of ASL—and other sign languages, as well—is its characteristic "oral" nature (even though it is a language used and developed primarily by deaf people, who are typically not at all "oral" when using it).[15] While it does not make use of the mouth or speech as its location for locution, ASL does take place, as other "oral literatures" have and do, in present, real-time, embodied linguistic interaction. ASL also takes place in space—a dimension no other written/print based language occupies.[16]

In fact, this "orality" and its nonprint existence in only visual-spatial dimensions has often operated to keep ASL out of the circle of accepted "modern" or "natural" languages, a point I make in the second chapter of this book. Even today, the literary possibilities of ASL are still often questioned by faculty and policymakers who have tried to determine whether ASL can be used and accepted to fulfill a "foreign/modern language" requirement in high schools and colleges in the United States. In an attempt to answer this question, Sherman Wilcox, of the University of New Mexico, and Joy Kreeft Peyton, of the Center for Applied Linguistics (CAL), have built a Web site and a working paper that address the ways in which ASL is (and isn't) a "foreign language." One issue that ASL continually faces when being evaluated as an option for "foreign language" credits or requirements at schools and colleges is the myth that there is no "literature" in ASL. The development of a digital anthology would illustrate and make accessible the rich and diverse body of authors, events, texts, and tropes that constitute the ASL literature, and perhaps that would put this question and issue to rest.

Yet, a digital anthology of ASL literature has more purposes than just to address doubts about the validity and features of the language itself to "outsiders" who have often not attempted to learn the language. Such a collection would also be a valuable learning tool for ASL classes that are already in existence at schools and colleges across the United States. As discussed in chapter 2, enrollment in ASL classes is up an astonishing 432 percent over a six-year period (1996–2002), as measured in a survey of foreign-language enrollments by the Association of Departments of Foreign Languages (Welles). These new courses need materials specifically related to *literature* in that language, especially at the more advanced levels of instruction, so that they do indeed match up with other modern language instruction and emphasis. There are several—although not many and surely not enough—DVDs and VHS formats that present ASL literature, particularly storytelling and poetry/performance.[17] But there is no resource that unites the history, breadth, and depth of ASL literary works.

Such a resource would not only be valuable to students learning ASL as their second language but also reflect back into the community of ASL authors, performers, storytellers, and poets, encouraging even more literary production in this visual-spatial language. Almost one hundred years ago, the president of the National Association for the Deaf (NAD), George Veditz, made use of the emerging technologies of film to both record and advance his native language, ASL. The year was 1910, and Veditz amassed $5,000 (no small sum at that time) in order to produce the "Sign Masters" series. Roughly a hundred years later, a project that would claim much the same mission as Veditz's 1910 vision is needed; the aim in this new project would be to "fix and give" ASL a distinct literature of its own by means of digital technology and thereby to produce the equivalent of "books" and "literary works" in this unique visual-spatial language.

The Modern Language Association (MLA) has itself recently shown an interest in American Sign Language. A special three-session event, "ASL, MLA, and the Academy," at the 2004 MLA convention, in Philadelphia, was designated as the "Presidential Forum" for that convention. Development is also currently under way to create an "ASL Discussion Group" within the MLA Governance and annual convention structures and to make the American Sign Language Teachers Association (ASLTA) an affiliate of the MLA. In sum, the time for the development of a significant literary research and learning tool like "The Digital Encyclopedia of American Sign Language Literature" seems to have arrived.

Other national (American) developments over the past two decades have all been building toward such an anthology. In the mid-1990s, Gallaudet University established a Department of ASL and Deaf Studies. In March 2006, it hosted a phenomenally successful conference, along with the Gallaudet University Press Institute, called "Revolutions in Sign Language Studies: Linguistics, Literature, Literacy." Students at Gallaudet University grow up with technology in and on their hands (and some, with cochlear implants, in their heads, as well), and established scholars at Gallaudet University, both deaf and hearing, are often devoted to the study of deafness, Deaf culture, deaf community, deaf history, deaf education, and sign languages both national and global. Both students and scholars there are naturally positioned—even poised—to engage in and lead on the development of this project.

While Gallaudet has developed its own Department of ASL Literacy and Deaf Studies in the past two decades, other universities have also recently established ASL courses for "foreign-language" credits, Deaf Studies minors and majors, and even, in three cases, teacher-training programs for ASL instruction. The American Sign Language Teacher's Association (ASLTA) has also recently formed its own independent organization (remaining connected to but now also separate from the National Association for the Deaf), and it oversees certification and professional development of ASL teachers, lobbies for state bills to have ASL recognized as a language, and addresses questions about the appropriateness of ASL as a "foreign language" in secondary and higher education.

"The Digital Anthology of American Sign Language Literature" project suggested here in some way parallels the development of the Multimedia Dictionary of American Sign Language that Dr. Sherman Wilcox has been leading on for years and the new *Gallaudet Dictionary of American Sign Language* (Valli), published in 2006. It might also take as its digital inspiration the ASL Shakespeare Project led by Dr. Peter Novak.

The development and use of a digital anthology of American Sign Language literature has significant potential to impact many specific and general academic fields. The project would, for example, advance research and scholarship in ASL and the "triple L": linguistics, literacy, and literature. We have no comprehensive resource of American Sign Language literature to date. We have no single text to tell us about key events in ASL literature (e.g., the National Technical Institute for the Deaf's first ASL Literature conference at Rochester Institute of Technology, in 1991) or to give us collected bios of and significant texts from ASL storytellers and poets as diverse as Nathie Marbury, Mindy and Theron, Manny Hernandez, the Flying Words Project, Ben Bahan, C. J. Jones, and Werner Zorn (but a few examples). We have no history recorded of ASL literature—other than the nine-page "Timeline of ASL Literature Development" offered as an appendix in Bauman, Nelson, and Rose's *Signing the Body Poetic* collection (241–50). Scholars and critics who have done some research in ASL storytelling, poetry, or performance have discussed such things as "cinematic technique," "classifiers," "metaphor," "rhyme," and "frame" and how print English literature has influenced any given ASL author. But these studies have never been gathered into one resource or at one location for the average audience, student, or scholar of ASL to explore and enjoy. The implications of the lack of such a literary resource on ASL literacy should be obvious, but allow me to press the point with a simple comparison: how would we talk about literacy in English without literature in English from which to draw and build that literacy?

Imagine, too, teaching ASL as a language without also having a literary reference resource. The potential for a digital anthology of ASL literature to further enhance ASL instruction, particularly at the advanced level, is considerable. Courses in advanced ASL literature do exist (e.g., at Gallaudet University; one is being developed at Ohio State University)—but they are rare. And sometimes one can run into a workshop on ASL literature (often given by Sam Supulla, Ben Bahan, or the now deceased Clayton Valli). But, again, no comprehensive text exists to guide (or alter or advance) such instruction.

Finally, broader fields will gain and grow from this encounter with ASL literature. For example, a digital anthology of ASL literature will have much to offer the broader field of digital media studies as the predominantly hearing/speaking people in this field work to engage, capture, digitize, edit, and frame the utterly visual, spatial, and three-dimensional domain that is American Sign Language. This is far more complex than mixing audio tracks or dubbing or clipping frames, and even the daunting challenge of getting the frame and angle of any signed and silent utterance "best" (let alone "correct") will surely usher in some new approaches and critical awareness for those who work in digital media. Through contact with and awareness of an encyclopedia of ASL literature, the larger fields of literary, language, film, and rhetorical studies (not just those focused on ASL) will also have the potential to engage new and changed ideas about concepts sometimes used in the critical lexicon of these fields, such as "vision," "voice," "visual literacy," "space," "frame," "the gaze," "presence," "embodied language," "utterance," and "identity." "Literature" itself might even change, reinvented perhaps as *sign-ature,* a new word and construct on the language-yielding hands of the ASL author.

4

Narrating Deaf Lives

Placing Deaf Autobiography,
Biography, and Documentary

Both Jan-Kåre Breivik (*Deaf Identities in the Making*) and I (*Lend Me Your Ear; Literacy and Deaf People*) have recently suggested that deaf lives and "writing" placed together, particularly in relation to their own life stories, have not been common or even probably condoned. Breivik summarizes the risks, reward, and resources deaf people face when narrating a deaf life via writing—using a language often not their "own" or not entirely comfortable or successful for them—and points out that deaf people are often "engaged in identification processes where the stakes are high. To succeed in their identification endeavors, they are often restricted to a limited number of alternatives . . . because literacy has been and still is less than widespread" (2–3). Some of the standard earlier written autobiographies of or by deaf people came from postlingually, well-educated, literary-minded deaf people—the English poet and professor David Wright's *Deafness: An Autobiography* (1969) and the former *Chicago Sun-Times* journalist Harvey Kisor's *What's That Pig Outdoors?* (1990), for example. (These are also by white men.) And, as Brievik points out, "their stories often highlight the faculty of reading and writing as a specific trait of their lives and as a means of connecting to or 'making it' in the hearing world" (3). In highlighting such connections and traits with writing, the work by deaf autobiographers like Wright and Kisor constitutes the way in which "writing is always the hero of writing," a clever point made by the literacy scholar Thomas Newkirk (1997) in a study on the performance of self in student writing.

Yet things are changing—and processes and products for literacy, as well as ways of expressing life experiences and stories, are among those changes. Digital media, video, and film documentary are all technologies increasingly used to convey life stories. These new and increasingly visual ways of auto-expression mark what Breivik claims is an "autobiographical trend |that| is both a global trait of modern life . . . and reflects the specific transformations within the Deaf worlds" (3). The "Deaf Lives" series that I instigated and edit for Gallaudet University Press aims to capture, reflect, and "publish" these new, diverse, and innovatively expressive ways of narrating deaf lives. The series and a conference hosted by the Gallaudet University Press Institute in November 2004 on "Narrating Deaf Lives" (some of the papers from that conference were later published in a special Winter 2007 issue of *Sign Language Studies*) all gesture toward inclusive and innovative ways of placing deaf lives in multiple genres, formats, and purposes. These placements are, often as not, *between* places as the authors typically write their way through the anxieties of identity and identification (with their deafness, with the deaf community); they work to identify the anxieties of their very betweenity.

The "Deaf Lives" series and the "Narrating Deaf Lives" conference celebrate and illustrate deaf lives of interesting and infinite variety.[1] As the first volume in the "Deaf Lives" series, Oliva's text is *her* story, her own autobiography, but the collected and contextualized narratives of nearly eighty other "solitaires" (as she calls them) are mixed in. Oliva's book, *Alone in the Mainstream: A Deaf Woman Remembers Public School* (2004), innovatively blends personal narrative with interview-based qualitative research and addresses the need to have the effects of mainstreaming deaf and hard-of-hearing students explored by the adults who have long since been through that process. When Oliva's manuscript first arrived at Gallaudet University Press, it was not a historical biography and not really a memoir or autobiography, in the strictest sense of the terms. It was not clear-cut academic research, either. It fell between many cracks. The "Deaf Lives" series was conceived as a place for these crack-dwellers—as well as for more traditional biography or autobiography about, or involving, deaf lives.

The "Deaf Lives" series, the November 2004 "Narrating Deaf Lives" conference, and the special Winter 2007 issue of *Sign Language Studies* that explores the development of new deaf autobiography, biography, and documentary all aim to create a space where it is imagined and hoped that deaf lives will no longer be—or will no longer be writing from—"alone in the mainstream." It is a place where, as the anthropologist Frank Bechter has recently claimed in a discussion on "the deaf convert culture," "the world is made of deaf lives. The task of deaf narratives, or perhaps of deaf culture itself, is 'to see deaf lives' when others—even one's deaf friends—do not" (2008: 60).

In the six sections that follow, this chapter takes up that task as it offers a view of deaf narratives and a sighting (and citing) of deaf lives. The
chapter begins with an extended rhetorical analysis over the (authorial)
production and (audience) reception of a controversial Public Broadcasting System (PBS) documentary, *Through Deaf Eyes*. Following from
the tensions of documenting a (deaf) subject, the second section takes
up the between space of deaf biography—as a cultural and/or individual
narrative—where identity politics between who "tells" the narrative of a
deaf life and who reads or receives such a narrative makes every (deaf)
biography fraught with anxiety. In the third section, the haunting subject
of Helen Keller—a subject that is autobiographically and biographically
blended, both deaf and blind—serves as a specific site and case of rhetorical anxiety over identification. Creatively, (deaf) writing also anxiously
works the hyphen between self and other. Working this hyphen is a place
that three (deaf) fiction writers find themselves in as they explore, in the
fourth section, the kaleidoscopic possibilities of placing selves and subjects, autobiographical or fictional, in "a world where people are made up
of Deafness, or in one where Deafness is made up of people." Whichever
world the deaf subject writes from or appears in, the diversity of deaf lives
becomes even more apparent when deaf narratives flourish; such diversity
is the subject of the fifth section. Finally, in the sixth section, I turn to the
future possibilities both of and for author, audience, and subject in narrating deaf lives.

Lava in the Cracks: The *Through Deaf Eyes* Documentary

The "Narrating Deaf Lives" conference in November 2004 ended in a very
hot place. I will begin there. Larry Hott of Florentine Films, the producer
and director, took the stage at the end of three days of presentations and
readings on biographical and autobiographical narratives of deaf lives.[2]
Hott was accompanied by Jean Bergey, his chief adviser and the curator
of the Smithsonian exhibit "History Through Deaf Eyes"; Dr. Harry Lang
(NTID-RIT), a consultant from the Deaf community; and some key ex-
ecutives from WETA (a Washington, D.C. PBS station) and The Corpora-
tion for Public Broadcasting (CPB). Surrounded by friends and associates,
only one of whom was deaf (Harry Lang), Hott proceeded to chronicle
the development of a planned two-hour PBS documentary on "history
through deaf eyes"; in his presentation, he included sample themes, issues,

and even some potential footage from the film that was just then beginning production. His remarks, as reproduced in the Winter 2007 issue of
Sign Language Studies, centered on the question "How do we approach a
film about the history of deafness?"

The answer to this question became the subject of an intense and often controversial barrage of follow-up questions and comments from the
audience in Gallaudet University's Swindells Auditorium that Friday afternoon in early November 2004. And this heated discussion also characterized many of the issues and elements—ethical, logical, emotional,
cultural, historical, scholarly, and attitudinal—that had pulsed throughout
all the sessions and discussions of the three-day conference. Yet, the pulse
ran considerably hotter and more urgent during this closing session, as
indicated by the anxious, and sometimes angry, comments and questions
from audience members about largely representational issues surrounding the "documentation" of deaf lives in this film project: who represents
whom; the potential lasting impact the film would have (how deaf people would be "seen" through it); the role of the film's advisory board; and
what it meant for a (hearing) filmmaker to document (deaf) lives.

In a senior research project completed for the annual Ohio State University Undergraduate Research Forum (May 2005), my student advisee
Jessica Stewart conducted an interpretive study of the texts and transcripts
from the "Narrating Deaf Lives" conference. This student added yet another layer of representation, and another between space, as a young adult
who had recently lost a significant amount of her hearing and who was
writing both critical and autobiographical texts. She attempted to engage
material (through transcripts) from an event that she had not attended
but for which she still believed herself to be an audience.

Working as a Comparative Studies major and a Disability Studies minor, she created a project, "Interpreting Deaf Lives," that won first prize
in the Humanities division. Stewart's analysis focused on three texts/
sessions at the conference;[3] for her audience presentation at the forum,
she created a "skit" from the transcript of the final Friday session where
Mr. Hott outlined the development of the "History Through Deaf Eyes"
film. The skit she created merits reproducing here because it offers context for not only Hott's presentation that day but for other issues that
threaded throughout the three days of the conference concerning the
promise and politics of "narrating deaf lives." Here, with her permis-
sion, is the skit she wrote based on the captioner's transcripts from the
conference session:

HOTT'S HISTORY: A SKIT IN TWO SCENES
Scene I: Setting the Stage

Harry Lang: Good afternoon, everyone. The "History Through Deaf Eyes" exhibit started back at the first Deaf Way in 1988. We really began with just three core ideas. We wanted to get the notion of the language, identity, and struggle that Deaf people have experienced. The project became the center of controversy, so we developed four conceptual ideas as time went on to accommodate the many requests and ideas that were pouring in about how the project was being handled.

The revised key concepts are: formation of community, language, and identity, community building, awareness, access and change.

Letters like these came from all over the United States. . . .

Audience Member 1: "Please don't exclude my child, please don't exclude me."

Audience Member 2: We should be focusing more on the future! Stop dwelling on the past!

Audience Member 3: I'm concerned; I don't feel that this exhibit should dwell on the oral, [or] Total Communication issue.

Harry Lang: I'm now going to introduce you to our esteemed director, Mr. Larry Hott. He has won countless awards, including Emmys, Academy Award nominations, a Peabody, a Fulbright, to name a few. He has worked with PBS on many films and documentaries before this, and we are honored to have him collaborate on this project with us as well. Larry?

(Applause)

Larry Hott: Thank you, I am pleased to have this opportunity. When WETA asked me to do this, I was honored. Projects like this take years to put together. I live close to the Clarke School in Massachusetts, and I know a little about Deaf Education, and so I knew that the story was bound to contain drama, tension, characters, and emotion. In fact, I was well aware that if we were not careful, we could be stepping into a hornet's nest. Of course this sounds like good television to me. It's the classic American saga—complete with plot points; the rise up and the sudden fall and resulting crisis and the final triumph, with the new threat at the end.

Narrator: At this point, Larry begins to show clips from various TV shows like *Magnum, P.I.*, *Picket Fences*, to some rare footage from George Veditz in 1913. For the most part the audience remains attentive and quiet, but it's when Hott introduces a Deaf filmmaker, Renee Visco, that they begin to shift in their seats. When the clip ends, the audience erupts in applause.

(Applause)

Hott: (stunned) *This* is now my favorite clip.

Harry Lang: OK, now we have some important people from our public television station here in Washington, and we've planned to conduct a focus group of sorts. I'm going to introduce Mary Stewart, the vice-president of communications for WETA.

Mary Stewart: Good afternoon. Publicity is about bringing folks to the screen, but outreach is about bringing hearts to the issues.

What should this film do, beyond the air?

We have a specific publicity project aimed at making sure that the Deaf community is aware of the program; here again we need your help in making sure our plans are extensive and appropriate. If you would like to make comments, come down to the center of the room, and tell us what your viewing habits of PBS are, i.e., musical, historical, etc.?

Scene II: "Not Exactly What Was Supposed to Happen"

Audience Member 4: I'm confused. What are we talking about here? The film or outreach to the community? I commend your work, Mr. Hott, but I think you need to determine your audience. For example, is the content of the film being portrayed for the hearing to hearing, or Caucasian to Caucasian audience? This is problematic.

Hott: That is an excellent question. Both hearing audience and the Deaf audience will be profiled. We don't want to make the mistake of saying this is a history as told by hearing people.

Audience Member 5: I teach a course entitled "The Images of Deaf People in the Media." This is your opportunity to do it right for the first time, and I hope you're not doing this just because it's the first time. The titles may need to be revised, that is, the issue here is that the movie will describe us as opposed to us describing ourselves.

You have an obligation, a responsibility to us. You may make a profit, you may receive rewards, but we have to live with how you describe and define us.

I need to know that Deaf people are involved at every level of the project; this is what is important to us.

(Applause)

Hott: Thank you, and I agree with everything you've said. I am working with an advisory committee at Gallaudet, which is headed by Harry Lang. There are over 30 people involved. We can't satisfy everybody. By the same token, we don't want to make a film by committee, which becomes bland and boring. Our hope is to make an exciting document that opens up the Deaf world, the Deaf culture, to the rest of America.

PIERCE COLLEGE LIBRARY

> *Audience 5:* I'm not sure if, pardon the pun, you're really hearing us. You really need to work side by side with a Deaf person to really understand the Deaf world, the conflicts, the history. Not a hearing person who knows a lot about the Deaf culture—that's not going to cut it.
>
> *Hott:* Could I get a stiff martini up here? So, as I was saying . . . I will be working with Harry Lang and . . .

Although he never got his martini, Hott's documentary film *Through Deaf Eyes* was successfully released and aired on many national PBS stations on March 21, 2007. And Jessica Stewart's ethnographic skit continues to write itself as the heat and anxiety around deaf/hearing identity politics generated from this early conference preview and discussion about the documentary in November 2004 still ripples through the (deaf) blogosphere. DeafRead.com collects commentary from (largely, though not entirely) deaf bloggers (in printed English) and vloggers (typically in American Sign Language and sometimes, though not often, with English glosses); upon release of the *Through Deaf Eyes* documentary, DeafRead.com hosted a contest for the top ten blogs and vlogs responding to the film (http://www.deafread.com/blog/?p=109). Commentary among the "finalists" for this contest echoes the anxious quarrel about who "owns," narrates, and represents for, about, and through deaf lives.

For example, a DeafRead.com finalist's comment, titled "A Hearing Person's View of *Through Deaf Eyes*" and posted at "Deaf Pagan Crossroads," argues that "this program was intended primarily for a hearing audience in order to bring about more awareness of Deaf history, culture, and communication, and in that it was well balanced and informative" (http://deaf-pagan.com/2007/03/26/a-hearing-persons-view-of-through-deaf-eyes/). This blogger identifies the documentary as a film "through deaf eyes" but apparently for the viewing pleasure (and edification) of hearing people.

In a similar view, Mark Drolsbaugh's blog, "Deaf Culture Online," features a response entitled "*Through Deaf Eyes*: This Is Only the Beginning," in which he suggests that "the PBS documentary *Through Deaf Eyes* was a groundbreaking success" but goes on to qualify and clarify his judgment on the basis of the perceived accuracy of the representation of deaf people as "normal" in the film:

> Yes, I know there are complaints galore. Yes, I know there were factual errors and omissions. Yes, I know that the pathological approach towards deafness ate up a significant chunk of time, especially at the end.

Regardless, I give this show two thumbs up. Not just for what it accomplished, but mostly for what it *started*.

First and foremost, I was doing cartwheels because this was the first time in recent memory that I recall seeing Deaf people portrayed as *normal*. (I can't stomach any of those sappy, patronizing, "Aw, look-at-the-poor-deaf-kid" stories.) (http://www.deaf-culture-online.com/through-deaf-eyes.html)

Also riveted by the portrayal of "normalcy" presented in the film, an anonymous blogger, "*ist*," who identifies as "sociologist, socio-historist [*sic*] and an epistemologist studying law and its circumstances" and whose blog is titled "You Are You and Your Circumstances," signifies relieved praise for the film. This anonymous blogger's praise is based not only on a sense of rhetorical identification ("through deaf eyes") but perhaps, just as tellingly, on how well the reviewer believed the film addressed "our society's much-needed understanding on Deafness." Identifying the documentary as educational and a good representation, *ist* wrote that:

I applaud the National Endowment for the Humanities for making this film a reality and especially everybody who contributed to this film. It is a wonderful balance of diverse Deaf people expressing their testimonies, experience, and their Deaf 'way' . . . said a little prayer that this film will be a good representation and understanding of, for, and with, the Deaf culture. It is been too long.

This film has given me a sense of relief. . . . The film brought a smile to our society's much-needed understanding on Deafness. The film truly has captured its true intent; through deaf eyes. [italics mine]

And so, bringing "a smile to our society's much-needed understanding on Deafness," the chorus continues: while this is a film represented "through deaf eyes," educationally, it is *for* hearing people.

Still another finalist blogger in the contest points to the collapse of deaf/hearing identity or history that he believes was achieved in the film. David Evans, from DeafDC.com, suggests that one rhetorical goal of the documentary becomes perhaps to demonstrate the world not just "through Deaf eyes" but also, and just as important, "through American eyes":

I thought overall "Through Deaf Eyes" accomplished quite a bit. The one objective I thought succeeded for both deaf and hearing audiences alike was the demonstration, whether through the historical/cultural narratives of Douglas Baynton, John VanCleve, and John Schuchman, or the anecdotes of the Gannons and Garretsons, *that you cannot separate deaf history from American history.* The overarching themes of religion, nativism, civil rights, and education are all parts of the American story. I think too often people see American history and don't know anything about Deaf history, or they know quite a bit about Deaf history, but fail to see the connections to the bigger picture. Whether it's AG Bell and his involvement with education, eugenics, and the 19th century backlash against immigration (which probably will come as a big surprise for hearing viewers who only know Bell as the father of the telephone), or Lindbergh taking people on "deaf rides," or the segregation and linguistic differences between blacks and whites (whether the language is English or ASL), Deaf history is American history, and vice versa. (http://www.deafdc.com/ blog/david-evans/2007-03-22/through-my-eyes-a-not-so-brief-critique-of-through-deaf-eyes/) [italics mine]

The rhetorical power of American history, nationalism, and myths as now double-visioned "through Deaf Eyes"—and therein deaf people's capability to carry what W. E. B. DuBois famously termed a "double consciousness"—also does not escape another finalist blogger, Carl Schroeder, of "Ka'lalau's Korner." In his bold and brief commentary, Schroeder speculates, in just one hundred words:

Through Deaf Eyes is itself a new myth, a metaphorical way of giving authority to a particular story. More importantly, it is an expression of the particular tradition's notion of metaphysics. Manualism (the use of American Sign Language) and oralism (the use of speech language), its major spin-off, both imagine the world as division. Our major stories are Deaf people who broke with the status quo. From our perspective on top of the wall we can see things through our eyes. We can see both sides of the wall. We can switch between both sides and understand many things. (http://carl-schroeder.blogspot.com/2007/03/written-critique-in-100-words-through.html)

The between space of double consciousness and the ability to see "both sides of the wall"—to see "through deaf eyes" but also to relate to "a hearing audience"—constructs a common place for deaf people's responses to this documentary.

Also suspicious of the myth of the deaf lives that are narrated through the "eyes" of this documentary, and perhaps working to read the film from a double consciousness, is the blogger from "*todos la vie*." Anonymous (in an Anglicized name) but with a picture that identifies her visually, this blogger titles and opens her commentary on the film with a quotation from Anais Nin: "We don't see things as they are, we see them as we are." We identify not just *what* but also *as*, we see. She goes on to explain:

> I never thought that I was deaf first but the show, "Through Deaf Eyes," PBS put that to the forefront with a banner "You have a disability, yet look at our progress we've done through the years for ya." . . .
>
> They discussed the Milan conference forcing the dark ages of deaf education in America and sending off sign language to the trash bin only to bring it back out of respite. The medical viewpoint of deaf people exists only in the world of people who do not know what/ who deaf people are. They only know what they see (and hear), and that doesn't necessarily mean they see or hear us. They still think that we are to be fixed, and that's the underlying projected tone of the whole program. . . .
>
> Through deaf eyes, grasping us as a whole, also means seeing accomplishments that we saw and linger in, but I saw none. What the producers did was put a shine on "shared experiences," of American deaf history in the perspective of the obvious questions asked of the producers off stage, "are you okay that you are not hearing in the ear and speaking in the mouth?" (http://blog.deafread.com/deafdiscourse/2007/03/24/we-only-see-what-we-are/)

For this anonymous (in written signature but not in visual space) blogger, the act of identification of, and through, shared experience—as represented in the documentary—masks the anxiety of deaf people's not-quite-normal placement in the world.

Finally, even Bobbie Beth Scoggins, president of the National Association of the Deaf (NAD), posts an official vlog at the NAD Web site that scripts the very "progress" myth that *todos la vie* attempts to smudge the shine on:

> I am delighted that PBS deemed the program *Through Deaf Eyes* an important historical documentary worth airing nationally. . . .
>
> NAD and its members hope that this documentary brought forth a greater understanding and awareness of deaf culture and history to the

general public, and gives us as a community another opportunity to look at ourselves as a rich and diverse group. The film inspired each of us to determine how we can work together to provide a more positive synergy as we move forward in defining ourselves as both a culture and as individuals.

That is very relevant to the NAD theme, "Together we move forward!" (http://blogs.nad.org/president/?p=6)

Moving forward, then, there is much lava flowing in the cracks of contemporary deaf identity; the ways this heat will shape the landscape in both the present and future will also be likely to shape the ways we think about, write about, and produce narratives of deaf lives in the way that NAD president Scoggins suggests here at the dawn of the 21st century—"as both a culture and as individuals."

Deaf Biography as Cultural and Individual Narrative

Identity politics around who produces and "tells" the narrative of a deaf life—as well as who the audience for such narratives might be—concerned many of the other presenters, as well, and consumed entire sessions, especially those on biographical work, at the "Narrating Deaf Lives" conference. Perhaps better than almost anyone at the event, the historian and biographer Harry Lang (who also played a role in the "Hott's History Skit" presented earlier) summarized the intricacies and elements of biographical research and writing that involve deaf subjects—as individuals or as cultural cases, or both. In his essay for the special "Narrating Deaf Lives" issue of *Sign Language Studies (SLS)*, Lang offers his "reflections on biographical research and writing" by taking us briefly on a chronological trip through the development of his four currently published biographies: *Silence of the Spheres: The Deaf Experience in the History of Science; Deaf Persons in the Arts and Sciences: A Biographical Dictionary* (with his wife, Bonnie Meath-Lang); *A Phone of Our Own: The Deaf Insurrection Against Ma Bell*; and *Edmund Booth, Deaf Pioneer*. Lang's essay in the *SLS* volume also makes use of three current biographical projects he has under way: about the Deaf teacher-poet and leader Robert F. Panara; about the Hispanic Deaf educator and leader Robert R. Davila (written with Oscar Cohen and Joseph Fischgrund);[4] and about the Civil War as reflected through many different "deaf eyes" of the time.

In his discussion of his own past and in-progress work, which also incorporates a discussion about how he teaches his students to write (deaf) biographies, Lang effectively outlines many ethical, scholarly, emotional, and physical advantages and limitations in the construction of deaf biography. He addresses, for example, the necessity of considering one's purpose and "writing voice" for narrating a deaf life; the politics of publishing with presses and editors who are—or, more often, aren't—familiar with Deaf culture and history; the use (and abuse) of potential secondary sources; the complexity of representing and identifying "Deaf experience" in either individual or community frames; the gift (and curse) of using media and technology in one's research around deaf lives; the risks and cautions of influence and interactions, particularly with oral histories; the place of visual material (e.g., photographs) in biographical narratives; the fine, and often anxious, line between fact and folklore; and the importance of finding a good lead and angle for your narrative about a deaf life. As a professor of math and physics and a research faculty member at the National Technical Institute of the Deaf (NTID), part of the Rochester Institute for Technology (RIT), Lang's own career as teacher, researcher, historical biographer, speaker, and leader in the Deaf community offers an excellent lead and angle into the intricacies—and sophistication—inherent in constructing biographical narratives of deaf lives.[5]

Susan Plann also attends to the cultural and individual nature of biographically narrating deaf lives, but her focus is on the nineteenth century, specifically on Spanish deaf girls and women at the Spanish National Deaf-mute School. Her essay in the *Sign Language Studies* special issue offers a few "portraits" from her recent book from Gallaudet University Press, *The Spanish National Deaf School: Portraits From the Nineteenth Century*. Her biographical work in attempting to paint these portraits begins with an admission that it is "difficult to learn much about the lives of [these] Deaf girls" because they were simply not considered important at that time—both because of their gender and because of their deafness (168). The overlay of their identities matters here as it doubly places them in cracks between dominant worlds. Their individuality is thus largely lost, and Plann must work to construct their "collective lives." In her construction of these collective lives, Plann offers such details as a typical schoolday and week for a 19th-century deaf girl enrolled in *labores* classes at the Spanish National Deaf-mute School. We learn, for example, that not only did these girls learn a variety of labor skills, but they performed much labor for the school itself (sewing, washing, ironing) while they also spent about eighteen hours per week in academic subjects.

We also learn of one important figure, Marcelina Ruiz Ricote, who has provided a source and historical insight into the lives of these Spanish deaf girls; Ruiz Ricote was the school's only woman teacher (and hearing), and she once delivered the commencement address at the school's graduation ceremony. In her commencement address, Ruiz Ricote, whom Plann argues was quite visionary and ahead of her time, made clear her displeasure with the deaf girls' instruction and their training solely in base labor skills (*labores*); she offered suggestions that they be trained in more "useful, marketable skills," such as drawing, lithography, painting, sculpture, and printing (also skills that made the young deaf girl more attractive for marriage). We come to see some of deaf girls' lives in a 19th-century Spanish deaf school through the institution's collective record of its daily and weekly activities (but not through records of its individuals) and, ironically, too, through the spoken words and progressive vision of one of their female hearing teachers.[6] These deaf lives come to us, then, as do many in history, through only institutional records or "as told to," via the lips, and pens, of (typically hearing) others.

A Haunting Subject: Helen Keller

While some deaf subjects are arguably hard to locate or document or have stories that come with considerable controversy surrounding such issues as who tells them (who author-izes them) and who receives them (who their audiences are), Helen Keller is an autobiographical and biographical "deaf" subject whose authority, audience, and mere presence in the larger landscape of deaf lives has perhaps been overwritten. It is hard to discuss the narration of deaf lives without running into, through, or around Helen Keller. She haunts the biographical, autobiographical, and documentary halls of the house of deaf lives. There are many mirrors in these halls as well.[7]

An entire panel at the "Narrating Deaf Lives" conference was devoted—although with some ironies—to Helen Keller, the universal, if not also omnipresent and omniscient, icon for both deaf and blind people since the 19th century. Rachel Hartig's essay in the *SLS* volume begins with a central question: "How does the person living with a difference most effectively cross the cultural divide and explain himself/herself to mainstream society?" (177). Hartig takes this as the central question raised by the French author Yvonne Pitrois in her biography of Helen Keller, published in 1922: *Une nuit rayonnante: Helen Keller* (A Shining Night: Helen Keller). Pitrois herself was also deaf-blind and fairly well known in her own country, and she engaged in social service and biographical studies throughout her lifetime. Hartig explores the unique biographical exchange between Pitrois and Keller, documenting Pitrois's affinities and agreements with Keller, as well as her ethical disagreements with Keller's performances on vaudeville stages.

It was Pitrois's own concern, characterized as sometimes harsh, about Keller's vaudeville profile to which Keller herself responded in a letter she wrote to Pitrois about the 1922 biography. Considerably different emotions and ethics are expressed about Keller's theatrical presence by these two deaf-blind women on two continents in the early 20th century. And it is these differences that allow Hartig to examine the way in which the particular individual and cultural contexts of Keller's and Pitrois's lives might have led them to different stances on the value of theatrical performance in acquainting, if not also educating, early-20th-century audiences with disability and difference. As both audience and author, then, Hartig offers her own biographical reading of an interesting biographical exchange in which the biographical subject can (and does) "talk back" to the biographer and their cultural and experiential differences are shared as they "dialogue on diversity." Hartig's essay constructs a remarkable and dynamic triangular biographical framework for reading Helen Keller's life, yet again.[8]

Georgina Kleege also offers a dynamic and provocative biographical framework for viewing and reading Helen Keller's life. Kleege's text in the *SLS* volume, "Blind Rage: An Open Letter to Helen Keller," defies simple generic categorization, however.[9] It is biographical in that it recounts elements of Helen Keller's own documented life. But it is also considerably autobiographical in that Kleege (who signs off as "GK")—as a blind writer, teacher, and scholar—writes a letter to Helen "because I'm having a bad day." The bad (snow) day offers Kleege a chance to explore her own position in the "overcoming" and "cheery cripple" role that she blames Helen, in large part, for having left her with as a successful, albeit blind, woman. The trials of negotiating a typical day at an urban university with snow blanketed over it provide Kleege with an angle into an interrogation of Keller's own life, while it also supplies a wedge into her own life. Kleege's "letter" to Helen Keller layers fiction with performance, mixed flavorfully with dashes of biography and autobiography.

At the center of this multiple-genre text sits rage—blind rage—as Kleege deftly negotiates the metaphor:

> So what I'd like you to tell me is this. What did you do with the rage, Helen? Because you must have felt it. There must have been days when you woke up and all you wanted to do was pull the covers over your head and say, "I surrender. This is too hard. Someone please take care of me." There must have been days when you wanted to shred the sheets with your teeth. (190)

Helen, of course, can not write back to Kleege's rage (as she did to Pitrois's denunciation of her vaudeville performances). But, given the power of Keller's haunting presence in the lives of many people with disabilities (not just those who are deaf, blind, or deaf-blind), Kleege invokes the lasting biographical and autobiographical impact of Keller's life on others who are "like" (but also unlike) her: "I don't know, Helen. I sense there's more you would tell me if you could. Feel free to elaborate. A word, a sign, a dream vision, a shudder of recognition—whatever means you have at your disposal. I'd really appreciate it. Hell, I'd even be grateful" (194). The elaborate, elaborating, and imaginative possibilities of re-writing "deaf" lives are raised by Kleege's innovative text.[10]

Creative (Deaf) Writing

A panel of three Gallaudet University English professors—all of whom study, as well as create, "creative writing"—took the stage for a session at the "Narrating Deaf Lives" conference. Together, Christopher Jon Heuer, Kristin Harmon, and Tonya Stremlau offered even more innovative, imaginative, and elaborating possibilities for creative (deaf) writing.

In Christopher Jon Heuer's essay from the *SLS* issue, "Deafness as Conflict and Conflict Component," he provides a critical and creative exploration of the role that deafness can play as a "conflict" in narrative—whether deafness is *the* conflict itself or is just one aspect of many in the conflict-components of the total story. "What is the fundamental relationship *between* deafness and conflict?" (195), he asks; this question is central, in its betweenity, for placing deafness in narratives both about and by deaf lives. Heuer explores possible answers to that question, particularly in the realm of deaf autobiographical and biographical narratives, because these, he argues, "are at least in some sense about deafness, and because no au-tobiography and biography can ever be complete unless it captures the conflict inherent in the subject's life" (195). He uses one of his own charac-ters, Daniel Tallerman, "a hard-of-hearing teenager struggling to survive the abuses of a violent alcoholic father as well as the abuses of both the Hearing and Deaf communities" (195), as his primary subject and site for excavating "conflict" in narratives about and from deaf lives. (As a char-acter, Tallerman is yet another between space—both autobiographical, Heuer claims, but also fictional.) Using two specific scenes from two sto-ries about Daniel Tallerman, "Listening for the Same Thing" and "On the Bottom," Heuer illustrates how deafness (as condition and identity) can be both the central conflict of a scene or event in a deaf life and yet also outside the center of conflict, as just one of the many possible "themes" in a story:

> Deafness as a social identity is one such theme. Coping with a parent's alcoholism is another. Violence as a way of life is yet another. All of these themes, at one point or another throughout the course of these two sto-ries, become the central conflict itself, as well as components of the dis-cord. Sometimes they become both. (198–99)

Much like Kleege's autobiographical approach to her own blindness and her narrative about having a "bad blind day" when she writes a (fictional) letter to Helen Keller, Heuer thus employs Daniel Tallerman both auto-biographically and fictionally to "walk a fine line," he says, between the various roles that one's disability or difference can play in a fictional, bio-graphical, or autobiographical narrative. Provocatively, Heuer concludes with a (questioning) point that further extends the one made by the (hear-ing) anthropologist Frank Bechter earlier—that "the world is made of deaf lives. The task of deaf narratives, or perhaps of deaf culture itself, is 'to see deaf lives' when others—even one's deaf friends—do not." Expanding the ways we might "see"—as well as ways we create and read—such deaf lives, Heuer goes on to ask: "Are the subjects of our autobiography or the characters in our fiction living in a world where people are made up of Deafness, or in one where Deafness is made up of people?" (199).[11]

Moving the focus from character and conflict roles in narratives about and by deaf lives, Kristen Harmon considers the ethical, political, liter-ary, emotional, logical, and expressive uses of language—or, rather, of lan-guages in the plural—in "Writing Deaf: Textualizing Deaf Literature." Like

Heuer, Harmon begins with a key question, but hers is concerned with issues of transliteration, hybridity, representation, and the inherent oppression in the relationship between American Sign Language and written English: "What does it mean to transliterate American Sign Language (ASL) and the visual realities of a Deaf life into creative texts written in English?" she asks (200), much as she had also asked during the ASL Literature and Digital Media Project forum discussed in chapter 3. She then maps some of the terrain of "postcolonial possibilities for textualizing Deaf lives and sign language" in creative written texts (composed then in English) (202); as markers on her map, she makes use of several samples of her own students' creative writing (at Gallaudet University). She illuminates a potent paradox in the writing of her (deaf) students, arguing that their writing "represented a mimesis of hearing phenomenology," although they "considered themselves to be culturally-entrenched in the Deaf World" and "used ASL with pride and awareness." "So, in print," Harmon suggests, "the people of the eye did not exist" (203). And so, too, the chorus of commentary about the *Through Deaf Eyes* documentary comes back again: it is as if her students write somehow "*through* deaf eyes" but still, mimetically, *for* hearing people. Their identity—especially on a written (English) page—shifts anxiously between the locations *through* and *for*.

In an attempt to discover, or at least make evident, these lost "people of the eye" in her creative writing class, Harmon introduced her students to the photographs of Maggie Lee Sayre.[12] She then challenged her students "to imagine writing [Sayre's] snapshots in sensory, visual, tactile ways that revealed what they knew and experienced in their lives and could also imagine in Maggie Lee Sayre's life... I asked them to write as Deaf writers" (203). Harmon then marks the way her students' creative responses to this challenging exercise do—and don't—"evince textual strategies of postcolonial writers as they recognize their own erasure from English . . . abrogation, or the denial of privilege to English . . . and appropriation, or the process by which the language is taken and made to bear the burden of one's own cultural experience" (204).[13] She points out her students' uses of "interlanguage" that involves ASL gloss, fingerspelling, and typographic features "that locate the writers and characters within [their linguistic] difference," and she illustrates their "hijacking" of English in order to "create non-standard, hybrid forms" that are not clearly Deaf or Hearing, English or ASL (206). A new form of written English thus begins to appear, as if perhaps from a magic embodied and visuospatial pen, of "bilingual, bicultural people living in a diglossic subculture" (207).[14]

Also concerned with bi-bi betweenity in a diglossic subculture, Tonya Stremlau, in her essay "Narrating Deaf Lives. 'Is It True?' Fiction and Autobiography," focuses and spins on that very question of veracity, particularly potent in authorizing deaf lives in a largely hearing world. As her case study in authenticity, she reviews her own short story "A Nice Romantic Dinner," published in the *Deaf Way II Anthology*, which she edited for Gallaudet University Press in 2002. Stremlau explains that she is often asked by people who have read this story whether it is "true"—meaning they want to know how much it is, or isn't, autobiographical. From that "is it true?" query, she then points to several scenes in the story that are essentially—but still not totally—autobiographical. These almost-auto-biographical scenes remain only "essentially" so because the pseudo-self character in the story, Sara (who perhaps mirrors "Sara" in *Children of a Lesser God?*) does things that Stremlau herself admits she might like to, but would never, do—like signing "bastard" to her insensitive husband in a public place. Writing fiction, Stremlau thus suggests (much like Heuer), is possibly autobiographical at its roots. But, it is also, in the seeds it might sprout, "an opportunity to create a new self, to try on new identities" (209) and thus, to embellish (fictionalize) the otherwise nonfictional.

The role of "distancing" (or bringing closer) one's authorial self is a role Stremlau is very aware of when she writes. Because she claims she is always negotiating how much of herself she wants to put in her writing—always considering how close or distant to come to the character, conflict, or plot of the story—she quips conclusively that even the writer she has been describing in this piece "is a persona." From this personified role she also discusses common "subjects" for her stories that often bring out "inherent conflict," as she writes about what she calls "the borderland that exists wherever there are deaf/hearing relationships" (209). Once again, the border—the between space—of deaf identity constructs deaf lives and narratives as they anxiously shift in deaf/hearing relationships. Finally, from this between space, Stremlau turns to the important rhetorical but also necessarily neglected question of *audience* in narratives about and from deaf lives: "What kind of audience would want to read stories about a deaf kid in a hearing family?" (211). Yet, even as she poses it, she also then admits that she must resist this question, not wanting to "limit myself" by predetermining certain audiences or second-guessing those audience's potential reactions. Like Heuer, Stremlau ends her essay with honesty: "if the story is honest, it should 'speak' to both [deaf and hearing] audiences" (211).[15]

Getting a (Diverse) Deaf Life

As I have already discussed, Gina Oliva's book, *Alone in the Mainstream: A Deaf Woman Remembers Public School,* is the first book published in the "Deaf Lives" series from Gallaudet University Press. Oliva's narrative is an excellent example of an honest story (about deaf lives) that also "speaks" to both deaf and hearing audiences. In fact, Oliva prefaces her book excerpt in the *SLS* issue by telling us that she had considered her audience to be "parents, teachers, and counselors, who may not have a clue about this information" (largely hearing people who are in contact with deaf people/kids) but also "my own brothers and sisters . . . the average reader, mainstream Americans" (212). Again, then: *through* deaf eyes, but *for* a hearing audience—those "average readers" and "mainstream Americans." From this wide—and largely hearing—imagined audience base, her excerpt goes on to recount slices from the life stories of her "relationship with two very special young women who are now both students at Gallaudet University"—Jessica and Summer (212).

In telling Jessica's story, Oliva focuses on the young woman's astonishing creative and expressive facility with American Sign Language (Jessica is DOD, Deaf of Deaf), even as a very young child. In recounting a few specific scenes of toddler Jessica's impressive skills with ASL, Oliva confesses that "Jessica made a believer out of me . . . my knowledge and respect for ASL went from almost nonexistent to profound" (214). In short, through the eyes, expressiveness, and energy of a four-year old, Oliva (as an adult) came to see, and believe in, "firsthand the beneficial effects of a Deaf child growing up in a bilingual environment" (214).

But Oliva also encounters Summer Crider, another deaf child, who makes her "realize that while I could identify with Jessica for her deafness per se, I did not identify with her in another very important way" (214). What she shares with Summer is the experience of growing up as a deaf child among a hearing family and being "mainstreamed" in largely public school environments. Oliva chronicles the many schools Summer attended in her (hearing) family's quest to find the right fit for their (deaf) child: a local elementary school; a private school; a "lab school" affiliated with the state university; and then (now), Gallaudet University. Oliva also chronicles how her observations of Summer in each of these settings was "hard to describe what I saw because I did not like what I saw. . . . I couldn't even see her capabilities during those years and worried for her future" (215). Summer's mother, Linda, has now collaborated on an essay with Gina Oliva about young deaf women and their issues of mainstream acceptance, appearance, and academic and social success. Because of Oliva's biographical experiences with Jessica and Summer—added to her own experiences as a deaf child "alone in the [hearing] mainstream"— she ends with a crack-dwelling note that deaf and hard-of-hearing children "deserve to be exposed to two equal and parallel worlds—each with its own opportunities—both respected by the adults around them" (219). Thus, although Oliva's biographical/autobiographical work in *Alone in the Mainstream* takes a decidedly political tack in her candid advice about what must be done in educating deaf and hard-of-hearing children, her excerpt also provides us with a unique blend—and purpose—for narrating deaf lives in a way that best illuminates their betweenity.[16]

Also centered on the education of deaf and hard of hearing children (and herself as one of those children), Bainy Cyrus's narrative from the *SLS* issue is an excerpt from one of three memoirs included in the "Deaf Lives" series' volume, *Deaf Women's Lives: Three Self-Portraits*.[17] Cyrus took the stage at the "Narrating Deaf Lives" conference with her first visit ever to Gallaudet University; in a comment she made on the floor in the concluding session, she marveled over how "comfortable" and "at home" and "included" she felt because of the first-rate captioning provided throughout the conference. (This kind of ultimate ease of access for deaf and hard-of-hearing students is one of Gallaudet's strongest selling points for recruitment.) Although Cyrus's educational and experiential identification, as one who was orally educated, remains largely in and with the hearing world, much of her story is clearly "deaf." For example, she writes of her predominantly oral education, beginning at the Clarke School, one of the premier and longest-standing oral-deaf institutions in the United States. She writes poignantly of her (delayed) language development as a deaf child in the 1960s and 1970s, working hard to comprehend the nuances of structure in both spoken and written English, despite her struggles to achieve literacy equal to that of her hearing peers at the time. Cyrus's story always remains positive and forceful in her recognition of not just what she is missing (from environmental sounds, from human voices, from print literacy) but also what she already has and excels at. Deaf people, she tells us, are "all eyes." And, with their eyes, they "read" much.

So it was that Cyrus herself stood before an audience in the Gallaudet University Conference Center auditorium in November 2004 and read to us some of her writing from her (then-forthcoming) book. In her reading at the "Narrating Deaf Lives" conference, she took up the challenge of speech (and, following from it, the challenge of reading and writing) as she threaded together several passages from her memoir, *All Eyes*. Her reading that day delighted us with her humor and made us not only marvel at, but also be thankful for, the fact that Cyrus had herself now become "a writer." Her stories about misreading English/American idioms such as "paint the town red" and "elbow grease" were all the more poignant when we realized that she had herself now managed to "paint the town red" through the successful completion of her memoir. She has also surely applied some "elbow grease" in that creation and completion. As the French feminist theorist Hélène Cixous has suggested, writing may be "too high" and "reserved for the great men" and even at times "silly" for women—but it is also obviously, in Bainy Cyrus's terms and (deaf and female) hands, a communicative act that is possible, potent, and promising.[18]

In his memoir, *Deaf Hearing Boy*, R. H. Miller also presents a portrait of communicative acts between deaf and hearing worlds that is potent and promising—but problematic. In his memoir about growing up as the oldest hearing son of deaf parents in the 1940s—and about being painfully sandwiched at times between his parents' own hearing parents and his deaf parents—Miller presents a powerful crack-dwelling, between kind of memoir. Fronted with a preface by Robert Hoffmeister, the founder of Children of Deaf Adults (CODA), Miller's own CODA narrative walks the thin but meaningful line that links communication options, family interactions, adult/child positions, autonomy, and public perceptions about deafness, which are all part of his particular era and place in American life. As someone who came to occupy a position of relative linguistic and cultural success—professor and chair of an English department at an American university—Bob Miller tells a story about the deaf/hearing relationships inherent in deaf lives that harkens back to Tonya Stremlau's point that such relationships are always the site of "conflict." Yet, Miller navigates this between space and its conflicting relationship with poise, power, promise—and also a fair number of problems. There is little sugar-coating here as Miller moves from his grand and eloquent literary epigraphs (culled from many works of great literature, such as Shakespeare's plays) to the considerably less grand but no less important scenes of negotiating an exchange over his own school behavior with a teacher and his deaf mother.[19]

Madan Vasishta's memoir published in the "Deaf Lives" series, *Deaf in Delhi*, offers a valuable international, cultural, religious, spiritual, educational, and experiential angle on growing up deaf or hard of hearing in the second half of the 20th century. For the *SLS* issue, Vasishta selected two excerpts from his book to convey this unique experience. Vasishta, waking up from a long illness as a young boy in a rural Indian community and finding himself "deaf," recounts his "panic in silence" as mirrored largely through what he already knows (and fears) the community does— and does not—imagine for and expect from a deaf person. Twelve years later, he goes for "the interview of my life" for a major position as a photographer at the National Physical Laboratory. He gets the job—and tells a thrilling tale of it—and he eventually also finds his way to the United States and to Gallaudet University, where he receives advanced degrees, takes up important leadership and directing positions, and comes to write this remarkable narrative. "I realized," he tells us both frankly and freshly in his conclusion, "that deafness was going to stop me from going up in life only if I wanted it to" (241).[20]

Growing up deaf also did not stop Emmanuelle Laborit, a French actress and author of the memoir *Cry of the Gull*. Laborit's acting and stage credits are already considerable: the prestigious Molière Award for best actress in 1993 for her role in the French version of *Children of a Lesser God*; acclaim in the award-winning 1997 German film *Jenseits der Stille* (Beyond Silence); roles in half a dozen European films; a starring performance in the short film produced by the French director Claude Lelouch that is part of the *11'09"01—September 11* film; and a starring role in *Stille Liebe*, her first movie as lead actress. Laborit, in her keynote presentation about "writing my life" at the "Narrating Deaf Lives" conference, simply brought down the house thanks to her mesmerizing narrative performance—articulated through French Sign Language (LSF), via international interpreters, and with plenty of American Sign Language (ASL) and International Sign Language pidgin signs mixed in. In recounting some of the major events and decisions in telling her own life story, Laborit capably also summarized some of the key issues for "narrating deaf lives" that had been discussed in the two days before her presentation: deciding why (and how) to write a book about your (deaf) life; considering collaborative writing and interpreting for getting your narrative out to both deaf and hearing public audiences; the relationship between "writing" and "signing"; using writing as/and analysis of one's life; writing as a way and form of identity; writing as access to information and education; and the role of theater, performance, and the arts in deaf lives.[21]

Laborit's book, *Cry of the Gull*, arises from—and returns to—the importance of deaf lives leading deaf lives. She tells us that when she was young, she would always ask her (hearing) parents, "Where are the Deaf people's books, and where are books written by Deaf people?" Laborit's narrative—both her memoir and the narrative she offered in the volume from her live performance at the "Narrating Deaf Lives" conference—centers on the paradoxes and promises of deaf/hearing relationships and the multiple ways of approaching, recording, producing, capturing, imagining, arguing for, and finally, placing deaf lives.

Placing Future Deaf Lives

At this writing, eleven narratives of deaf lives have been placed in the "Deaf Lives" series (three of them appear together in the volume *Deaf Women's Lives*).[22] In the next few years, four or five more will appear, and these next volumes in the series will include even more diversity and further representation of the complex relationship between deaf and hearing people. They will also offer even more interesting illustrations of the intertwined, and sometimes knotted, nature of individual and collective identities within "Deaf culture" or "the Deaf community." Anxiety over identity and place in "deaf world" and as a deaf subject will pulse through each of them, much as it has for the first five volumes and eight narratives.

Recently published or forthcoming in the "Deaf Lives" series are:

- A "double-deaf" biography authored by the historian and biographer Harry Lang on the subject of Dr. Robert Panara, *Teaching from the Heart and Soul: The Robert F. Panara Story* (2007)
- Another forthcoming "double-deaf" volume in which David Kurs, a 1998 Gallaudet University graduate (and president of Gallaudet's Student Body Government in 1997–98) edits a collection of the writing (speeches, poems, newspaper articles) of Larry Newman, a former president of the National Association of the Deaf (NAD)
- A memoir by Elizabeth (Liz) Thompson, native of central Ohio, titled *Day by Day: the Chronicles of a Hard of Hearing Reporter*, a story that includes, among other things, her (early) mainstreaming experience in Ohio public schools; her work among hearing people at the Battelle Institute in Columbus, Ohio; her entry into the central Ohio deaf community (where she learned sign language); her (fairly recent) cochlear implant; and samples of her energetic newspaper columns, "Day by Day," published in many suburban newspapers in central Ohio

- A double-volume set, *Deaf Lives in Contrast: Two Women's Stories*, that focuses on deaf lives as told through the eyes of women family members. These two are both largely autobiographical accounts and also incorporate biographies of deaf family members. The first, by Dvora Shurman, is a CODA narrative that moves from "turn of the 20th century Jewish immigrant culture" in Milwaukee to Shurman's own "double helix, around the core of Deafness and society, and my duality in the Deaf and hearing worlds." The second is the story of Mary Rivers, a determined Louisiana (Cajun) mother and Army wife, who raised a deaf son, Clay—along with four other children—during the 1960s and 1970s at a time when ideas about ways to educate deaf children in America were undergoing considerable changes.
- The second volume of Madan Vasishta'a memoir, this one, tentatively titled *Deaf in DC,* focusing on his "adult" life in America.

And, beyond these volumes, I am sure there are more.

Out there on the horizon, I often also imagine what more, or most, I would want for the future of narrating, placing, and "publishing" deaf lives. Although "vision" is always a shifting, shaping, and relational thing for me, I come quickly to at least two answers. First, and foremost, I hope to see more documentary, film, and digital media development of narratives from and around deaf lives. And, while I think a YouTube.com video is as fine a place as any for the young (or middle-aged, or old) deaf narrator to set down (and potentially share) his or her story, I want further to find ways to best encourage and develop high-quality and carefully mastered and edited biographical and autobiographical narratives in sophisticated, visually based mediums. As "people of the eye" (McKee)—a phrase borrowed meaningfully from NAD president George Veditz's famous 1910 "Sign Masters" speech—deaf people probably also have much to contribute to the innovation of elements and effects in documenting lives through digital media.

Perhaps in conjunction with the creative capabilities I believe that digital and visual-based media offer for collecting deaf identities and placing deaf lives, I want, second, to see greater integration of the *collective* work of deaf narratives. Rachel McKee's collection, *People of the Eye: Stories of the Deaf World,* which collects "several generations of Deaf voices" in New Zealand that "reflect both common and diverse Deaf experiences," serves as an example of the kind of integrated collection I am thinking of; events like the "Narrating Deaf Lives" conference in November 2004 and the special issue of *Sign Language Studies* focused on that conference's proceedings, along with "set" collections in the "Deaf Lives" series that feature more than one narrative are other examples. To be sure, an individual life rendered in a singular biography or autobiography is a powerful and meaningful thing. But I suspect that all deaf people—whether they are native signers with deaf parents, orally educated with a cochlear implant, rural or urban, young or old—know some, if not all too well, of the "alone in the mainstream" phenomenon Gina Oliva documents in her first volume for the "Deaf Lives" series. The tyranny and paradox of both autobiography and biography are that, while both genres attempt to represent and somehow "mainstream" an individual's experience, they also create isolate that individual as a representative of his or her "kind." They cut away from the fabric of "folk."

To help hold together or quilt that fabric, I would also want to see, third and last, the development of community and school/university-based workshops that bring deaf and hard-of-hearing people together to work on manuscripts and documentaries about their lives and to collectively learn the crafts of biography, autobiography, and documentary. In this learning they would also be likely to change and re-create the very technologies and genres they work with. In keeping with my vision of "integration," I best imagine these workshops as including those in close relationships with deaf people who might also have stories to tell of their lives, interwoven with deaf lives, who are also part of the fabric that places, though perhaps always a bit anxiously, a deaf identity. As the poet and memoirist David Wright begins his own memoir, *Deafness*:

> About deafness I know everything and nothing. Everything, if forty years' firsthand experience is to count. Nothing, when I realize the little I have had to do with the converse aspects of deafness—the other half of the dialogue. Of that side my wife knows more than I. So do teachers of the deaf and those who work among them; not least, people involuntarily but intensely involved—ordinary men and women who find themselves from one cause or another, parents of a deaf child. For it is the non-deaf who absorb a large part of the impact of the disability. (1)

To some, Wright's claims here may seem dated (especially since they do come from 1969) or even oppressive in the modern age of current identity politics, since they relinquish some of the power and perspective in narrating a deaf life to the voice and vision outside the direct experience of a deaf life. But I think, instead, that Wright simply offers us a complex relational narrative frame that, in fact, conveys the collective nature of any (falsely) assumed "individual" life. For, while I want a future that indeed has "deaf lives leading deaf lives"—a future where more deaf people have reason and recourse to narrate their own lives, collective or individual—I also want a future that fairly represents the full fabric, a future that places deaf lives in all the between contexts, relationships, and frames possible.

5

Deaf Eyes

The Allen Sisters' Pictorial Photography,
1885–1920

"The Misses Allen," they were most often called—personally, by those who knew them in Deerfield, Massachusetts, and also professionally, by those critics who wrote about their photography at the time.[1] And although their names do appear singly in relationship to a few of their photographs, more often than not they appear as a unit, Mary (Figure 5.1) and Frances (Figure 5.2) Allen together: The Misses Allen. For nearly fifty years, they were companions in art, work, communication, and everyday life.

In this essay, I work from five different contexts. And, although I move through these contexts one by one, I must also confess that this movement and my established contexts serve as an artificial organizational design for painting a portrait—taking a picture, as it were—of the Allen Sisters and their photographic art. The Allen Sisters and their photography is a subject that I have found to be quite complex, in fact. The five contexts I want to work around, in, and through overlap at many junctures. First, I want to focus on just the sisters themselves and develop a mini-autobiography—a sketch, as it were—of them before I begin discussing additional images and contexts. Second, I move out of that close-up autobiographical frame and briefly discuss another concentric circle surrounding their lives and work—the context of Deerfield, Massachusetts, during the period of their photographic work, 1885–1920. Third, I offer some background about women and photography in general during this particular period in American (and international) history. Fourth, sandwiched between the third and fifth contexts, I take a visual break as we look at examples of their photography and place these examples in several kinds of (again often overlapping) categories. This categorizing work I do with the Allen Sisters' photographic images is greatly influenced by contexts of gender, history, and disability.

5.1 and 5.2 Frances Stebbins Allen & Mary Electa Allen. Photographs courtesy of the Pocumtuck Valley Memorial Association, Memorial Hall Museum, Deerfield, Massachusetts.

Then, finally, fifth, I end with the part of my essay that serves as my main title: "Deaf Eyes." In this last part, I want to conclude by re-viewing some of the context of the gender and history section (the third one) with a "deafness" lens or filter laid over it, as well. *What would it have meant to have been deaf, and a woman, and a professional photographer at the turn of the twentieth century?* I do not propose that the Misses Allen hold the answers to all the parts of identity posed in that question. But I do think that exploring some of their history—looking, in particular, at their multiple contexts and between placements—and placing that exploration alongside their photographic images can develop and frame some interesting pictures for us as we reflect on that question.

Frances and Mary Allen: A "Well-Rounded Life in the Chiefest of Things"

Born to a successful farmer, Josiah Allen, and his wife, Mary Stebbins, in the town of Deerfield, Massachusetts, Frances and Mary were joined by two brothers, as well.[2] Frances was the oldest child, born in 1854, and Mary, four years younger, was born in 1858. The Josiah Allen family was an extended one, with numerous close relatives always stopping by. The family also housed many boarders during the children's younger years—especially young, unmarried, female teachers for the local school. In the fall of 1874—when Frances (often called "Fanny" at that time) was twenty years old and Mary (known sometimes as "Mame") was sixteen—they began, together, a two-year program at the State Normal School teacher's college in Westfield, Massachusetts. Upon graduation from the normal school, Frances spent the next ten years, from 1876–1886, teaching school. Mary's health was reportedly poor during this period, so her teaching was sporadic.

By 1886, their hearing loss had proven great enough that they both gave up teaching. The specific source of the loss is as yet unknown, but their deafness does not seem to have surfaced as a significant problem until they were in their early thirties. The best medical guess we have today is that their loss might have been the result of otoschlerosis, a hardening of the bones of the ear. This condition, once thought to be the result of chronic ear infections or the toll of typical childhood illnesses, is now known to be largely genetic. And true to the pattern of the Allen Sisters, it may not appear in a significant way until the middle years of a person's life. We know that in 1893—when they would have been thirty-nine and thirty-five, respectively—the two sisters took a hundred-mile trip by train to Boston to be examined at the Massachusetts Eye and Ear Infirmary. It was determined by the doctors there that Frances would not even benefit from surgery on her ears but that Mary might. Thus, surgery was performed on Mary but proved unsuccessful. Mary Allen apparently made use of an ear trumpet for some time (see Figure 5.3). Yet she eventually complained that it did not work very well, and so she gave it to her neighbor, Lucy Andrews, who was also deaf (and who had ten children). Even with two owners, the ear tube—which was sold as a "Conversation Tube" in the 1902 Sears, Roebuck catalogue—survives, apparently in excellent condition (Flynt 56). Those of us who have used hearing aids and found that they offered the same lack of overall utility as that experienced by Mary Allen and Lucy Andrews and who have therefore eventually retired these devices to our sock drawers might well imagine Mary Allen's "conversation tube" nestled among the knickers of either of these two women at the time.

In 1897, after they had already embarked on their second "career" as photographers, Mary—who wrote many letters—corresponded with her friend and cousin Ellen Gates Starr about their position and life in

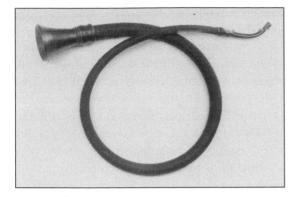

5.3 Mary Allen's ear trumpet. Photograph courtesy of the Pocumtuck Valley Memorial Association, Memorial Hall Museum, Deerfield, Massachusetts.

relation to their hearing loss.[3] Starr responded with words that I find remarkably wise and forward-thinking, given the reality of what it must have been like for two single women who had just lost their first careers (one of the few careers available to women at all during this time): "No, it isn't a maimed life. It is a difficult one—hard & trying often; but those who having eyes see not & having ears hear not, they live the maimed life. Yours is a well rounded one, in the chiefest of things" (Flynt 22).

Although their hearing loss could not have been heartening, the fact remains that it did foster their new careers in photography just as it added to their mutual support. While the official historical records state that Mary and Frances "remained single" all their lives, nothing, in fact, could be further from the truth. Carroll Smith-Rosenberg argues that "an abundance of manuscript evidence suggests that eighteenth- and nineteenth-century women routinely formed emotional ties with other women" and, further, that "such deeply felt, same-sex friendship were casually accepted in American society" (1). Not only did Mary and Frances Allen have each other in an obviously rich and rewarding nonsingular relationship, but they also had thick and multiple relationships with their Deerfield neighbors, their extended family, and several key women of the time—most notably Ellen Gates Starr and the social reformer Jane Addams, who co-founded the Hull House in Chicago, and Frances Benjamin Johnston, a leading photographer and critic of the "pictorial" school of photography that was becoming so popular at this time. Finally, out of their deafness and their close relationships, a kind of "life of the eye" through the lens of photography was generated. I will come back to this point in my last section and context.

Frances and Mary Allen had apparently first been exposed to photography by their brother, Edmund Allen, who often took photographs for his job as a civil engineer in the 1880s, as the sisters were going deaf and leaving their careers as teachers. Edmund himself began using the camera outside his engineer's job when his four daughters were born, between 1888 and 1895. And, by at least 1884, Frances and Mary were photographing with the use of a view camera and creating albumen prints. There is, for example, a wonderful image taken by Frances of Mary standing beside a view camera in 1885, which would have been at the very beginning of their photographic careers.[4]

The Allen Sisters had been taking pictures, using photography as both art and income, for nearly fifteen years before their moment of national and international fame came. Brought along with thirty other American women photographers to be featured in the 1900 Universal Exposition in Paris, the Allen Sisters found themselves the center of considerable attention when the exhibition organizer, Frances Benjamin Johnston—herself a well-known photographer and critic—declared the sisters two of "The Foremost Women Photographers in America" in a July 1901 issue of *Ladies Home Journal* (Flynt 42).

Despite their popularity as photographers even in their local area (neighbors reported having to put signs on their own doors warding off lost Allen Sisters visitors),[5] and despite their considerable artistic and competitive success, when they did choose to exhibit their work in larger public exhibits and contests, the Misses Allen remained remarkably modest about their work. In a March 1894 article in the photography journal *The Photo-Beacon,* the sisters present a quite unpretentious "Prize-Winners' Account of Themselves." This account contextualizes well the sisters' own vision of their work and is worth repeating, at least in part:

> Our methods are too simple to have much interest for the skilled amateur photographer who tries all the new processes. We use the camera simply as a quick way of sketching, and regard all the technical part, which comes after the exposure is made, as a necessary evil.
>
>   . . . In pictures, artistic excellence is usually entirely at variance with what is called a perfect photograph. The eye cannot focus itself on every object in its field of vision at the same time. If a photograph does this, the effect is hard and unnatural. But there must be method in this madness. A picture is not necessarily beautiful because it is blurred, and there's need of all one's technical skill, even after a negative is made, in adapting the print to its peculiar individual qualities.

The merit of posing, which you kindly give us credit for, belongs rather to the models. Our chief virtue is in letting them alone. We usually have better success with children who are not too highly civilized, or too conventionally clothed, or who are too young to be conscious. We give them a general idea of the picture we want, and then let them alone until they forget about us and the drop catches an unconscious pose. They consider it a game, and we are always ready to play at it. (Flynt 27)

As their modest comments on their art demonstrate here, their particular success at the kind of art "pictorial" photography being made popular at this time was chiefly with children, while they also excelled—as I'll soon further demonstrate—at photographing colonial re-created scenes of work and home, local citizens at work or play, and local landscapes. Throughout their photographic career, Mary repeatedly described their work as somewhere between "art" and "craft."[6]

She may have placed their work in a "between" space in part because it did serve at least a dual function for them as both artistic expression and source of basic income. For, even while their photography gained due attention in competitions and art-focused publications, the Allen Sisters also used it as a source of income in two significant ways: via portrait photography and sittings arranged for people who traveled to have their portraits done by the sisters and through commissions for photographic illustrations for magazine articles of the time when this new technique began to replace wood engravings.

They opened their own formal studio in 1901 by converting one bedroom upstairs into their darkroom, while the parlor downstairs became the salesroom. Here the conversion of a typically "hearing" social space, the parlor, into their salesroom, a place now dominated by the eye—a space centered around visual communication via their photography—seems particularly appropriate when viewed through "deaf eyes." This conversion of a private parlor to a commercial parlor place was, however, quite unusual. Although it was common for photographers of this era to imagine, furnish, and advertise their studios as "parlors," they were actually rarely in a private home (Grier).

In 1904, the Allen Sisters began publishing catalogs of their images. Their last catalog was published in 1920. Mary apparently went on with some of the business throughout the 1920s—well into her 60s—but Frances' sight began to deteriorate considerably during that decade. Now both deaf and blind, Frances was known to continue her gardening and to have

5.4 Deerfield Society of Blue and White Needlework as photographed by Mary Allen. Photograph courtesy of the Pocumtuck Valley Memorial Association, Memorial Hall Museum, Deerfield, Massachusetts.

stepped out the rough equivalent of a mile, which she would walk each day on their front porch. Frances died first, at the age of eighty-seven, on Valentine's Day, February 14, 1941. And always but always together, Mary died only four days after her, on February 18, at the age of eighty-three.

In a Community: The Arts and Crafts Movement in Deerfield

Some part of the Allen Sisters' success at photography—whether as art or craft, income or aesthetics—was due to their local historical circumstances as citizens of Deerfield, Massachusetts, at the turn of the twentieth century. Deerfield was a town deeply engaged in the local arts and crafts movement that swept much of America at that time, and it was well regarded, by one account, for "its four-fold aspect which makes up the background for human happiness,—rural peace and plenty, historical associations, artistic expression, and intellectual alertness" ("Deerfield," *Handicraft* 5, no. 4 [July 1912]: 53).

Mary Allen herself was one of the original four members of the Deerfield Society of Blue and White Needlework; in fact, she designed its trademark—a blue "D" within a flax wheel. The sisters also recorded the

history of the needlework society through photography, as we see in Figure 5.4. This society of embroiderers was held up as a kind of model community for arts and crafts at the time, as was noted by the *Chicago Daily
News* in 1897:

> The Deerfield Society of Blue and White Needlework is a national prod-
> uct of our awakened interest in things colonial and in handsome things
> rather than in those turned out by the dozen from machines; it is also an
> example of the Ruskin notion of establishing village industries and pro-
> moting rural crafts. (Flynt 32)

In fact, for a number of years, Mary was often torn between embroidery
and photography. For example, in 1898, she wrote to Francis Benjamin
Johnston that the two "still elbow each other, . . . I'm no nearer deciding
which master to serve" (Flynt 33). But, by 1900, when Francis Benjamin
Johnston convinced the Allen Sisters to exhibit their photography in the
famous Universal Exposition in Paris, photography seems to have become
the dominant elbow for her. Yet the relationship between the two—their
photography and the larger arts and crafts movement—was still often
two-handed, as their biographer Suzanne Flynt has noted: "Frances and
Mary Allen served two critical, but distinct, roles in the Deerfield Arts
and Crafts movements: their handcrafted photographs were among the
town's artistic offerings and their images of craft workers publicized the
town's activities" (Flynt 33). The photographic work of "the Misses Allen" was always handcrafted, aesthetically pleasing, subtle, careful, and yet
simple. And these qualities matched and advanced those of the overall
arts and crafts movement in America at the time.

What is more, their location in Deerfield, Massachusetts, was crucial to
the content and composition of their photography, as they made the most of
their local subjects. The Allen Sisters excelled, for example, at four overlapping kinds of photographic compositions that all made use of local scenes
and subjects: (1) capitalizing on the still potential nostalgia for farming in
the area; (2) re-creating colonial life (another form of nostalgia of the time)
through the willingness of local posed subjects and annual pageants; (3)
composing nature's paradoxical grandeur and simplicity; and (4) centering
on the simple yet rich lives of children. I will return to these four compositional and content categories for their photography in my fourth section.

For now, let me conclude on the context of Deerfield, Massachusetts,
by also dwelling on its relevance in relation to their deafness. Deerfield is

located only twelve miles from Northampton, Massachusetts, home to the famous Clarke School. The Clarke School for the Deaf was founded in 1867 as the first permanent oral school for the deaf in America, and it remains, to this day, one of the premier oral-focused educational centers for deaf and hard-of-hearing children in America, if not the world. Mabel Hubbard Bell (Alexander Graham Bell's wife) and her father, Gardiner Hubbard Bell, provided much of the financial backing to start the school; Alexander Graham Bell himself once served on the Clarke School Board of Trustees. I will return to the importance of this influence in the last section when I discuss, more specifically, the context of "deafness and disability" in the life, work, and art of the Allen Sisters. Let me just note here that we do know that the Allen Sisters both took lipreading lessons at the Clarke School. Yet, we also know they did not do well at them, and, although Mary continued to work at lipreading, Frances—who was also apparently more deaf than Mary—abandoned lipreading and oral efforts altogether and relied primarily on writing to communicate with others. (There is a wonderful image, for example, taken by Mary Allen of her sister, Frances, exchanging a written note with one of their young nephews.) But, given that the oral-dominated method of educating deaf children (and adults) was significantly in favor at this particular time, their proximity to the very center of American deaf oral education would have certainly impacted the way they went about being "deaf" and interacting in a hearing world.

Women and Photography: A Turn of the 20th-Century Snapshot

Alfred Stieglitz, father of the pictorial movement in photography and instigator of the renegade "Photo-Secession" movement at the turn of the twentieth century, wrote to Frances Benjamin Johnston in summer 1900 that "The women in this country are certainly doing great photographic work & deserve much commendation for their efforts." Commendation was indeed quick in coming as Johnston organized, on very short notice, the history-making exhibit of thirty-one American women photographers at the Universal Exposition in Paris in both 1900 and 1901. The exhibit was so successful that it went even more international when W. I. Sreznewsky of St. Petersburg commissioned the exhibit to travel to Russia, as well.

Johnston herself was a formidable figure in American photography. She compiled a string of impressive firsts: the first White House photographer; the first female member of the Washington, DC, Camera Club; and the

first woman really involved in underground photography; she was a pro-
lific critic and author on the subject of photography and art, as well (Curtis 24). For the Universal Exposition in Paris, Johnston is known to have
particularly sought out and encouraged women who were doing what she
deemed "art photography." Records of Johnston's correspondence further
indicate that she believed that the inclusion of professional photographic
work by three American women photographers in particular was essential
to the exhibit: Zaida Ben Yusuf, from New York; Mabel Osgood Wright,
from Connecticut; and the Allen Sisters, of Deerfield, Massachusetts.

From the outset, photography developed as a field that offered women
multiple and previously unmatched possibilities. Here, at some necessary
and illuminating length, is how the contemporary photography scholar
Verna Posever Curtis explains these possibilities in an essay about Francis
Benjamin Johnston's role in "staking the sisterhood's claim in American
photography":

> It was true that the field of photography, in particular, offered women
> life-fulfilling possibilities. The will to experiment in a promising endeavor
> motivated those seeking their independence in the last quarter of the
> century. Photography allowed women to show their mettle in socially ac-
> ceptable ways without being bound to predominantly male patronage or
> to the academic tradition of the fine arts. Qualities that were advanta-
> geous to the picture-taking, developing and mounting processes—such as
> deftness, attention to detail, good taste, patience and perseverance—were
> regarded as innately female, or at least were reinforced through train-
> ing in such household arts and crafts as spinning or needlework. Indeed,
> mastery of photography required what was then expected of the female
> sex. In photographic portraiture, to cite one area, women who radiated
> graciousness and tact were at a great advantage with sitters. (29–30)

What I am most struck by in Curtis's own observations is how the list of ad-
vantageous qualities for success at photography mirrors, in essence, those
we might deem as most desired for teachers: deftness, attention to detail,
good taste, patience, and perseverance. Yet, teaching was clearly a hearing
vocation (at that time, if not always) whereas photography, quite conveniently, could facilitate the deaf and "silent," but ultra-observant, faculties
of the photographer's "eye." Photography, as an art and craft then open to
women, could supplant their other gendered profession of teaching. Yet,
photography, unlike teaching, was a fairly deaf-friendly occupation.

The Misses Allen, trained first as teachers, used to making their own income and maintaining their independence, and educated well, found themselves in their 30s struggling to communicate in an oral and aural world. In fact, when Johnston wrote to the Allen Sisters early in 1900, requesting that they submit some photographs and a biographical sketch for consideration as part of the Paris exhibition, Mary Allen responded modestly about their work and their biographies. And, while Mary hints at the role of their deafness in their coming to photography, she does not, of course, directly name it:

> I will send you a few prints to show what sort of work we have done in a few days. I should be glad to compose an autobiography also, but you know already all there is to know. We have no "methods" and no "conditions." We have had not training either—technical or artistic—and we have no theories. We take what work comes to hand—and it fits itself as it can into the intervals of other duties, for it still has to take a secondary place.
>
> *We took to it [photography] ten years ago as a resource, when we were obliged to give up teaching.* (Flynt 39) (Italics/emphasis mine)

As this passage from Mary Allen's own letter indicates, they were talented and resourceful, yet they also lived with the limitations in career options imposed upon them as members of the female sex at this particular time and place. Quite artfully, however, they found their place and success behind the shutter of the camera's eye. With a camera in their hands and an artful eye, the Allen Sisters passed in a hearing world.

Embodying the Sisters' Work

Here I want to pause for a kind of illustrative break before I move to my final point. I have already outlined what I believe to be the four dominant compositional and content categories of the Allen Sisters' photographic work. First, they often capitalized on the particular nostalgia for farming in the area, as can be seen in images like the award winning "Sharpening the Scythe" (Figure 5.5). Although this image seems natural, it is, in fact, posed. It features one of their favorite subjects, the Deerfield citizen William Stabbings, with a long gray beard and dressed in simple but traditional black and white that matches his serious countenance, posing in a field of some kind of flowering and grassy growth. He grasps in his left hand the sickle of a scythe while his right hand holds the sharpening stone. His eyes gaze intently at the blade itself. The photograph is indicative of other staged colonial photographs of its kind.

Second, as the Deerfield, Massachusetts, Museum indicates, the Allen Sisters also re-created general colonial life (another subject of nostalgia at that time) through the willingness of local posed subjects and annual pageants. Many of these posed "colonial" images were not of farming but rather of domestic and community life. In "Betty at the Churn" (Figure 5.6), for example, "Betty," clad in "colonial" garb, works butter in an old-fashioned churn while sunlight (from the right of the image) streams in on her face from a window and a cozy cat laps cream from a bowl at her feet.

In another classic "colonial"-pose photograph, "The Letter of the Law," the Allen Sisters disturb somewhat the pastoral, homey nature created by images like "Betty at the Churn." In the "Letter of the Law" image (Figure 5.7), an apparent Puritan minister, frowning deeply and clad all in black, with a stark white collar, holds open a (white) book to which he points with his square, strong, white right hand. His image sits predominantly in the right half of the frame; the left half is consumed by blackness, which also then leaves one half of his face (the right side) deeply shadowed, while the left half shades into light. When I show this image to students, I call it the "Scary Puritan" photo.

Far less scary and even, in fact, amusing and ironic is a late photo of the Allen Sisters that reflects re-created colonial life in the community by documenting a scene from a local pageant. "Anachronism" (Figure 5.8) records the image of a (costumed) "Indian" standing in front of a fall cornfield. This "Indian" holds a camera, and he is taking a picture of a woman dressed like a Puritan, who is standing next to a man also dressed like an "Indian." The ironic and playful distance of one of the sisters capturing this anachronistic scene and presenting us then with a photograph within a photograph makes this image a classic example of the "between" space the Allen Sisters occupied in their community and art.

In the third category of their photographic art, the sisters also use distance yet presence—conveyed in tandem, and in juxtaposition, through their cameras—to compose nature's paradoxical grandeur and simplicity in their own back yard. In "Red Winter Sunset" (Figure 5.9), for example, the Allen Sisters make a scene familiar to, yet distant from us. This image, taken literally in their own backyard at the end of their photographic careers, features the play of light and dark on bare trees on a snowy bank against a half-iced lake. The scene captured is devoid of human presence, and, in its wintry chill, it seems to shun such presence.

5.5 (top left) Sharpening the Scythe, 1900.
5.6 (top center) Betty at the Churn, 1904.
5.7 (top right) Letter of the Law, 1906.
5.8 (above)Anachronism, c. 1910–1916.
5.9 (right) Red Winter Sunset, 1920.
Photographs courtesy of the Pocumtuck
Valley Memorial Association, Memorial
Hall Museum, Deerfield, Massachusetts.

At the other end of their career, in 1895, they also froze a winter frame for us. This one, in "Snowstorm," from 1895 (Figure 5.10), does include human presence in the cluster of black but white snow-topped buildings featured its center. Yet, the heavy blanket of snow-covered trees and the field of white in the foreground make the buildings seem empty. Nature herself is clearly the living subject of this image.

And, finally, in images that they were perhaps best known for, they centered on the simple, yet rich lives of children. "Making a Dam" (Figure 5.11), for example, creates a triangle of three children, nestled in the V of a small stream valley, attempting to build a dam for the stream. Much like construction workers of contemporary times, one child has his hands on the rocks (the builder), while another child simply points, directing what the builder/worker must do, while a third child (the youngest one) stands with his hands clasped behind his back and merely observes. Even more passively—distant but somehow engaged—we also observe this building scene.

Likewise, in one of my favorite of all the Allen Sisters' images (Figure 5.12), we become the passive but engaged observers as the motherly figure of Eleanor Brown Stebbins, bent on her knees, washes a child's right hand while the child's left hand (no doubt sticky) reaches up, lovingly, for her face. This image perhaps comes close to the "Cult of True Womanhood" (http://www.pinzler.com/ushistory/cultwo.html) and suggests a kind of religious, baptismal scene.

In another evocative, "little woman" posed scene, "Little Girl and Doll at a Tea Party" (Figure 5.13), the Allen Sisters represent a young girl (as a little mother) overseeing her doll on a high chair at a posed tea party. Here, of course, the little girl is quite young (her chair still fairly overwhelms her), but she poses as an adult.

Deaf Eyes: The Allen Sisters as Deaf/Women/Photographers

I am not a historian. My work is primarily in rhetoric—the analysis and production of persuasion through discourse (and visual images certainly count for such discourse)—and in Disability Studies and Deaf Studies as they intersect with issues of identity, persuasion, and motivation. Many of my closest colleagues in these fields are historians, however, and so I am acutely aware of the dangers involved in transferring one's own sense, self, and standpoint into some situation now long past. Context really matters.

5.10 (right) Snowstorm, c. 1895.
5.11 (below) Making a Dam, c. 1900.
5.12 (below right) Eleanor Brown Stebbins Washing a Child's Hands, c. 1905.
5.13 (bottom) Little Girl and Doll at a Tea Party, c. 1900.
Photographs courtesy of the Pocumtuck Valley Memorial Association, Memorial Hall Museum, Deerfield, Massachusetts.

Yet, I have been watching the Allen Sisters closely for some time now, taking my own pictures of them as I've watched them passing, with the "aid" of photography, in a hearing world. Can I mark, plot, point to the specific illustrations of "deaf" in their photographic images? Can I see and unmask the "deaf eyes" on the other side of those images? No, I'm not entirely sure I can.

But then again . . . I grew up very hard of hearing (deaf wasn't a word we would allow ourselves) in a rural farming community in western Kansas during the '60s and '70s. We had no arts and crafts community really to boast of (although the baking and gardening arts were fairly apparent at the county fair each year), and, to be honest, I was interested in none of that. I was born exactly one hundred years after Mary Allen. I was also like Mary, I suppose, in some of my communication abilities and choices—fairly skilled at lipreading, very skilled at writing, possessing a direct gaze (as is evident in the portrait photo take of her by Frances and shown in Figure 5.2), interested in teaching yet daunted by what that would mean for someone whose ears worked like mine did (or rather, like mine didn't).

So, instead, I turned to art. My art at the time (and now) was writing. The Misses Allen passed in the hearing world with some success through and in their photographic art; likewise, I have passed in the hearing world with some success in and through my chosen "art"—writing. The most beautiful thing about a book or even just a written sentence, I have always told (and written to) people, is that it never minds if you say, "Huh? What? Can you repeat that, please?" Words on the page—like images captured through a lens to photographic paper—yearn to be read again and again. Our "deafness" in never really "hearing" them complete or perfect is, in fact and irony, what makes them endure.

Can we ever really say that my writing is—or isn't—"deaf writing"? Can we ever really say that the Allen Sisters' photography was—or wasn't—"deaf art"? I don't think we can. Yet, in the fall of 2004, when the opportunity to deliver a lecture at the Columbus Museum of Art that would coincide with an exhibition of the Allen Sisters' photography was proposed to me, I can say for certain that my "deaf eyes" were definitely drawn to their "deaf eyes."

And here is what I saw.

The Allen Sisters grew up in a unique period and place in American deaf history. It was also a hard place, to be sure. The first half of the nineteenth century had been, for deaf people in America, a significant period of educational and social growth, as the first school for deaf children, the

American School for the Deaf (ASD), opened in Hartford, Connecticut, in 1817. Education for the students at ASD was delivered and encouraged in both oral English and manual sign language—a method that not only worked to meet with the linguistic capabilities of all the students but also allowed deaf adults to become teachers of deaf children. But, by midcentury, things began to shift considerably. By the mid-19th-century, oral education had once again become the favored method of education. The first major oral school in the United States, the Clarke School for the Deaf, in Northampton, Massachusetts, —just twelve miles from Deerfield, where the Allen Sisters lived—opened in 1867. And, while the first college for deaf and hard-of hearing people in the world—then known as the Columbia Institute for the Deaf, in Washington, DC, and now as Gallaudet University—also opened in 1864, oral education was fast taking hold as *the* method of instruction for deaf children in the United States.

The influence of Alexander Graham Bell was substantial in these oral-focused efforts. Bell's mother and his wife, Mabel Hubbard Bell (Ma Bell), were both deaf, and, in fact, Bell began his adult career as an oral educator for deaf children. Mabel had been one of his students. He stumbled onto the telephone—his most famous invention—because he was looking for a device that would help deaf people hear better and that would help him use, with more success, a method of teaching deaf pupils that he and his father had developed called "Visible Speech." Bell also developed the first audiometer—the prototype instrument for the measurement of hearing loss. Furthermore, Bell was also known as one of the leading eugenicists of the day, and he even wrote, and published, a eugenicist tract, *Graphical Studies of Marriages of the Deaf*, attempting to prove that when deaf people marry other deaf people, they often produced deaf children; therefore, Bell went on to reason from the logic of a "positive" eugenics philosophy that he had helped make popular, deaf people should be greatly discouraged from marrying other deaf people.

The eradication of sign languages and the support for, and dominance of, oral/speech-based means of communication and education for deaf people was crucial to Bell's eugenicist argument. For it was believed that, when deaf people had sign languages to share with each other, they were all the more likely to associate exclusively with each other and find, alas, their way to marriage. Raised orally, it was thought, deaf children would be all the more likely to mix and mingle and marry in the hearing world, thereby eventually decreasing (if not eradicating) the number of deaf children. At a famous international conference on the subject of deaf education, the Milan Conference of 1888, Bell himself spoke strongly in favor of oral-only education. And, when the vote was taken at the Milan Conference regarding what was called the oral-manual debate, sign language was declared forbidden as a viable method of educating (or communicating with) deaf children.[7]

The Allen Sisters grew up in the middle of this period when significant stigma was attached to deafness, when strictly oral methods were dominant in the education of deaf children, and when eugenics "science" declared deafness (and, thereby, deaf people) an aberration worthy of eradication and not deserving of marriage, particularly if the cause of deafness was unknown (as it was for the Allen Sisters) and potentially genetically transmissible. Perhaps they felt the stigma even more palpably because they were well educated and well off financially, because they began young adulthood with a career that depended significantly on their hearing, and, too, because they lived in such proximity to the nation's premier (and elite) school for oral education, the Clarke School. (And we do know, as I pointed out earlier, that the Allen Sisters both took some lipreading training at the Clarke School.)

One impact of the focus on oral education was that deaf women found themselves without employment opportunities at a time when America's women were entering the teaching force in great numbers. While deaf men, being men, had other kinds of work they could do, the possibilities were quite limited for deaf women. And once teaching—along with the focus on oral education—was taken from them, the limits were staggering. As the historian and Deaf Studies scholar Susan Burch has put it in her study of American Deaf History from 1900 to World War II, the combined trends of oralism and the overall feminization of the teaching force in America

> ultimately displaced educated Deaf women to an even greater extent, depriving them of both educational and career opportunities, as well as of social choices. . . . Thus, as oralism and other reform movements opened more opportunities for women in general, they closed doors for Deaf women. (19)

If deaf Americans overall were the subjects of "illusions of equality"—as the historian Robert Buchanan suggests in his book *Deaf Americans in School and Factory, 1850–1950*—deaf women were not even allowed the illusions, it seems.

Yet, clearly, Mary and Frances Allen had something more than illusions. They had a camera; failed careers as teachers and new time on their hands; a knack with children; a sensitivity to the soul of a pose; an educated and worldly sense of art and culture that was quite forward-looking, along with a strong sense of local flavor and understanding that also centered on saving and savoring the past (nostalgia, we might call it); and a community that embraced them and their work. And, of course, they had each other. With two pairs of deaf eyes, they looked out for each other. We know, for example, that Mary especially assisted Frances, whose hearing loss was considerably greater, when they traveled and also when they met with people to do their portraits.

When I look at their remaining images—both those on display in the traveling exhibit that came to the Columbus Art Museum in early 2005 and the roughly fifty more I could find digitally online via the Deerfield, Massachusetts, Memorial Hall Museum—I note that, as time went on and the sisters aged and became even more deaf (Frances was also mostly blind in the last ten years of her life), their photos move back and away from their earlier people-centered and posed portraits. These portraits would have surely been hard to do well as their deafness overtook them. Frances especially withdrew and communicated less and less with people in Deerfield; while Mary would still sometimes do actual portrait-taking or posing, Frances would complete the technical work and focus on other business-related tasks. In the later years, especially in the last five, 1915–1920, most of their photography was either of landscape—something they would not really need to listen to or interact socially with—or images that position them as the distant history-recording observer who chronicled the many pageants and events in the Deerfield community. From these positions, their camera and their photographer's eyes—deaf eyes—allowed them to remain in the scene, however distant. Yet, whether they were watching and recording from close up or afar, the deaf eyes of the Misses Allen behind their cameras were serving, in effect, as tools of communication and social interaction, art and income, history and hope. Through the (deaf) eyes of their camera lenses, the Allen Sisters, deaf but deftly, negotiated their way in a larger hearing, male-dominated world.

6

Posting Mabel

Postcard 1: Calling the Dead

6.1 "Telephone a nuisance—radio a joy to Alexander Graham Bell." Photograph courtesy of the Library of Congress.

Dear Mabel:

I confess, I have found my way to you through your husband, Alexander Graham Bell.[1] I suspect I am not the only one who met or wrote you through this channel. Your presence first appeared to me in a poem I once wrote to "Alec" himself. The poem began like this:

> *Call to A.G. Bell*
> *Got some quarters*
> *so I call you up on the telephone*
> *ring-ring-ring*
> *but only your wife and mother are home,*
> *so no one answers.*
> *You are out charting and graphing*
> *marriages and progeny*
> *of the deaf,*
> *while only your wife and mother*
> *—deaf—*
> *are home. (ringed in)*

Using my literary license, I tried to phone Alec back through the ages. Rumor has it, however, that he was never very fond of the phone himself.

The image on the front of this postcard is from a photo dated May 5, 1922—just three months before his death and the last clearly dated photograph of him in the U.S. Library of Congress collection. It shows him sitting in front of a radio, wearing headphones and holding his pipe. I know how much the keeping of records and the legacy of your husband and his work mattered to you, Mabel; you were, after all, the primary reason we even now have such extensive records of his letters, your letters, and all these photographs. I thought you would be interested to know that the record of this last living image from the archives has a caption attached to it that is uncharacteristically interpretive when compared to many of the other more plainly descriptive captions in the entire collection of A. G. Bell images. This caption tells us: "Telephone a nuisance—radio a joy to Alexander Graham Bell."

I hope it is not a nuisance that I am writing postcards to you now. These seem a more useful way for me to approach you than, say, a séance. I'm an academic, after all, and not given much to spiritualism— table tipping, channeled voices, near-dark rooms, or automatic writing (although that might come in handy for university paperwork). What good are those to a deaf person anyway? I have enough trouble just communicating with the living.

I'm deaf, but, like you, Mabel, I'm also a very skilled "speechreader." My deafness is genetic. I'd like to write to you again. May I? BJB

Postcard 2: Communicating With Alec

Dear Mabel:
There is no image on this postcard. You'll just have to imagine. I think you can. Current copyright laws won't let me get this picture to you; it's too complicated, too anachronistic, too much creative license. It's "too-too," as we would say these days. Following on Hamlet's first soliloquy, if I could show this image to you, then perhaps this "too too solid flesh would melt." Things might unravel.

I took an official portrait of the great A. G. Bell in his later years, and I played with it using Photoshop. In the portrait, Alec is quite fleshy. I know you worried much about his girth. I can see why. It doesn't seem to be the kind that would melt easily. On the image, I've applied some shading and an antiqued filter, using an overlay of brown and orange tones, to give the

6.2 A "postcard" without an image.

image more depth and warmth and also to offer an even more stately, perhaps even an ominous, tone as I channeled him forward into my era, an age of awesome digital media technologies. (Maybe I'm interested in séances after all?) I've also worked in various newer telecommunications devices and embodied him with them (or is it *them* I've embodied with *him*?) A little image of a TV, with another image of me playing on the screen, has been placed, perhaps telepathically, on his forehead; an AOL Instant Messaging screen nestles in his impressive white beard, right below his mouth; and a BlackBerry is tucked in where his jacket pocket would be.

He is indeed prepared to communicate.

And yet, as you know, he often didn't. You and he lived your lives in an ironic dance of communication. He once wrote to you, some thirteen years into your marriage, that:

> *I feel more and more as I grow older the tendency to retire into myself and be alone with my thoughts. I can see that same tendency in my father and Uncle in an exaggerated degree—and suppose there is something in the blood. My children have it too, but in lesser degree—because they are younger I suppose. You alone are free from it—and you my dear constitute the chief link between myself and the world outside. (May 5, 1890)[2]*

Three years later, in another letter, he repeats this characterization: "*You are always so thoughtful of others—whereas I somehow or other appear to be more interested in things than people—in people wholesale, rather than in persons individual*" (June 2, 1894).

Others who were close to him remarked on the same tendencies. Shortly after Alec's death, your own son-in-law, David Fairchild, said of him: "Mr.

Bell led a peculiarly isolated life; I have never known anyone who spent so much of his time alone" (Bruce 307). And even early in his life, a Scottish friend, Marie Eccleston, wrote to him just as he was leaving for America in 1870 (at the age of twenty-three): "Don't get absorbed in yourself—mix freely with your fellows—it is one of your great failings" (Bruce 308).

Yet even you, it seems, could not save him from his self-absorption. Did you ever find peace with that? Or was it one of the shadows that followed your marriage, longer and darker then shorter and lighter in varying seasons? He worked alone late at night and into the early morning and then slept through most of the regular morning hours when others, including you, were bustling about. You hated this. You worked hard—and often with some anger, it seems—to keep him social with others, as well as yourself.

In 1895, after eighteen years of marriage, you wrote to him, again apparently frustrated with his "deaf mute business" (which always seemed to chafe you) but also scolding him about his aloofness: "*Your deaf mute business is hardly human to you. You are very tender and gentle to the deaf children, but their interest to you lies in their being deaf, not in their humanity, at least only in part*" (July 9, 1895).

Did you sometimes also think that you, Mabel, were of interest to him only in your being deaf and not in your "humanity"? That would certainly be something like the "slings and arrows of outrageous misfortune," now, wouldn't it?

That same year (1895) you wrote to him from Paris, and, even in your absence, you were most concerned with his way of being absent when present with others: "*I cannot bear to think of you living all alone, shut in yourself, holding no communication with your neighbors. Please please don't go back to such a life. . . . Please try and come out of your hermit cell. . . . I want you to succeed in your experiments, but not to lose all human interest in the process*" (July 9, 1895). You seemed then to understand keenly the role you played in keeping him present, engaged, communicative. But that understanding was not ever really acceptance, was it? And it must have been hard (perhaps even a bit self-absorbed?) work at times. Even after thirty years of marriage, your discomfort, perhaps even disdain, with him spills from your pen: *You have lived too much by yourself. You've talked about nature and solitude and all that, but you haven't been in the crowd at all and that's what you need* (March 10, 1907).

So, while he chose isolation and seemed even to seek it, to embrace it, you only endured its imposition. What rankled you most, Mabel— that Alec's isolation would often become yours, as well? Or that Alec was hearing, and, as such, he had the *choice* of aloofness, noncommunication, and isolation, while you often did not? Where exactly did your hurt on this matter come from? Or go to?

The irony is almost too much to bear, isn't it? His biographer, Robert Bruce, claimed that "no one word covers all his activities, but the one that covers most is the word 'communication'" (307). Yet the inventor of the telephone, a teacher of the deaf, the developer of an instructional method known as "Visible Speech"—the need and apparatus for communication apparently etched everywhere in his consciousness—finds himself locked in his own reclusive tendencies while his deaf wife pounds on the shell of his diving bell. Yet, bear it you did. Perhaps this was your own personal communication legacy?

I'll admit, I'm curious about all of this because I dance similar steps with my own husband. I have a recurring nightmare that I can remember having even when I was a teenager. In it, the people sometimes change, but the scene and script stay the same, like an old record caught in a scratched groove. In this dream, I am trying to communicate with someone. Sometimes I am naked, as well, and not comfortably so. But that someone not only doesn't seem to hear me, they don't seem to see me. I don't seem to exist. It is as if my too too solid flesh has melted. They are there—right there before me—but I am alone. I cry, I beg, I spew angry words to incite a response, ask rhetorical questions, contort my body to draw their attention, flap and flop around as if my head has been cut off in the yard. They do not communicate back.

If I have the dream again, I think I will write to you when I wake. Please don't let me melt.

Yours in communication, BJB

Postcard 3: Writing

Dear Mabel,

I have found this lovely photo of you. It comes from the summer of 1922, shortly after Alec died, and it was taken by your son-in-law, David Fairchild. You are sitting at your morning room desk at Beinn Bhreagh, the estate at Cape Breton, Nova Scotia. A very small table with a typewriter is before you, and you are engaged in writing; your right hand is on the carriage, and there is a fresh piece of paper just rolled in. You sit in a wicker chair, and light from both windows, in front of and behind you, floods your back and face; it must actually then be close to midday.

6.3 Mabel Hubbard Bell
at her writing desk, 1922,
Beinn Bhreagh. Photograph
courtesy of the Library of
Congress.

Now, first, let me say that I think you should get a different chair. This one must be very bad for your back. I hope you at least have a pillow wedged at your lumbar area? And that desk is so small you have no place to put your water, your tea, your wine, a piece of toast. Can you really write without food or drink?

I've been reading, and rereading, your letters, Mabel—trying to get a handle, a glimpse, an impression of your life through the words you left on pages to others. You loved letters, didn't you? Everything about your posture and composure in this image says that. You lean slightly forward, not pained but both sturdy and relaxed in the kind of engagement that seems not intense yet seriously attentive. Your hand is ready at the carriage wheel—ready to roll your day, your thoughts, your very self into written words. Your profiled face seems serene yet studious, eager but not inappropriately zealous, about the correspondence ahead of you.

I wish you would write to me!

You were always begging Alec to write. . . .

> *Your telegrams never say anything of yourself, how you are and what you are doing. I can't stand this silence much longer—I must have a letter no matter how busy you are. Have you really no desire to make me share in your thoughts and feelings? (June 27, 1888)*
>
> *No word from you today, I wish there were. I think your lambs could spare you long enough to indite a telegram at least. (April 21, 1891)*
>
> *I want to thank you so much for your kind letter received today. It is so nice to get a little petting and sympathy from you Alec dear. (November 23, 1896)*
>
> *Still no word from you. . . . (May 29, 1898)*

> *I did not think it was a very kind or gracious thing for you to tell me that to write to me properly was to steal time from your thoughts and experiments. Surely your wife has a right to a few minutes of your time and thoughts once in awhile? (May 20, 1899)*

And, at the end of this same letter:

> *Good night, I have sat up late to write all this. Will you read it at all? I know your abhorrence of long letters, but I forgot it until just now. Will not bother you again in this way. I find however I like typewriting. It does not tire my hand the way a pen does, and I fancy you prefer it to my penmanship. You have no old fashioned preferences for something your wife's hand has touched and which bears the mark of her individuality! (May 20, 1899)*

Yet, Mabel, your letters clearly did seem to bear the mark of your individuality. I see that mark in this late photograph of you. How the light shines when you are writing your letters. How your "morning room" could eclipse into noon and you would still be, at peace, writing.

You remind me of something I once wrote in an essay on "passing": *Writing is my pass, writing is my passageway, through writing I pass.*

I will write again soon, BJB

Postcard 4: Passing

Dear Mabel,

There you go, passing again. I have found an image of you in a canoe with Alec—you in front, he behind—on Bras D'Or Lake near your home, Beinn Bhreagh, at Baddeck, Nova Scotia. Now, they say sound carries especially well over water, but I still don't think that's going to help you "hear" and lipread Alec from behind. Perhaps that's convenient for both of you?

I've been wondering how you actually *did* lipread (or "speechread," as you called it) Alec in the first place? Now I don't know about you, but I am generally pretty skilled at this lipreading thing. In fact, I'm so good that most of the time I even fool *myself* into thinking that I can "hear" what someone is saying . . . until that frightening moment when, say, someone walks between me and the person I am lipreading and the whole slate of conversation just goes utterly blank for me then. It's like someone

6.4 Mabel Hubbard Bell and Alexander Graham Bell, Bras D'Or Lake. Photograph courtesy of the Library of Congress.

bumped the Etch-a-Sketch drawing I had going and sent me right back to the empty gray screen.

But I have skills. I pass pretty well. I've been going to my department's faculty meetings for fifteen years now and passing through them without a captioner or interpreter. (There are reasons why I've made that choice for these particular meetings even though I use a captioner in all my classrooms and at other university committee meetings these days . . . but that's another letter for another day.) Oh, sure, I miss things. But I don't seem to have missed that much. One person in my department knits throughout the meetings. I like to imagine then that I too am knitting the little yarns of the conversation that I can grab hold of into something useful. Maybe a shawl for the days when my office is too cold?

Except, alas, I have no patience (or skills) for knitting, real or imaginary.

This letter is an example: I started by wanting to ask you how you could ever really lipread Alec? But I have followed a thread elsewhere. . . .

My point was that there are two situations that make lipreading (and, therefore, passing) very hard for me: men with full facial hair and people speaking English but doing so with a strong foreign accent. The latter just form their words differently, the consonants don't cluster the same, the vowels veer off from the patterns I so patiently learned. But the former, the hairy-faced men, well, I might as well try to have a conversation with my cat. There's hair. And a mouth that moves a little, a slip of pink tongue, the point or glint of a tooth . . . something that looks like it might be sound. But there isn't any sense of it.

How did you do it? Did you ever ask him to shave it all off? Did you ever tell him you were tired of passing?

The only accounts I can find, through your letters and also from that famous piece you published in *The Atlantic Monthly* about "speechreading," tell me, over and over again, that you really had no trouble whatsoever "listening" to your husband. In his biography of A. G. Bell, Robert Bruce remarks that you managed to lipread "so well that none of the family thought of her as deaf" (321). Well, of course they didn't. You wouldn't allow it. Bruce also notes that Alec "never needed to use finger spelling with [you] as he had with his mother [and Helen Keller]. Lipreading was enough" (321).

You even wrote in that 1895 "Subtle Art of Speech-Reading" article of your clear reading of Alec's lips: *It is no uncommon occurrence for my husband to talk to me perhaps for an hour at a time of something in which he is interested. It may be on the latest geographical discoveries, Sir Robert Ball's Story of the Sun, the latest news from the Chinese war, some abstruse scientific problem in gravitation—anything and everything. Very rarely do I have to ask him to repeat.*

Well, I have to tell you, if he talked to me for "an hour at a time," I don't think I'd ask him to repeat much either. But, aside from that, I still doubt you here. I need more context for this passing, listening, lipreading thing you did, Mabel. Especially with Alec.

Did you only row the boat and look out on your own private waterworld on outings like the one here?

In a 1906 letter to a friend, you agreed with Helen Keller about whether deafness or blindness were the "worse" of the two, when you claimed that: *I have always declared I would sooner be blind than deaf . . . the blind through their ability to hear are able to be the centre of everything, whereas it is extremely difficult for a deaf person to be kept or to keep himself in close touch with the intimate family life going on around him* (March 15, 1906). Yet, you also, in that same letter, played your passing card well: *From my power of speech reading I have been able to overcome much of the difficulty and am, I believe, nearly as much the centre of my home as any hearing mother can be* (March 15, 1906).

"As any hearing mother can be." Ah, yes, I understand all too keenly the deaf person's position of always but always being stuck in that unequal comparative script. But what, then, of any hearing wife? You do not look much at "the centre" in this rowboat.

You wanted, and you worked very hard, to pass. Bell's biographer, Robert Bruce, notes that not only did you have to contend "with [your] handicap in understanding others but also with the deficiencies in [your] speech that made it difficult at first acquaintance for others to understand her" (Bruce 321). Alec himself once publicly defended your speech after a talk you had given: "The value of speech is in its intelligibility," he reminded the audience, "not in its perfection" (1892; Bruce 322).

Intelligible, intelligent, yet imperfect. I suppose, then, you were just human after all? And, however "imperfect" you or others might have judged you for your hearing loss, it seems that you rarely gave up your passing, rarely owned your difference. Waite's biography of your "romance" with Alexander Graham Bell, *Make a Joyful Sound*, records that only near the end of your life did you really offer "a glimpse into the lifelong struggle behind [you]" in a letter to your niece, Helen Bell: *All my life I have tried my hardest to have you children and everyone else forget that I am not the same as your mother, for instance* (259). With regard to your hearing loss, you always "tried my hardest" to have others forget what your difference was, working to claim a place and identity, as you said, "nearly as much the centre of my home as any hearing mother can be."

In a letter to a family friend, a few months after Alec's death and a few months before your own, you stated directly your credo on this matter: *I shrink from any reference to my disability and won't be seen in public with another deaf person* (1919). Yes, it's harder to pass when you are with those you don't want to look like. As my colleague Tobin Siebers has written, with some humor, in his own credo-essay, "My Withered Limb":

> The solitude of the disabled is crushing. We are barred from gathering among ourselves by the laws of human physics, which declare that gravity exerts five times its influence where two cripples stand in one place, ten times its influence where four of us gather. All objects slump close to the horizon and threaten to crash to the earth where the burden of weight finds its final rest. (25)

Given the gravity of your own desire to pass and "shrink," I wonder, then, if you would have been seen with me? For myself, I would have enjoyed very much a canoe outing with you. I am never more comfortable than when I am on, in, or around water. I like the rhythm of rowing and the way sound is indeed magnified on water. I would have turned to face you in that boat, rowing backwards, our lips both ready for the reading.

The view is just as good from the rear as it is facing forward when you are on water, I think. We could have passed the time of day there, together. Passing, rowing, reading.

Yours in passing, BJB

Postcard 5: Oh, Brave New Technology!

Dear Mabel,

I would like to introduce you to Shelby. Shelby is one of the "supporting actresses" in a remarkable documentary film, *Sound and Fury,* that aired on PBS first in 2000. Shelby is not actually the star of the show in this film—that honor would go to Heather, the young deaf girl whose deaf parents (and grandparents, both deaf and hearing) are embroiled in cultural and familial controversy over whether or not Heather, age five, should get a cochlear implant (C.I.). In trying to make this decision, Heather's (deaf) family visits several other families whose children have C.I.s, and they also take Heather to several schools where children with C.I.s are "integrated." Shelby is someone Heather visits both at home and school. Shelby's parents are hearing, and she apparently does not associate now with deaf people, either adult or peers, at all; she does not use sign language. She is "successfully integrated" into a "regular" school, even though her teacher has to wear a special individual microphone that connects directly to Shelby's implant, and this would also then mean that Shelby is always tuned in and turned on to her teacher but not necessarily to her peers. Now there's a lesson in learning.

Really, though, it is not so much Shelby, the person, as it is Shelby's technology—that cochlear implant surgically placed in her head and wired to a transmitter at her waist—that I wanted to introduce you to. Alec himself would likely be more interested in Shelby's technology than in Shelby herself; he was, at your own admission in a letter you once wrote to him, more interested in his "deaf mute business" and the *deaf children [because] their interest to you lies in their being deaf, not in their humanity* (July 9, 1895).

In fact, I think Alec could have invented the cochlear implant; feel free to show him this image of Shelby and share this postcard with him, if you'd like. I'm sure he would be interested. The C.I. would have been right up his inventive alley, and it would have certainly helped carry out his twinned dreams—that there would be a device that would help deaf people speak better (the thing he was looking for when he invented the telephone) and that something could perhaps prevent deaf people from having too much exclusive contact and forming what he wrote strongly against, "a deaf variety of the human race." In his full eugenics frame of mind, he argued, in his 1884 treatise, *Memoir Upon the Formation of a Deaf Variety of the Human Race*, that "Those who believe as I do, that the production of a defective race of human beings would be a great calamity to the world, will examine carefully the causes that lead to the intermarriage of the deaf with the object of applying a remedy."

Never mind that he more or less assigned you a defective human being here (and also saved you from the "calamity" of "intermarriage" to the deaf?). Instead, I want to focus on the cochlear implant as an object of his desired applicable remedy. But it is, of course, only one of many such modern technological objects. For, while the deaf community itself currently spends a good deal of its anxiety and attention on the cochlear implant as a potential tool for cultural "genocide," the unfolding terrain of communicative and technological options for deaf people in the 21st century now not only makes it possible for deaf people to interact more and perhaps better with their hearing peers but, ironically, also puts them in better touch with each other. The social and cultural fabric of a thing called "Deaf culture" or even of "the deaf community" is currently quite durable, strong, and tight knit—and much of its present strength comes from technologies that are just as pervasive as cochlear implants.

Indeed, in a five-page position statement the National Association of the Deaf (NAD) issued about cochlear implants in October 2000, it too acknowledges that the C.I. is one of many powerful "technological advancements with the potential to foster, enhance, and improve the quality of life for all deaf and hard of hearing persons." Yet, the rhetorical exigency the NAD must have felt surrounding the cochlear implant is evident in the care given to developing a five-page public position statement about this surgically implanted, outrageously expensive bit of biopower; in such an exigency, while they acknowledge the C.I.'s anxious place in the lives of 21st-century deaf cyborgs, they also follow that with a list of cautions:

> Cochlear implantation is a technology that represents a tool to be used in some forms of communication, and not a cure for deafness. Cochlear implants provide sensitive hearing, but do not, by themselves, impart the ability to understand spoken language through listening alone. In addition, they do not guarantee the development of cognition or reduce the

benefit of emphasis on parallel visual language and literacy development.
(http://www.nad.org/site/pp.asp?c=foINKQMBF&b=138146)

Now, that's some "surgeon general's warning," don't you think?

I also think you would not have been daunted by these warnings. Am I right? I think you would have welcomed any tool you could really use in some, or any, forms of communication. Yet, I'm not as sure, and I suspect you aren't either, that it would have really changed any of your forms of communication with Alec himself.

And there's the rub, isn't it? He would have no doubt been proud to invent this tool. It would have been every bit as useful as that breathing pump he revived a drowned sheep with (which later became the iron lung that some polio victims learned to live out their lives in). And surely every bit as useful—and a nuisance—as the telephone.

I want to picture you then with a cochlear implant, e-mail, and the Internet at your disposal, daily blogs to sift through, a listserve to log onto. If nothing else, these all might have made your yearning—no, your torment—over Alec's lack of attentive communication less palpable? And maybe, too, they would have made you feel differently about Alec's paradoxical aloof obsession with his "deaf-mute business"?

The part of my "Call to A.G. Bell" poem I sent you in an earlier postcard was the opening. At the end of this poem I go on, in fact, to consider all the other available means of communication and applicable remedies we might now use to connect:

> *No, wait—*
> *I'll fax you the facts;*
> *I'll send a video,*
> *documentary of my life,*
> *captioning and all,*
> *interpreter on standby;*
> *or perhaps a vlog, video relay service,*
> *an e-mail, or instant message even—*
> *coming through.*
>
> *Let's "talk."*
> *But oh—*
> *now that I've gotten my medium,*
> *I've forgotten my message.*

I guess, Mabel, that sometimes having the tools doesn't necessarily make the communication happen, let alone make it become meaningful. Sometimes, the methods alone aren't much of a message. Do you think we should let Alec in on this wisdom? BJB

Postcard 6: Women and Children

This image appears, reappears, replicates itself in virtually every book I have found about A. G. Bell, about you and Mr. Bell, about just you. It is an official family portrait from 1885. It makes me anxious. Yet I also can't stop staring at it. The girls are young, Elsie at age seven and Daisy at age five. You have also recently lost two sons who both died shortly after their births—Edward in 1881 and Robert in 1883. I think their ghosts haunt this portrait.

I have never lost a child. But my youngest sister has lost two—and two boys at that. Even today, with her one beautiful daughter now married and happy with a successful career, my sister's character always seems a

6.5 Alexander Graham Bell family portrait, 1885. Photograph courtesy of the Library of Congress.

bit anchored down—ever on the verge of a deep sigh, and with a slightly dulled tinge from those losses surrounding her.

There is space in this portrait for Edward and Robert; they inhabit, in their absence, the triangular place cut between you and Alec, the space behind where Daisy, their younger oldest sister, sits. It is this space you are gazing toward—a space past (or through?) Alec himself.

You are in this portrait. But you are not. Your girls and Alec all face the camera, their eyes aimed at one object together. You are not with them. You are smaller even than your daughters! The tight angles of your body match the slant of your gaze, which travels in the direction of Alec, to your left, but then goes right past him somewhere into infinity. Into ghosts.

There are angles everywhere. You predate Picasso's own "weeping woman." Your eyes angle slightly downward as if ready to avoid Alec's eyes should they move to meet yours. Or perhaps your eyes angle downward as if to look at subjects smaller than you. The only thing that anchors you in this portrait is your elbow, so angular and stiff, locked into Elsie's hand. In fact, Elsie, whose seven-year-old form is far more substantial than yours here, holds you up; your fragile, slight, angular, corseted frame edges against her arm. The corset itself traps you as a triangle. The bent of your arm with Elsie's locked through it creates a harsh right angle that is anything but right. The deep V and gulf of ghost-white space between you and Alec dominates, in angularity, the center of the portrait. The inverted triangle from your shoulders to your bound waist reverses the one of your head with your chin tucked tight against your neck. Elsie's legs are crossed at her ankles, another triangle, with her knees held tight against each other, while Daisy's legs are in a more relaxed pose (and less lady-like, perhaps, but, then again, she was only five) with her knees wide apart, although her ankles also come to a crossed position; another triangle, then, is captured in the pose of Daisy's legs and dominates the central foreground of the picture. Your right hand extends from the right elbow angle that is held by Elsie and comes to rest, just lightly, on Daisy's shoulder. Without the girls, you would collapse to the floor or drift, spirit-like, up out of the image. They anchor you; they shore you up. The three of you, a woman and her children, form your own triangular unit.

Alec alone is square. Alec is alone.

And he seems to realize this in 1885, as well. In a long, anxious, and effusive letter to you on December 12, 1885, written to you from New York—approximately two years after you lost David, your second son—he begins by confessing that in your eight years of marriage he has largely offered you "words—without soul—like too many of the letters I have written to you of late years." His letter is filled with memories of how he wooed you and then near-desperate claims of his debt, respect, and love—"All that I am to-day I owe to you and yours. I love you darling more than you can ever know." But then, following on these anxious endearments, he wonders, first, "whether it is best for you that I should return just now" and then turns that wonder into his own clear opinion on the matter: "I do not believe that anything short of our complete separation for a time will secure to you that perfect rest that I am sure you need to make you well." In the longest paragraph of the letter, near the end when he declares your "complete separation" necessary, he comes, finally, to the real heart of the matter—the loss of your two sons and his own guilt over those losses:

> And when death came and robbed us of the little ones we wanted so much you forgot your own suffering to try and comfort me. Dear—dear Mabel. My true sweet wife—nothing will ever comfort me for the loss of these two babes for I feel at heart that I was the cause. I do not grieve because they were boys but because I believe that my ignorance and selfishness caused their deaths and injured you. In the first child's case one cause seems clear both to you and me. After his death I prevented you from fully recovering and gave you another child before you were well. You have not even yet completely recovered and I believe you never will until you have had a complete and prolonged rest. (December 12, 1885)

In an undated letter you write to Alec that seems of the same period, you also bring up the loss of your son and, in the very same short breath, your additional sense of your own lack as a mother. Here, your hearing—its loss—haunts the text, forms the cross of your own burden that you try to share with (or shove upon?) him:

> I believe in God, perhaps the reason our boy was taken from us so early was that we have not done our duty by the children we have, perhaps we may never have one until we prove that we are able and willing to give our children proper care. Why was our wealth given us if not to give you time to make up to your children what they lose by their Mother's loss. They need to be better cared for now, for by and by they will have to act more for themselves than other more fortunate mothers children. (undated)

"What they lose by their Mother's loss" . . . if only they were "more fortunate mothers children." I hardly know what more to write now, Mabel. This portrait, these words—they drive a wedge through my own heart.

You end this letter as "your loving but distressed wife" and set down, the weeping woman, a sentence that swirls in pain: "Alec I am frightened and don't see what we are coming to." In this portrait I can hardly see you. I am frightened too.

Distressed but loving, BJB

Postcard 7: Making your World

Dear Mabel,

I think many of my posts so far have been a little gloomy, critical, doubting. Maybe that's the academic in me again. I want to try now a more positive angle on your life. Let me go then to Beinn Bhreagh.

The first ten years of your marriage seemed "loving but distressed" as you began to raise (largely by yourself) two daughters who were apparently quite a handful (judging from some of the accounts you give of them in letters to Alec), lost two sons at childbirth, and learned to cope with your husband's fame, indulging his many idiosyncrasies (such as working through the night and sleeping late in the mornings) and enduring his absence, always his absence—even when present but also because he did travel much in those earlier days. And, although you had wondered, in frightened words set down in an undated letter to Alec, what you were coming to, you did eventually come to much. You began to make your way in the world and even to make your own world.

6.6 Beinn Bhreagh. Photograph courtesy of the Library of Congress.

You and Alec found, quite by accident on your way to Newfoundland, a place in Cape Breton Island, Nova Scotia. This was in the summer of 1885, the same year as that haunting family portrait—a hard and strained time after the death of your two sons in 1881 and 1883. It was love at first sight; you wrote in your journal, on your first encounter with Baddeck, that there were "forest-covered hills, undulating valleys with trim, well-kept fields and neat little houses pretty streams. . . . Baddeck is certainly possessed of a gentle restful beauty, and I think we would be content to stay here many weeks just enjoying the lights and shades on all the hills and isles and lakes" (September 17, 1885; Bruce 300–1).

My reading of various biographies of your husband tells me that the place also suited Alec for its Scottish flavors and as a perfect summer retreat, since the heat of Washington, DC, had a tendency to cause him significant headaches and heat rash. The following year, in 1886, the two of you bought fifty acres on the point and a cottage and then proceeded, over the next seven years, to buy out all the farmers on the headland. In 1893, your estate, Beinn Bhreagh Hall, in Baddeck, Nova Scotia, was completed. As the "Beautiful Mountain," it sat on an imposing cliff over Lake Bras D'Or. For the next thirty-six years, largely in the summer months, from April–May until November, it became your home, and you made your own way there.

From some of the photos of the main house sitting up over a formidable cliff, it does not always look like a very friendly place to me, but, then again, I can understand why you would have flourished here. In Washington, DC, I am sure your deafness mattered much more. While the oppressive swamp-like heat bothered Alec, I would think that the demand of social events in the nation's capital, and even the very "advanced" cultural pressure of being deaf in America at that particular time (and married to the particular man that you were), would have been much harder to negotiate than the rural life of Beinn Bhreagh in remote Cape Breton Island, Nova Scotia. I doubt you were anywhere near as "deaf" at Beinn Bhreagh as you were in the eastern United States at the turn of the 20th century.

Now I grew up in western Kansas. I know all about this. Out on the rural plains of Kansas where there are more cows than people, I was easily "mainstreamed" in a time before mainstreaming became standard educational practice. I didn't even really know how "different" I was until I went to college at the University of Kansas, seven hours across the wide state from my own hometown. And although those first two years of college were ones of outstanding social isolation and I admittedly over-studied for fear of all I was not getting from those lecture halls where I sat with 250 other students. In the end, the university life suited me very well. At college—deeply engaged in books, ideas, and writing—I began, as you did at Beinn Bhreagh, to make my way in the world and even, to make my own world.

There are at least a dozen pictures of you and Alec on walks, holding hands, at Beinn Bhreagh. A dozen more of you near or on the water with him and always then looking peaceful, sometimes even smiling. Hundreds with your children and grandchildren gathered about you on the grounds, the porches, the shores. Your first grandchild was born there, in 1902. You arranged grand dinners and themed banquets for both the locals and visitors who were often working with Alec on his experiments and projects—with sheep, with flight, with boat-building during World War I.

And since there was very little of the "learned society" you were used to in America, you just created your own at Beinn Bhreagh—began, that is, to invent your own world. You were no longer bound, I think, by what society decided you could and could not do (given your deafness). There you became more of a partner in Alec's experiments with sheep and kites and aviation, deeply interested in this work on the slopes of your "Beautiful Mountain" in a way that you had never been engaged with either his "deaf mute business" or the telephone's invention in America. You started Baddeck's first public library, set up the "Home Industries of Baddeck" to display and sell the handiwork of the local women, established The Young Ladies Club of Baddeck (modeled on the Washington Club of which you were a member), which brought women—and men—together to discuss books, art, travel, local and world events, brought the first Victorian Order of Nurses (VON) to Baddeck to improve health care in the area, formed what was essentially the first Canadian parent-teacher educational association and the first Canadian Home and School Association, and founded the Children's Laboratory at Beinn Bhreagh Estate, which was Canada's first Montessori school.

Such a busy bee! You created a fortress against the loneliness and distress you had formerly felt with Alec, didn't you? And, apparently, ironically, it seemed to have only drawn him in and closer to you. What a clever girl!

You made yourself not just the object of his affection but indispensable to him in many ways. At Beinn Bhreagh, you took over all the accounts and maintenance of this vast estate and much of Alec's affairs.

He would send you telegrams and letters that were really only scientific notebooks—lists, for example, of the latest results of his study with twin-nippled sheep. You would keep the records for him. You wrote to your mother one October at Beinn Bhreagh that "If Alec is well it is by my care; he is nearly as irresponsible as a baby. He always was, you know" (October, undated; Bruce 328). At Beinn Bhreagh he seemed to become more exclusively your baby, and the care you extended there—where the rest of the modern world could not distract him so much—knitted you back together, didn't it?

Yours in busyness, BJB

Postcard 8: Flights and Fancy

Dear Mabel,

If the family portrait of 1885 scares the hell out of me, this one reassures me. In fact, it delights me. It is from 1903, now twenty-six years into your marriage, and taken at Beinn Bhreagh. Alec is in the triangle this time.

The caption with this particular image placed in a photographic biography by Dorothy Harley Eber, *Genius at Work: Images of Alexander Graham Bell*, quips, "Testing the virtues of aluminum kite frames." You are standing inside a tetrahedral aluminum frame, surrounded by it and holding it up much as you might hold up your skirts crossing a puddle.

6.7 Testing the virtues of aluminum kite frames; Alexander Graham Bell and Mabel Hubbard Bell. Photograph courtesy of the Library of Congress.

Alec stands outside the frame and with his body half twisted to the side, his head reaching into the frame for a kiss; you lean slightly forward to give—or to receive—a kiss. You might be the woman in Klimt's famous 1907–08 painting, *Der Küss*, except that, instead of having circles patterned on your clothes, you stand enclosed and adorned by triangles while Mr. Bell's big square frame—much like the man in Klimt's painting—reaches toward you, Mr. Bell's head tipped at a considerable right angle.

Alec was said to have been always interested in flight, even when he was inventing the telephone, but his interest flew to obsessive heights once the expansive grounds and cliffs of Beinn Bhreagh were available to serve his fancy for flight. And, just as in this image, you were right there with him, making yourself now the object of his interest and desire. You made yourself, literally, a part of his experiments. It was your financial backing, in fact, that formed the Aerial Experiment Association (AEA) in 1907. Thirty-five thousand dollars of your own money! For this, you definitely deserve a kiss!

We might think of you, then, as the first lady of aviation. Yet, I suspect what it really meant to you was a way for you to work outdoors with Alec and to be together with him, rather than stuck, alone and frightened, on the other side of his aloofness, his egocentricity, his tendency to become so singlemindedly absorbed in whatever experiment, project, or work he was currently taken with that you would slip right out of not only his figurative mind but his literal lipreading range. You wrote to him in 1894 after a visit to your parents that *I realize as I see Mamma and Papa, Grace and Charlie together how little you give me of your time and thoughts, how little willing you are to enter into little things, which yet make up the sum of our lives* (May 28, 1894).

And so, it seems that you began to discover that if he could not be made to enter into the little things of your daily life or your children's daily lives, then you would have to find more ways to enter into his and to break through the barrier of an utter absorption that he even admitted to. Writing to you about a kind of second honeymoon you took in 1895 to Mexico, he confessed: *I meant to give you pleasure, but pleased myself instead. I meant to devote myself to you, but the scientific men and old mines, etc. were all for me. I fear that selfishness is a trait of my character. I can see it very clearly in others, but I do not recognize it in myself until too late* (May 20, 1895).

You worked hard to overcome that selfishness, it seems to me; perhaps even harder than you worked to pass or overcome your hearing loss.

Writing to him about the "in common" bond you felt with him even in the earliest summers of your time at Beinn Bhreagh, you wondered:

> *do you ever think of me in the midst of that work of yours of which I am so proud and yet so jealous, for I know it has stolen from me part of my husband's heart. . . . I lie in hope that you will not quite forget me, and that we may pass another summer like the last when we had thoughts and interests in common. (December 3, 1889)*

If he will not think of you in the midst of his work, why not then bring yourself into the midst: simply don one of his inventions, that light aluminum tetrahedral kite, and watch him then flutter, like a moth to the light, toward you? Brilliant, my girl.

I salute you, BJB

Postcard 9: Language and the Garden

Dear Mabel,

This is one of me that I am sending you. I thought it only fair to give you an image back after spending so much time scouring through yours. I think you will know instantly why I have chosen it. Many of the biographies remark on your love of, and skill with, your gardens at Beinn

6.8 Brenda Brueggemann, Columbus, Ohio, August 2003.

Bhreagh. This is me from my backyard garden in Columbus, Ohio. I'm probably not half the gardener you were. But I do have both a passion and knack for it.

My mother did, as well. Every year, she would turn our semidesert western Kansas yard into a veritable oasis. From May until October, she would spend every nonworking moment after her 5 p.m. day job ended as the town's city clerk, out in the yard. We three daughters would fetch "jelly sandwiches" for ourselves while she labored, in love, with flowers that were shamelessly exotic in western Kansas. She alone might be responsible for the nearly complete draining of the already dreadfully low water table in western Kansas.

I don't get that carried away. But I do seem to have an eye and hand for growing up the green things. But, mostly, I have just always been happiest when I am outdoors. And in the sun.

So, when my university's alumni magazine wanted to do a feature story on me and how I had developed the American Sign Language program and also a Disability Studies program at Ohio State and they came around to take my picture, I suggested doing it in the sun, in my own backyard, in my garden—even though it was late August and the garden was beginning to get a little raggedy. They titled the piece "For the Love of Language."

The book in my hand is actually one my husband was reading and had left out on the patio. He is always reading—always but always reading. Now, I like books a lot, too. But my time and interest with books compared to his is probably something like the time and interest you took in Alec's fancy with flight as compared to Alec's actual time and interest in that work. I think I have loved books more as a way to lead me to writing—as a means to an end. But my husband loves books, I think, for the books themselves and the ideas therein. I read to write. I believe he reads to read. And to think. And then to read some more. He jots down ideas he has in a small notebook as he reads. But I read often only enough to get me writing—and not just notes in a small black bound book. Okay, I confess—I get carried away with writing.

Et tu, Mabel?

But this is no betrayal, is it? The letters, the words and feelings exchanged on the page—this love of writing could sometimes serve you, and save you (and serve me, and save me) from the hearing loss. You would sometimes even leave Alec a letter *before* you (or he) parted from the other. And it was from your insistence and care that the legacy—through so many of your letters and his letters—remains for us today. You knew these pieces of written exchange would not betray who you—and he—really were in the way you suspected a biography might. Several months before Alec died, you wrote to Gilbert (Bert) Grosvenor, your son-in-law, that

> *My husband is so much to me that I know the very best account of him that could be written will seem to me wrong in some way. It would praise him perhaps, but in ways that did not seem to me true, and I would hate to have things attributed to him that were not so. He is big enough to stand as he is, a man, very imperfect, lacking in things that are lovely in other men, but a good man all the same. . . . But I would never say this publicly, it would seem disloyalty, and one of us would either, I think, which would mean that the book would be inadequate. (May 4, 1922)*

Loyalty, perfection, adequacy; disloyalty, imperfection, inadequacy. The yin and yang of any human character that could be captured, controlled, crafted on the page. You knew that so well, didn't you?

In an essay I wrote for my first book, an essay I might as well have written for you, Mabel—like another letter perhaps—I write about (almost) passing. I write about writing:

> *If nothing else, I could always write about it, read about it. I had been doing literacy, and doing it well, all my life as yet another supremely successful act of passing. In all those classrooms I disappeared from as I drifted off, when my ability to attend carefully was used up and I wafted away to what my family called "Brenda's La-La Land," I made up my absence by reading and writing on my own. If nothing else, I could always write about it, read about it.*
>
> *. . . She wasn't deaf when she was reading or writing. In fact, she came to realize that we are all quite deaf when we read or write—engaged in a signing system that is not oral/aural and is removed from the present.*
>
> *How many times must she have written—to herself or to someone else— "it's easier for me to write this than it is to say it; I find the words easier on paper." On paper she didn't sound deaf, she could be someone other than herself—an artificer (thus fulfilling Plato's worst nightmare about the rhetorical potential in writing). On paper she passed. (Lend Me Your Ear 96–98)*

And so, Mabel, as an artificer in potential community and communication with you, I post you these postcards.

Yours, BJB

7

Economics, Euthanasia, Eugenics

*Rhetorical Commonplaces of Disability
in the Nazi T-4 Program*

In the summer of 2004, I packed my rusty and rudimentary German skills and went back to the Fatherland, *mein Vaterland*. There, I joined twenty other scholars from Germany, Canada, and the United States—and from fields as diverse as medieval history, pediatric medicine, cultural anthropology, physical and occupational therapy, bioethics, social work, cultural studies, performance studies, women's studies, creative writing, sociology, and school and counseling psychology—in a four-week-long institute sponsored by the Einstein Forum at the University of Potsdam, a city just southwest of Berlin that was, during the Cold War years, part of East Germany and a long-standing intellectual center for all of Germany.

The title of our specific institute was "Disability Studies and the Legacies of Eugenics," and the center of our study and discussion was the Nazi "T-4 program." We worked to explore this topic from three connected angles, triangulating the topic, as it were: (1) studying the eugenics-influenced policies (both German and American) that led up to the T-4 program; (2) excavating the T-4 program itself—its sites and victims; and (3) discussing the continuing impact of the T-4 program on current German (and international) policies regarding prenatal testing, abortion, and the social and political rights of people with disabilities. My role within this experience was to focus on German deaf people in relation to T-4.[1]

T-4: A Synopsis

T-4 was achieved largely through the potent sociopolitical, medical, and rhetorical forces of economics, euthanasia, and eugenics. The T-4 program was born following upon the eugenics sterilization laws of the Third Reich (much like those in America) during the 1930s and then publicly endorsed through Nazi propaganda posters and films about those the Nazis termed "useless eaters" or "lives not worth living." Eugenicists believed that people with disabilities were wasting the country's precious and threatened resources. The program was instigated and officially signed into action by Hitler in a seized Jewish villa at Tiergarten-Strasse 4 in the heart of Berlin (where the new Berlin Philharmonic Hall now sits). T-4 took place within an eighteen-month span between 1940 and 1941, and it focused on six major psychiatric institutions as the sites for the transport and immediate "euthanasia" (mercy killing) of some 70,273 people with disabilities. That is the more or less "official" count from program documents. But the larger number, still not completely accounted for, sits somewhere around 240,000 because of more covert killing that was accomplished through starvation or drug overdoses once the official part of the program closed down. Children, I might add, were one of the first and biggest targets—for numerous reasons (Friedlander, 1995). These "lives unworthy of living" and "useless eaters" were killed in efficiently designed gas chambers built in the basements or outlying buildings of these six central institutions. Only a doctor at each institution was allowed to operate the gas controls for the chambers.

These gas chambers pioneered the killing technology that worked so well that it became the centerpiece of "the Final Solution." In fact, once T-4 officially closed down as an official state program, Hitler had most of the crematoria, the ovens, and some of the doctors and nurses from these institutions who had "firsthand" experience in the T-4 operations transported directly to the death camps in Poland. Following the officially declared end of the T-4 program, in 1941, the killing continued through a period now called "wild euthanasia," as doctors and nurses continued to kill patients through either starvation or drug overdoses. Figure 7.1 presents a view of the postwar cemetery at the Hadamar psychiatric institutions, where the graves of "euthanasia" victims, largely unidentified, are laid out in long, wide, and disturbing relief.

Why did the T-4 program close? Largely because of concern expressed by families that had members in such institutions throughout the Reich, as well as Hitler's documented fear that the Americans would find out about it and enter the war over it. There is also existing documentation of some resistance by both Protestant and Catholic church leaders in the state and by several directors of schools and institutes, particularly those for deaf children (Friedlander, 2002).

7.1 A cemetery of Hadamar "euthanasia" victims. These are the unidentified graves of victims who died
during the "wild euthanasia" period.
Photograph courtesy of the U.S.
Holocaust Memorial Museum. The
views or opinions expressed in this
book and the context in which the
images are used do not necessarily
reflect the views or policy of, nor imply approval or endorsement by, the
U.S. Holocaust Memorial Museum.

          The Nazi doctors in these insti-
tutions routinely engaged in significant falsification of their patients' records in order to quietly justify to the victims' families the (false) causes
of death. State-generated condolence letters routinely declared that each
patient's death was "merciful" given, alas, the (burdensome) condition of
his or her life as a person with a disability. The state explained further that
the family could not retrieve the body (it had been cremated for general
health purposes) and that, after filling out the necessary—and extremely
elaborate and burdensome—paperwork, the family could, if it wanted, receive an urn with the patient's ashes. The urn received, of course, would
not actually contain the ashes of the relative. The medical staff had already
harvested any gold dental work and the victim's organs, especially his or
her brain[2] (Friedlander, 1995).

    In this chapter, I first outline four major commonplaces that served the
arguments that led up to the Nazi T-4 program. I work to answer, at least
in part, the question: How did we get to this program in the first place?
Our study that summer—through our readings, our discussions with German scholars, and our travels to several of the T-4 killing centers—kept
turning up at least four major influences (or *topoi,* "commonplaces" as
they were known in classical rhetoric). Following on these commonplaces,
in two concluding sections, I bring my reader into the killing chamber
sites, citing the victims.

Commonplace 1: American Eugenics, Sterilization Laws

First, the legacy of the American eugenics movement and forced steriliza-tion laws for "the feebleminded" (as the master category) in the United States generated one very "available means of persuasion" (as Aristotle de-fined rhetoric) on which the Nazis could construct the T-4 program. State laws enacted in 1907 in Indiana were the first to require the forced and necessary sterilization of those deemed feebleminded. In the end, thirty states enacted sterilization laws, and just over sixty-five people in the United States were sterilized without their consent of that of their family (Eugenics Archive).

Perhaps the best-known U.S. incident surrounding these sterilizations is that of Carrie S. Buck, a citizen of Lynchburg, Virginia. Both Carrie and later her mother, Emma, were deemed feebleminded and were committed to the Virginia Colony for Epileptics and Feebleminded in Lynchburg at the age of seventeen. What's more, they were also judged "promiscuous," since they had both given birth to a child out of wedlock (while in that in-stitution). Carrie's daughter, Vivian, was determined to be "feebleminded" at just seven months of age, and, consequently, Carrie herself was ordered sterilized. The year was 1927. Carrie refused. And the case was carried all the way to the U.S. Supreme Court. Ruling for the forced sterilization of Carrie Buck, U.S. Supreme Court Chief Justice Oliver Wendell Holmes de-clared famously that "three generations of imbeciles are enough" (http://www.dnalc.org/resources/buckvbell.html).

While many notable geneticists had become critical of the eugenics movement even by the time of *Buck vs. Bell* (1927), eugenics was just be-ginning to gain substantial ground in Germany as a "science" that served both politics and economics well. Between the appearance of its first edi-tion, in 1921, and 1940, an influential "standard textbook" by three German geneticists, Erwin Baur, Eugen Fischer, and Fritz Lenz, was published five times. *Menschliche Erblichkeitslehre und Rassenhygiene* (Human Heredity Teaching and Racial Hygiene) is known to have been read by Hitler in its second edition in 1923, and he processed some of its essential ideas for *Mein Kampf* (Glass).

Another scientist and doctor, Alfred Erich Hoche, professor of psychi-atry and neuropathology at Freiburg, was himself honored by the Nazis as a pioneer in supporting the idea of "euthanasia," the mercy killing of peo-ple who were deemed unworthy of life (Friedlander, 2002). Hoche's co-authored (with Karl Binding) sixty-page book on the subject, *The Release of the Destruction of Life Devoid of Value: Its Measurement and Form,* was published in 1922. In this book, Binding and Hoche provided a cost-benefit analysis for psychiatric care and described sick and disabled people as "ballast existences," "elements of minor value," and even "mentally dead." When the book was first published, there are records that indicate it raised considerable alarm and opposition. However, with the worldwide depression that struck Germany particularly hard in the late '20s and early '30s, their ideas found more and more followers. Interestingly enough, by 1933 Hoche had distanced himself from his own ideas expressed in this book of a decade before.

Yet the seeds had been sufficiently sown. Germany was already, by the late 1920s, presenting arguments for its own sterilization laws, largely through a series of propaganda posters and some short films. Such propaganda would bring together eugenic "science" with economic crisis and sum those two in order to equal "euthanasia," a policy that Hoche himself had suggested would enact the "painless killing" of the "incurably" sick against their will. This is counting, of course, that we need to account for.

For example, in a 1936 issue of *Neues Volk,* a Nazi Party journal devoted to racial theories, a particular Nazi propaganda poster argued that Germany did not stand alone in its eugenics philosophies or practices. The poster's headline claimed, "*Wir stehen nicht allein*" ("We do not stand alone"). It portrayed a woman holding a baby and a man standing behind her, appearing to support her while he also held up a shield inscribed with the title of Nazi Germany's 1933 "Law for the Prevention of Hereditarily Diseased Offspring." The couple also stood in front of a map of Germany, and around the border of the poster were the flags of nations that had already enacted (to the left) or were considering the adoption of similar legislation (to the bottom and to the right) (Proctor 96).

The Nazis designated nine kinds or classes of disabilities that were to be the targets of their sterilization efforts: congenital feeblemindedness; schizophrenia; *folie circulaire* (manic-depressive psychosis); hereditary epilepsy; hereditary St. Vitus's disease (Huntington's disease); hereditary blindness; hereditary deafness; severe hereditary physical deformity; and severe alcoholism (at the state's discretion)[3] (Proctor). One of the many things that became painfully obvious to me during this experience and research is that no matter how much the contemporary American Deaf community might strenuously argue against its classification as or association with "the disabled," there were undeniably important moments in history that drew deafness tightly right alongside disability. Here on the

Nazi's "hereditarily diseased offspring" list, deafness clearly did not stand alone as a privileged, distant, or different cousin in relation to the eight other classifications. In the rhetoric, policy, politics, and medical world of Nazi eugenics and "racial hygiene," deafness was as dirty as its eight allies.

Commonplace 2: Economic Crisis

In an equation of eugenic science and economic crisis, disabled lives were represented, then, as not only a burden but a burden simply too heavy for the state—and its less burdensome individuals—to bear. Some of the Nazi propaganda posters of the time make use of arguments that employ emotional appeals (*pathos*), economic angles, racial perspectives, sociopolitical views, and even religious overtones with regard to the question of Germany's *Erbkranke* (genetically diseased).

Two posters especially emphasize emotional arguments that portray a life without hope, and existence only as a burden, for people with disabilities. (Figure 7.2 and 7.3). The first poster (Figure 7.2), *Leben nur als Laft* (Life Only as a Burden), shows two middle-aged men in white gowns standing over a row of beds that have high board sides, much like baby cribs; a few beds seem to contain patients who are adult size (although the image is not very clear).[4] In fact, the poor clarity of the image makes it uncertain to me, at least, whether the two men in white gowns are physicians looking over these patients or perhaps even patients themselves. One thing that is more certain, however, is that, even though the bright light of day floods in through the windows behind the row of high-board beds, the room itself seems quite dark. The light streaming in from the windows in the upper right cannot penetrate the deep shadow of the lower left, where the text glows in sharp relief.

The second image (Figure 7.3) shows a group of children and young adults photographed through a chain link fence. In the background is a "yard" where a few other children can also be seen. Apparently these are "*Erbkranke*" (genetically unhealthy) children or children in some kind of caregiving institution; many of them give the appearance of complete health, while a few appear to be possibly blind or developmentally disabled. What is interesting, however, about the emotionally charged message printed across the bottom of the image is that most of the children are smiling and do not seem at all "without hope." The caption line places

7.2 *Leben nur als Laſt* poster.

7.3 *Leben ohne Hoffnung* poster.

7.4 Ein Erbkranker geg. Eine Erbgefunde Familie poster.

Photographs courtesy of the U.S. Holocaust Memorial Museum. The views or opinions expressed in this book and the context in which the images are used do not necessarily reflect the views or policy of, nor imply approval or endorsement by, the U.S. Holocaust Memorial Museum.

Leben (life) against the background of the chain link fence, while *ohne Hoffnung* (without hope) appears in a black bar background at the very bottom of the poster.

Other posters rely more on a rhetorical appeal to logic, particularly a Nazi-esque logic grounded in economics. For example, one poster carries text that reads in translation: "The burden you carry, the losses you share: One person afflicted with a hereditary disease costs about 50,000 RM [Reichsmarks] for 60 years of life." The image on this poster is of a large-scaled, muscular, blond man standing against the backdrop of a city that is only half his size; his back and neck are slightly bent, and his face turns downward as he carries on his shoulder a bar upon which two other men—apparently men "afflicted with a hereditary disease"— are balanced on either side. Presented, and argued, in this image is the idea of economic burden foisted upon the "good" and "fit" citizen, who is even larger than his nation. The rhetorical chord of this image has always struck me as uncannily resonant and evident still today in much of the current American backlash against the Americans with Disabilities Act (ADA) (Colker).

Another poster of the era also centers on economic logic and, in fact, features the cost (60,000 RM) first and foremost. This poster from the 1930s promotes the Nazi monthly *Neues Volk* (New People), the newsletter of the party's racial office, and it is still widely circulated on Web sites and in various archives. Translated, its text reads: "This genetically ill person will cost our people's community 60,000 Reichsmarks (RM) over his lifetime. Citizens, that is your money. Read *Neues Volk*, the monthly of the racial policy office of the NSDAP." (See http://www.calvin.edu/academic/cas/gpa/posters2.htm.)

Yet another poster demonstrating the logic of the economic burden argument (Figure 7.4) pivots on the price of lives perhaps not worth living, calculating that cost daily and directly against the needs of a healthy German family. In this poster, a black box represents the daily cost of 5.5 Reichsmarks. The "*Erbkranker*" stands alone and in profile, supporting himself against the black box of his burden (the daily cost), while the "*erbgefunde*" (healthy) family of five features the father holding that black box with one hand while his other arm is apparently around his wife, who holds a baby and looks somewhat forlorn as another young child, her daughter, tugs at her arm. The family's young son stands ready for school with a textbook tucked in his arm. The text of this poster reads:

7.5 *Geisteskranker Neger* poster. Photograph courtesy of the U.S. Holocaust Memorial Museum. The views or opinions expressed in this book and the context in which the images are used do not necessarily reflect the views or policy of, nor imply approval or endorsement by, the U.S. Holocaust Memorial Museum.

"The hereditarily diseased person costs the State 5.50 RM daily: for 5.50 RM per day an entire hereditarily healthy family can live."

There were also posters aimed at the "genetically diseased" that used other strong social, moral, or religious arguments. Half of the poster shown in Figure 7.5 displays just a black box with white letter words in it that read: "Hereditarily diseased 'Negro' (from England) institutionalized 16 years costs 35,000 RM." Against this statement is a black man who appears to be standing in a line (there are the bodies of two others in line behind him) and holding an empty white (food?) bowl. His head is bald, and the fixed gaze of his eyes to his right indicates that he may be blind. What is most noteworthy, rhetorically, about this poster is its designation of its subject, the *Geisteskranker Neger* ("hereditarily diseased Negro")— someone who would have been doubly genetically and racially flawed in the National Socialist regime—as *not* a German citizen but, rather, as English.

Also chilling and distancing in its social rhetoric is the poster shown in Figure 7.6, which makes its case by employing religious rhetoric. Some unknown hand holds up—at a cold distance—an apparently "genetically diseased" baby. The text beside this image, which takes up two-thirds of

7.6 *Denn Gott Kann nicht wollen* . . . poster. Photograph courtesy of the U.S. Holocaust Memorial Museum. The views or opinions expressed in this book and the context in which the images are used do not necessarily reflect the views or policy of, nor imply approval or endorsement by, the U.S. Holocaust Memorial Museum.

the entire poster, claims: "When God won't take care of the genetically diseased and sick, these diseased and sick reproduce themselves."

There were films, as well. The Nazis produced a series of short propaganda films that played before the feature films in many theaters throughout the state. *Ich Klage An* (I Accuse), produced by Wolfgang Liebeneiner, in 1941, was one of the most famous ones and is still available, but only for research viewing, today. It was intended to prepare the public for the assassination by drugs and withdrawal of food from the "*Erbkranke*" (genetically diseased) that became the focus of the post-gas-chamber "mercy killing" of people with disabilities after the T-4 program was officially shut down. Interestingly enough, however, the film focuses not on a "mentally sick" or disabled person but instead on a physicians's wife who suffers from multiple sclerosis (MS). Her husband, who has apparently been encouraged by his wife to give her life-ending medicine, puts himself before the court and accuses himself. The film ends without a judgment. One critic claims that the film is "the most famous straightforward propaganda film . . . produced by order of the government as a response to the criticism of some sections in the German society to the psychiatric euthanasia murders which started in 1939. The film uses all the well-known eugenic arguments about 'life not worth living,' 'killing as healing,' and 'deliverance from misery'" (http://www.freedom-of-thought.de/film_program.htm). I was not surprised, but still distressed, to discover that some significant analogies were recently made between the original *Ich Klage An* film and the case of Terri Schiavo.[5] And, uncannily, a 2005 production/interpretation of the "I Accuse" film appeared in Germany.

I also want to point out that this eugenics-economic crisis and equation is what led the Nazis, in the other direction, to institute a radical program to produce "*erbgefunde*" (healthy) families. That is, much like eugenicists in America, they began by advocating for and practicing "positive genetics"— encouraging people to "breed" and reproduce in ways that would most likely bring forth the best of the next generation. At this time in Germany, there was a bit of a birth crisis (or so they thought): people were, by and large, not thought to be producing enough children—especially families of high economic, political, or intellectual standing. In the spirit of such "positive eugenics," the Reich thus instigated an award systems for mothers who produced, in significant numbers, healthy "fit" children (Weyrather).

The *Mutter Kreuz* (Mother Cross), for example, was awarded to mothers who were sufficiently fecund. In 1938, Hitler instigated a program to reward mothers who were "child-rich." A bronze cross was awarded for more than four healthy births and a silver cross for more than six "fit" children; eight genetically sound offspring brought a woman a gold cross; and twelve children without designated defects reportedly garnered the poor mother the gold cross plus a valuable china tea cup (as if she would ever have time to take tea). Apparently, the wearer of any "Mutter Kreuz" was also given "preferential seating" at public events. I imagine that this special seating was close to the bathroom, where diaper changes, crying babies, and various accidents could easily be taken care of.

Finally, the Economics of the *Erbkranke*, as I've come to think of it, was so widely part of propaganda and public knowledge that it appeared in German children's textbooks. One mathematics primer for thirteen- and fourteen-year-olds contained, for example, the following story problem:

> The costs for one hereditarily ill patient today amounts to 4.5–6 Reischs-mark (RM) per day. Calculate the total sum of the cost per day, per month, per year. . . . In the year 1930, approximately 1 billion RM were spent for the hereditarily ill. In contrast, only 730 million RM were spent for the *Reischwehr* in 1930 and only 713 million for the whole Reich administration. . . . How many farm settlements, of which each should cost 32,000 RM, could have been constructed with the amount used for the hereditarily ill? How many homesteads could have been erected with this

sum, if the aggregate building cost was 6,000 RM per house? (Rechen-buch für Volksschulen; Heberer, 57–58)

I have already calculated an answer to this (accounting) problem, and I confess that that it was the folksinger Bob Dylan who helped me with my homework:

> How many times must a man look up
> Before he can see the sky?
> Yes, and how many ears must one man have
> Before he can hear people cry?
> Yes, and how many deaths will it take till he knows
> That too many people have died?
> The answer, my friend, is blowin' in the wind,
> The answer is blowin' in the wind.
> (http://www.bobdylan.com/songs/blowin.html)

Commonplace 3: Medical-Psychiatric Professional Power in the 1930s

The Third Reich, the National Socialist regime, the Nazis, the 1930s—it was a good time to be a doctor. And psychiatry, in particular, had just taken off—thanks in part, to Sigmund Freud—and was quickly becoming big business. New medicines and treatments, particularly aimed at treating the kinds of patients who were commonly institutionalized in this era (both in Germany and in the United States), appeared on the medical-mental scene. Sulfinalamide, the father of the sulfa drugs, provided the first effective treatments for pneumonia, meningitis, and other bacterial diseases and greatly (positively) affected the mortality rate during World War II.

The Tuskegee Experiment to observe the natural history of untreated latent syphilis (on 399 African American men) in Macon County, Alabama, began in 1932. This experiment was tacitly sanctioned by the powerful twinned forces of racism and eugenics and was made possible by the architecture of modern psychiatric institutions, but, much like T-4, it would run counter to both the Hippocratic Oath and the ethics of modern medicine. Phenytoin was discovered in 1938 and established a new era of anticonvulsant neurotherapeutics that permitted greater control over not only epileptic seizures but also many general psychiatric patients in institutions at this time.[6] Also offering greater control over institutionalized patients, Egas Moniz of Portugal introduced lobectomy surgery to the United States in 1935 via his American colleagues, Walter Freeman and James Watts. This surgery, which severed or removed part or all of the temporal lobe of the brain to aid in controlling severe epileptic seizures, moved the boundaries of medicalized control over institutionalized bodies a significant step forward (or perhaps it was really backward). Finally, governments, both in America and abroad, became more involved with all medical care, especially with psychiatric care (http://www.aneuroa.org/html/c2ohtml/1930_1939.htm).

In Germany, in the National Socialist Party, being a doctor was a key political position. Hitler's success in the T-4 operation itself, as well as in the actions that predated and followed this official program, depended upon doctors and nurses—not military soldiers—carrying out his orders. The twenty-three doctors tried at Nuremberg served in both political and medical capacities. As Robert Lifton has documented, the (Nazi) doctors at such "clinics" as the Hadamar Psychiatric Institution (one of the six main killing center for the T-4 program) especially came to "take over" during the "wild euthanasia" period when they exterminated patients through starvation or drug overdoses (Lifton 95–114).

During the "wild euthanasia" period, which followed the official closure of the T-4 operation, in 1941, the doctors and nurses at Hadamar again began to murder disabled patients. From 1942 until the end of war, in May 1945, the facility claimed the lives of an additional 4,400 victims by lethal overdoses of medication (in addition to the more than ten thousand victims who had died in the gas chambers and crematoria during the official T-4 period). The Hadamar Trial (October 8–15, 1945) was the first mass-atrocity trial in the U.S. zone of Germany immediately after World War II. Apparently, American authorities were eager to try Hadamar physicians, nurses, and staff for the murders of the nearly fifteen thousand German patients killed at this institution, but they quickly discovered that they had no jurisdiction to do so under international law.

The second Hadamar Trial was held between February and March 1947 before the district court at Frankfurt am Main. In this second trial, twenty-five Hadamar medical staff were accused of having killed or helped to kill Germans in the institution. The second trial fell under U.S./international jurisdiction because it was discovered that almost five hundred Russians and Poles from the work camps in those countries had, in fact, been transported to Hadamar during the war and had also been victims of "wild euthanasia" there. In the final judgment, the physicians Dr. Hans Bodo Gorgass and Dr. Adolf Wahlmanh were sentenced to death for at least nine hundred assassinations. Both judgments were, however, commuted to imprisonment, and both men were then reprieved in the 1950s. The other defendants were sentenced to imprisonment for up to eight years.

Among those sentenced to eight years' imprisonment was the Hadamar head nurse, Irmgard Huber (Figure 7.7). Huber first claimed that she had never killed patients directly, and this claim was corroborated by coworkers and witnesses at Hadamar at that time; she was released. Later, however, the court ruled that Huber had assisted in selecting patients for murder and in falsifying their death certificates and that she also controlled the supply of drugs used to overdose the patients. Huber was then rearrested and tried with six others, and she received twenty-five years in prison for serving as an accomplice to murder. She was released from prison, however, in 1952, when American authorities issued amnesties and clemencies for many convicted Nazi perpetrators because of Cold War political pressures.

Karl Brandt, Hitler's personal physician and the one to whom Hitler's orders to begin the T-4 program were addressed, was found guilty of war

7.7 Portrait of Irmgard Huber, chief nurse at the Hadamar Institute, in her office. The photograph was taken by an American military photographer on April 7, 1945. Photograph courtesy of the U.S. Holocaust Memorial Museum. The views or opinions expressed in this book and the context in which the images are used do not necessarily reflect the views or policy of, nor imply approval or endorsement by, the U.S. Holocaust Memorial Museum.

crimes at the Doctor's Trial and was executed June 2, 1948, at Landsberg Prison, Bavaria. Philip Bouhler, head of the Reich Chancellery and the other person to whom Hitler addressed the T-4 order, committed suicide in 1945.

But where were the deaf subjects in this very anxious moment of history and identification? I saw for myself the records of some *taubtumme* ("deaf and dumb") patients at Hadamar and in the Bundesarchives (and elsewhere in relation to the T-4 program). The overlay of clinical diagnoses once a patient was committed to any institution (then as now) meant that clear-cut designations were not always possible. One could enter the institution as "deaf and dumb" and soon also become (labeled) manic-depressive, "epileptic," mentally deficient, or "dangerous." Any label could count, or cover, for another.

Commonplace 4: War as Cover

Perhaps the biggest cover for the T-4 program was the war itself. The T-4 order from Hitler (Figure 7.8), issued at the stolen Jewish villa in central Berlin, was given on the day of the invasion of Poland: September 1, 1939.

7.8 The T-4 order, signed by Adolf Hitler. Photograph courtesy of the U.S. Holocaust Memorial Museum. The views or opinions expressed in this book and the context in which the images are used do not necessarily reflect the views or policy of, nor imply approval or endorsement by, the U.S. Holocaust Memorial Museum.

Now, as the Romulans of Star Trek fame have taught us, there is nothing quite like a cloaking device. Given the immensity of the invasion on Poland, it was the hope of the Reich administration that no one would really notice the order for the "mercy killings" that had also now been enacted and was in full force. This force is quite the opposite, of course, of Spock's Vulcan greeting, "Live long and prosper."

There were precursors and signs on the horizon that presaged this ultimate act. On August 8, 1939, the Nazis had set some things already significantly in motion with a decree to register and record all persons with disabilities. The propaganda posters displayed throughout much of the 1930s (as I've illustrated) also pointed in this direction.

The T-4 operations, which were "officially" ended in August 1941, after approximately twenty months of official existence, were carried out in many more ways, in many more places, and with many more victims than occurred only at the officially designated sites of the six psychiatric institutions. The cloaking device of war had proven so effective that it shrouded much of what was to become later known as the "wild euthanasia" period and that was also often interwoven into the fabric of the concentration and death camps now established as part of "the Final Solution."

Entering the Sites, Siting the Victims

At the midpoint of our institute experience—after ten days of preliminary reading, bonding, and local events in the Potsdam/Berlin area—we took a one-week "field trip." We rented three vans, one of them accessible (which is in and of itself a minor miracle in a country like Germany), and we set out on a weeklong excursion to visit three of the killing center sites: Brandenburg, Bernberg, and Hadamar.

There were six psychiatric institutions that served as the key locations of the T-4 program. Moving out or down from Berlin, where the T-4 order was issued, were Brandenburg, Bernberg, Sonnestein, Hadamar, Grafeneck, and Hartheim. These six institutions were the primary "intake" locations into which people with disabilities who were actually at *other* institutions were "funneled" to be killed in gas chambers. At the other "feeder" institutions, lethal injections and starvation were the principal means of "mercy killing." Patients arrived at one of the six major killing centers in gray or brown buses with windows painted over. They did not stay long. They did not typically take up residency at this institution. They were, in fact, almost always immediately "processed" and sent into the gas chambers, which were, of course, designed to look like showers.

The "processing" usually involved stripping naked, placing clothes and other items in a pile, and standing—with others—in front of a table and a team of institute doctors and nurses who pretended to fill out intake forms and record vital information. In fact, what was being processed and recorded were possible and probable (but falsified) causes of death that could be recorded on the patients' death certificates and sent home to their family. This was rhetoric, as much as medicine, at work. For example, these doctors did not want to put down the cause of death as "appendix burst or acute appendicitis" when, in fact, the patient might have previously had his appendix removed. That might look a little suspicious to the family. Thus, these doctors and nurses looked for scars or physical features that would help them document the most plausible reason for the patient's death on the official–but, of course, entirely fabricated—death certificate. They also looked for features such as gold teeth (and patients who had them were marked with small X's on one of their shoulders) and interesting "features" that might prove worthy of autopsy and further scientific use. Many brains of the victims were removed, for example, and shipped to medical research centers such as the Kaiser Wilhelm Institute for Brain Research in Berlin and the Psychiatric Clinic of the University of Heidelberg.

The witness image in Figure 7.9 was taken with my own camera. It is from the Brandenburg T-4 memorial site, just south of Berlin. It illustrates the "processing" of patients/victims who arrived at the site. Of all the images and artifacts I saw or collected in my own memory during this experience, this one is the most memorable—and disturbing—to me. It represents a drawing made by a witness to the processing, Elizabeth Hempel; she has labeled herself in the drawing. She stands next to a table

7.9 Witness illustration from Brandenburg Institution Memorial.

of "authorities"—doctors and nurses—and she watches the children undress. She observes a nurse, directly in front of her, who has picked up a very young child by one arm and is throwing that child into the gas chamber (*Gaskammer*). Behind the witness and to her right is a table covered with paperwork and records that resemble medical files. In front of that document table is a pile of clothes (*Kleider*) and shoes *(Schuhe)*. The exit (*Eingang*), with deep, ironic bitterness, lies just beyond those shoes. All the elements of the T-4 apparatus are here in this testimonial drawing: medical staff in surveillance and control, (falsified) medical records, piles of material objects from the patients, patients who have become victims, an exit unused, the gas chamber. Only the witness seems unusual. And although we do not know *why* "E. Hempel" was witnessing this scene and not directly in it herself (she was apparently a patient at Brandenburg, as well), it is her presence in the very center of the drawing that makes this memorial truly now a part of my own consciousness and memory. I have, as it were, absorbed her *ethos* in my own witnessing.

The Nazi doctors and nurses involved in the T-4 program did not care so much about memory—false, apparent, real, or otherwise—of course. Not only did they falsify the *cause* of death, but these Nazi doctors almost always falsified the *date* of death. There were at least two reasons for this lie. First, to record a substantial number of deaths all on one day (the gas chambers typically held sixty to seventy-five people) might, once again, arouse suspicion. If Family A were to discover that its son, daughter, sister, aunt, or cousin had died of "heart attack" on X day when that person had no history of heart problems but also, interestingly enough, Family B just down the street also had a relative who was sent to the same institution and died on the same day of "consumption," well, questions could start to arise. The second reason was quite simply that money could be made—a once "useless eater" could, in fact, generate a few Reichsmarks for the state. Because families paid a support fee for the institutionalized patients—even if it was just 1 RM per day—the state could conveniently record a patient's death date perhaps ninety days past the day the person actually died, then bill the family for those days and receive back 90 RM for "caring for" a patient it did not, of course, actually care for.

So much hinged on circumventing suspicion—proof that all along those involved in the T-4 operations, from Hitler on down, understood the potential public revolt, not just a mere outcry, if all this were made known. The cloaking of the order itself on the day Germany invaded Poland, the multiple layers of deception around patient records, and even, finally, the official order to halt T-4 operations on August 24, 1941 (approximately twenty months after the order to begin operations was issued, in January 1940)—all were acts aimed at keeping the secret. Yet, the secret apparently became open quite quickly, and, thus, presumably fearing public and citizen unrest at a critical point in the war, Hitler declared an end to the official phase of "euthanasia."

The conservative estimates we have indicate that 70,273 patients died from the gas chamber apparatus during this twenty-month period. But, really, even those figures lie. T-4 was much more complex and comprehensive than just those twenty months and some seventy thousand lives. As another example of its reach and ravages, in the spring months of 1939, long before T-4 was an official program, Philip Bouhler and Karl Brandt began to organize a secret killing operation that was never given a name but was targeted at disabled children. According to the historian Patricia Heberer, "conservative estimates suggest that at least 5,000 physically and mentally disabled children were murdered through starvation or legal overdoses of medication at some thirty special pediatric units throughout the Reich" (60).

Other operations involving the base of these six psychiatric institutions throughout the war took place, as well. The best-known was Operation 14f13, also known as *Sonderbehandlung* (special handling) or *Invalidenaktion* (the Invalid Operation). Approximately ten to twenty thousand concentration camp prisoners between 1941 and 1945 were dispatched to Bernberg, Mauthausen, and Hartheim in what was considered a "solution" to the problem of ailing and severely injured prisoners in concentration camps, where forced labor was designed to produce only benefits. There was also "Operation Brandt," in which hundreds of geriatric and nursing home patients were dispatched to the killing centers in order to free bed space for military casualties and victims of Allied bombing.

In the Chambers

They called the spaces chambers, *kammer,* not rooms, *zimmer.* We must go in them now, my friends. I suggest we hold hands.

After the initial stop at the memorial site where the Brandenburg institution once stood—and where E. Hempel left her testimonial drawing—we traveled to Bernberg. Bernberg is still the site of an active psychiatric institution. The killing began there on November 21, 1940, with twenty-five persons from the mental home at Neuruppin, a *Zwischenanstalt*

7.10 Our group outside the Bernberg memorial and chambers.

(intermediate home) becoming the first Bernberg victims. Our group waited outside the building, in a harsh, cold drizzle, for the institution's staff to bring more assistance so that they could carry some of our group members who used wheelchairs down into the chambers. While we waited, we took pictures of the "silence is broken" memorial outside (see Figure 7.10). We were largely silent as we did so.

Bernberg serves as a model for the other five killing centers, and its memorial building carefully documents the process that patients were taken through once they entered the cellar and were funneled through the various chambers. On the ground floor, incoming patients were registered. Here patients were often undressed and handed over their valuables to the personnel; this scene would have been similar to the one drawn in E. Hempel's testimony. Next, a superficial inspection of the victims took place in order to see what plausible cause of death the Bernberg administration could pass on to the victim's relatives. Then the staff took photos of the victims. Following the photo taking, the patients went down into the cellar and immediately entered the gas chamber. After the gas chamber, the victims' bodies were further "prepared"—often with the removal of organs or teeth. Finally, the victims' bodies traveled to the crematoria, the ovens at the end of the room.

A few notes from my own journal entries following on the Bernberg site visit include the following. My notes accompany pictures I took with my own camera at this killing center site:

- The peephole in the heavy chamber door was set at optimal surveillance height for whomever was on the outside of the chamber, looking in.

- When patients came down the stairs at Bernberg and into the cellar after being processed on the ground floor, they filed immediately into the gas chamber, thinking they would be taking a shower. The heavy chamber door was propped open, hiding behind it the gas controls. Only a doctor was allowed to work the gas controls.
- The shower heads did not function, of course, as shower heads. No water ever came from them. The gas piped into the chamber actually came from very small holes in the mortar between tiles in the chamber.
- A mirror inside the gas chamber was placed in direct sight line with the door's peephole, thereby allowing the onlooker outside the door to survey the entire chamber from just the peephole view. From this point of surveillance, one could quickly assess the status of the victims inside the chamber.

At our third site, the Hadamar Institution, nestled atop a hill overlooking the sleepy little "Village of Princes," I stopped taking pictures. It no longer worked to hide behind the camera. It was July 15. My daughter, Esther, was turning ten back in Columbus. Here, on her birthday, in the middle of a Nazi killing center, I ached for her smell, for her spunky and ferocious character, for her lightly freckled face, her caramel brown eyes. Instead, there were only ghosts at Hadamar.

About one-third of the patient records from the official T-4 period remain. Hadamar has kept some of its own records, but the bulk of the remaining ones are housed in the Bundesarchives in Berlin, where I spent an entire day with five other colleagues from the institute, working to decipher the German doctors' handwriting and to piece together the largely falsified puzzles of these lives, now dead, in so-called medical files. The R139 files, as they are now called, literally crumbled in our hands as we handled them, so very carefully. When we packed up to go at the end of a long day, our work table was covered with tiny confetti, the disintegration of the paper palpably evident. So it is that records remain but largely can't be written about. It is the ultimate of ironies: even though these patient files are largely devoid of much information (the negligence of the institutions in the "care" they were entrusted with is quite evident in the absences inscribed—in vivid blankness—on the pages of a patient's file), and even though what is written there is largely, if not entirely, false, these are still "protected medical records."

My good friend and writer-colleague Steve Kuusisto has smartly suggested that I create fictional narratives based on some of the people in those scant records. But I have found that I can't. I just can't bring myself to create more fictions out of lives—and deaths—that were fictionalized enough already.

The people in the sleepy little village of Hadamar apparently knew much of what was happening at the institution set up on the hill. Multiple photos of the acrid smoke rising regularly from the crematorium chimney appear during that brief period in history. The children of the town teased each other about the buses: "If you don't behave, they'll put you on the death bus." Lines like these are recorded from several interviews with the older citizens of the village who were children at this time.

And written in the records of the institute: When the ten thousandth victim was burned at Hadamar, they celebrated with a round of champagne for the entire staff.

Back at Bernberg, which was before Hadamar, we shared a makeshift memorial service. (At Hadamar, our third site, we did not, we could not, bear to linger in the chambers.) From the cellar window at Bernberg, through the patches of original paint still remaining from the original T-4 period left on the windows, I took a picture of small yellow flowers growing on a bush outside the window. This is the last picture I took that week. Almost everyone in the group contributed something to this extemporaneous service at Bernberg. My friend and colleague Adrienne Asch was there. Adrienne is the Edward and Robin Milstein Professor of Bioethics at the Wurzweiler School of Social Work and Professor of Epidemiology and Population Health at the Albert Einstein College of Medicine, both at Yeshiva University. She is known the world over as an important disability studies scholar and activist. She is Jewish; she is blind. It was Adrienne, in her beautiful voice, who led us in singing "Blowin' in the Wind" there in that hot, close, and windless basement of Bernberg's main building.

> *Yes, and how many years can some people exist*
> *Before they're allowed to be free?*
> *Yes, and how many times can a man turn his head,*
> *Pretending he just doesn't see?*

Then, when Adrienne finished, I walked *backwards*, slowly but with great deliberation, out of those chambers, erasing yet also carrying the memories of these spirits and spaces with me. I walked backwards in order to go forward.

Notes

1. This question, "How useful is 'Deaf'?," was posed not so long ago on the international Disability Studies in the Humanities (DS-HUM) listserve. One (hearing) historian who works in Deaf history and studies, Rebecca A. R. Edwards, responded definitively that "Deaf" was still useful, and did still matter:

> The word Deaf still means something to me, personally and scholarly speaking. And the Deaf people I know are very clearly Deaf and not just deaf, though they are all deaf as well and must be. Hearing people are not Deaf. And we won't have a Deaf community to speak of anymore if we don't have deaf people. We might still have signing people, but we signers who are hearing are not Deaf. We have hearing eyes. Physical deafness matters. (May 1, 2007, DS-HUM)

My own reply to the question, which I also take up in the first essay in this volume, was far less certain:

> It may be somewhat like the change in "usefulness" for the term "gay"? But then again, it may not. Admittedly, I haven't thought this through well yet and perhaps someone else here on the listserve has deeper and more careful thinking about the use, and usefulness, of identity terms and adjectives that shift meaning historically?
>
> For myself, I just use "deaf" anymore. It's an adjective that is admittedly very (perhaps too?) powerful, to be certain. But it was what deaf people called themselves before "Deaf" began to appear, from out of a university classroom, in the early 70s. I also use it admittedly because I spend a lot of time writing now about people who are deaf (audiologically) but maybe not deeply involved in the deaf community or who would consider themselves part of Deaf culture (uh-oh, needed to use the capital letters again there). I am writing about people like Mabel Hubbard Bell, James Castle, the Allen Sisters, Vinton Cerf, some of the *taubstumme* (deaf and dumb), as they were designated, "patients" during the T-4 program, etc. So, I guess

you could say I am doing just little "d" deaf studies. Yet for all of these people, their deafness and identity as "deaf" —even just medically and especially in the way they communicated with and related to others and in their life professions/art/experience—really really DID (and does) matter.

gayly yours in identity and terms, Brenda (April 30, 2007 DS-HUM)

Perhaps the most succinct, yet still slippery answer to the question was offered by Lennard J. Davis as he quoted from an earlier post by Dirksen Bauman: "What we are talking about here is a multifaceted construction of fluid possibilities, hitting up against some embodied borders from time to time." (April 26, 2007 DS-HUM)

2. This question, whether or not deaf people could be considered an "endangered species," was actually provocatively posted recently on the "Gallynet L" listserve. One of the listserve's primary posters and founders, Slemo Warigon—who also often signs off as "Zendun, the Deaf and Dumb"—had prompted:

Greetings! Given technological and medical advances, should Deaf people be protected by the Endangered Species Act? Just curious… The U.S. Senate declared May 18, 2007, Endangered Species Day to encourage people "to become educated about, and aware of, threats to species, success stories in species recovery, and the opportunity to promote species conservation worldwide." (30 May 2007 Gallynet-L)

Following on this "curiosity," listserve members also debated the seriousness and relevancy of the question itself.

3. The question of the relationship between deafness and other disabilities also appears, like parentheses, in the first and last essays in this volume.

CHAPTER 1

1. Other, shorter versions of this essay appear in the following two volumes: *Open Your Eyes: Deaf Studies Talking*, ed. H.-Dirksen L. Bauman, University of Minnesota Press, 2008; *Signs and Voices: Deaf Culture, Identify, Language, and Arts*, ed. K. Lindgren, D. DeLuca, and D. Napoli, Washington, DC: Gallaudet University Press, 2007.

2. I turn to explore the commonplaces (topics of invention) for the Nazi's T-4 program against people with disabilities in the final chapter of this volume.

3. Here you can now imagine a Big D if you want, but for now I'm going to just let one term stand and use "deaf" or "deafness" (little d) to represent both the "deaf" and the "Deaf" positions since, as I have been arguing, no one really

seems to completely understand the differences and distinctions between the two terms to begin with.

4. These issues over American Sign Language in the academy and its relationship to "foreign-language" instruction were the subject of a three-session "Presidential Forum" at the Modern Language Association Annual Convention in Philadelphia, PA, December 27–30, 2004.

5. For more discussion on the consequences of the lack of contextually and culturally based approaches to scholarship in "deaf language and literacy," see the introduction to *Literacy and Deaf People: Cultural and Contextual Approaches*, ed. Brenda Jo Brueggemann (Washington, DC: Gallaudet University Press, 2004).

CHAPTER 2

1. See the Modern Language Association's Web site at http://www.mla.org/about.

2. William C. Stokoe Jr., Dorothy C. Casterline, and Carl G. Croneberg, *A Dictionary of American Sign Language on Linguistic Principles* (Washington, DC: Gallaudet College Press, 1965).

3. See the American Sign Language Teachers Association's Web site at http://www.aslta.org/index.html.

4. See Christopher Krentz on the "foreign" and "familiar" nature of ASL, especially within American universities, in "Proposal for ASL to Satisfy Foreign Language Requirements," at http://artsandsciences.virginia.edu/asl/t8.html.

5. Sheryl B. Cooper, "The Academic Status of Sign Language Program in Institutions of Higher Education in the United States," Ph.D. diss., Gallaudet University, 1997.

6. Even though this idea might be somewhat "foreign" to many people, as someone who grew up deaf/hard-of-hearing in the years right before "mainstreaming" became a popular form of deaf education, I could (and would) just as easily argue that I, for one, would like nothing more than if every speech pathology/audiology professional, every physician in training, and every special education teacher (indeed, every teacher, "special" or not) learned some basic ASL!

7. See Ohio State University's American Sign Language Program Web site at http://asl.osu.edu/.

8. Elizabeth B. Welles, "Foreign Language Enrollments in United States Institutions of Higher Education, Fall 2002," *ADFL Bulletin* 35, nos. 2–3 (Winter–Spring 2004): 7–26.

9. Some of the data we have collected from students who are enrolled in ASL 101 (the first-level course) over a three-year period show us that undergraduates enrolled in the ASL I class are students from the following colleges: (1) 56 percent from Arts and Sciences, including the Colleges of Arts, Biological Sciences,

Humanities, Math and Physical Sciences, and Social and Behavioral Sciences; (2) 15 percent from Health, Medical, and Biological Sciences; (3) 14 percent from Journalism and Communication; (4) 3 percent from Human Ecology; (5) 3 percent from Education; (6) and 6 percent other colleges. The student survey also indicates that, while 44 percent of the students enrolled in ASL 101 claim they are taking it primarily to fulfill their general-education language requirement, 56 percent of the students are taking it for other reasons and do not need it for their general-education requirements. Of those 56 percent who are taking it for reasons other than just to meet the language requirements, 39 percent claim they are taking it because of some "affinity" for the language because of an ongoing or previous personal interest in ASL and/or deaf culture; because they have a deaf friend or neighbor; because they have a deaf family member; just to learn more about deaf people and communicate with them; or because of their own current or partial deafness. In addition, 28 percent of the students taking ASL 101 say they have chosen it as an "alternative" to learning other languages because it is "interesting," "new/different," "nontraditional," or "unique" or because the student is a "visual learner."

10. Ibid., 8–15.

11. Welles, "Enrollments," 15.

12. See http://english.osu.edu/asldmp//default.htm.

13. See the American Sign Language (ASL) Literature and Digital Media Project, Ohio State University, at http://english.osu.edu/asldmp/default.htm.

14. See http://www.aslta.org/index.html.

CHAPTER 3

1. Search conducted in *MLA International Bibliography* on May 15, 2007.

2. For live examples of classifiers "in action" visit either of the following sites: the John Logan College Interpreter Training Program (http://www.jal.cc.il.us/ipp/ Classifiers/) or the ASL Shakespeare Project, "The Process: Challenges: Classifiers" (http://www.aslshakespeare.com/).

3. See http://deafness.about.com/cs/culturefeatures1/a/abcstories.htm.

4. Participants in this discussion forum included the following seven "authors" who create and perform ASL literature (e.g., stories, poetry): Flying Words Project (Peter Cook and Kenny Lerner); Cinnie MacDougall; Mindy and Theron (Mindy Moore and Theron Parker); Benjamin Jarashow; and Werner Zorn. Web sites or video production, if available, of any of their material is listed in the bibliography. The seven scholars/critics who have written about ASL literature who participated in the forum were Dirksen Bauman (ASL & Deaf Studies, Gallaudet University); Brenda Brueggemann (English & Disability Studies, Ohio State University); Susan Burch (History, The Smithsonian Institute); Michael Davidson (English, University of California–San Diego); Kristen Harmon (English, Gallaudet University); Christopher Krentz (English and ASL, University of Virginia);

and Peter Novak (Theater, San Francisco University). Selections of each critic's scholarship related to ASL literature are listed in the bibliography.

5. I will typically use the hyphenated term "author-performer" when referring to those who create stories, poems, mimes, and so on in ASL. I choose the double designation of the hyphenated term because they are indeed authors creating a literature in their language while also, of course, being performers who then present that literary creation to an audience (either live or through film and digital media). As with all hyphenated identities, I suspect there is also quite a lot going on in the between space of their two creative identities.

6. It will not escape the literary critic at large who might be reading this essay that much of the anxiety over both productive and interpretive control and the "death of the author" (Barthes) is ground well covered now in literary criticism. The ideas of reader response criticism, New Criticism, and Deconstruction seem to only be just appearing and becoming "a way of happening" (Rosenblatt) for ASL literature. In part, this is because the literature of ASL has not yet been "read" much, has not yet been "a happening" in the eyes of its audiences. No doubt, ASL literary criticism will have to undertake a fair amount of wheel reinvention as it begins to happen. Yet, in this reinvention, we readers of this embodied visual spatial literature will also likely come to "pattern out of the material that we bring to the work from our past knowledge of life and language" (Rosenblatt 341), and entirely new things will happen from those patterns, too.

7. The listing for the videocassette *Telling Tales in ASL: From Literature to Literacy*, produced by the Gallaudet University Distance Education Program in 1997, cannot be found in the Ohio State University Library, nor in the "OhioLINK" system, which includes 84 colleges in Ohio and also the State Library of Ohio, containing 45.3 million library items.

8. I use the term "accessible" in scare quotes here because, although this DVD is easy enough to find, purchase, and play, it isn't, in fact, completely accessible in terms of the language used in it. There are no translations in voice or caption (into English), and so only the viewer skilled in ASL can entirely comprehend it. And, even for the skilled ASL user, the signing of these turn-of-the-20th-century "masters," is sometimes substantially different—in style and lexicon—from what one might see from American Sign Language of the early 21st century; these signs are now nearly a century old! Padden and Humphries (2005) explain the "astonishing achievement" of these films in relation to their historical, linguistic significance:

> The astonishing achievement of the NAD films is not only that they were
> made at all, or that they were made so early in the history of film, but
> also that there was such a range of signing preserved for the modern day,
> from older to younger signers, from hearing to Deaf, across many different
> topics. The window into the history of American Sign Language through
> these films is, fortunately for us, a wide one.

The NAD films have given linguists a treasure trove of examples of how signs have changed over time. (60–61)

9. After several ASL linguists and members of the American deaf community created written (English) translations of Veditz's signed lecture (in part to caption the film for modern use), a written English version of the speech—created by Veditz himself—was discovered in what Padden and Humphries (2005) call a "wholly accidental and fortuitous discovery" (66). Padden and Humphries also acknowledge that those "sponsoring the film exhibitions were almost always Deaf people: alumni associations, local Deaf clubs, Deaf churches. This does not mean that there were no hearing people in the audiences" (70).

10. After Kenny Lerner's explanation of their translation process, Peter Cook himself went on to illustrate with a specific story of the control lost in the hands of other kinds of translators:

> Kenny and I do work together on the words, we try to come up with exactly what is a good word for this concept? We work back and forth, we feed off one another. And if I left it completely up to him, he would die if we did that. Trying to voice all of this is impossible. Like what happened recently. We have huge discussions and arguments about it, but I'm actually experiencing the story. We were at the RID [Registry of Interpreters for the Deaf] convention in Boston and there was a stenographer there, a lot of captionists. I was curious exactly what was being said that I was doing while I was telling the story about being thrown out of class because I farted. Well, I was going on with the story, and I kept using this sign. But when it was all said and done, the word that was being captioned was flatulence. I didn't use that word. No, farting is funny. The word "farting" is funny. Flatulent was not funny. Whatever word you put through, it was a fart, this is the way I had actually signed it. So there are some of those issues, and they always come up again and again.

11. We had set the room for the forum up in a manner that would allow all panelists visual access to each other and also create a visual space for the few audience members who were there and, importantly, the cameras and tech people recording the event. We knew there were 14 people participating—7 authors/performers and 7 critics—so we had placed 14 chairs in a V-shaped formation, with 7 chairs on each side of the V. The audience and cameras were at the top (open end) of the V. A team of interpreters stood behind each side of the V (thus, two teams of interpreters). What was interesting was that somehow all of the authors flocked to one side of the V, while the critics took the other side. (No one told them to do so.) In a very bad hearing cultural reference, I had quipped that we were enacting perhaps a challenging game of "Red Rover, Red Rover." Even in

the "translation" of this sound-based schoolyard game, the deaf members of the forum didn't "get it"—yet another lived experience of how much work translation still sometimes can't do.

12. There is an excellent sign for this "what do you do?" concept in ASL. It is called the "do-do" sign: *What do you do? What does it do?* is asked with the eyebrows scrunched, and the index finger and thumb of both hands repeating a snapping down move; visually, this repeated movement quickly collapses a fingerspelling of D-O, D-O.

13. See chapter 2 in this volume.

14. The original project at Yale University was directed by Peter Novak and involved 11 other participants (well, 12 others if you count "Snacks" the dog); its aim was to "document the process of translating Shakespeare's language, specifically that of *Twelfth Night*, into American Sign Language, with an emphasis on the history of gesture in visual representations of Shakespeare's plays" and to "serve as the 'text' for a full-scale production of *Twelfth Night* opening in October 2000 at Philadelphia's newly founded Amaryllis Theatre" (http://www.yale.edu/asl12night/project.html). The project was, even then, generously supported, listing seven major supporters at its Web site, including individual and family donor names, The David T. Langrock Foundation, The Elm Shakespeare Company of New Haven, Connecticut, and the Digital Media Center for the Arts at Yale University. The original Web site for this project still functions at http://www.yale.edu/asl12night/index.html. From there it was moved to a new site at the University of San Francisco, where Peter Novak joined the faculty in the Performing Arts and Social Justice Program. Recently, with funding from the U.S. Department of Education, the project has again relocated to an even more sophisticated—and ASL-visual—Web site at http://www.aslshakespeare.com/. The latest project is designed to be primarily educational, and the site offers many additional resources, lesson plans for ASL and deaf educators, numerous video clips of the process of translation and production into ASL, and even more video clips that sample from the performance itself and illustrate various literary concepts employed. Novak's DVD about the project, *William Shakespeare's* Twelfth Night *Performed in American Sign Language and English,* is also now available through Gallaudet University Press: http://gupress.gallaudet.edu/bookpage/WSTNbookpage.html

15. For scholarly discussions of the nature of "oral" literature that can be applied well to American Sign Language, see Bahan 2006; Davidson 1997, 2002; Edwards and Sienkewicz; Finnegan; Frishberg; Isidore; Ong; Peters 2000; Rose.

16. For discussions on the visual and spatial dimensions of ASL literature, see especially Bauman 1997, 2003; Batson 1987; Bragg; Brueggemann 1999; Davidson 2002; Frishberg; Krentz 2006; Lentz 1987; Maxwell; Padden and Humphries 1988, 2005; Peters 2000, 2001; Ree; Rose; Valli 1993, 1995.

17. See http://www.cal.org/resources/digest/ASL.html.

CHAPTER 4

1. Readers may view the "Deaf Lives" series publications—and have an opportunity to read reviews about and a sample chapters from each—directly online at: http://gupress.gallaudet.edu/deaflives.html.

2. For more information about Lawrence Hott and his film production credits and affiliates, see http://www.florentinefilms.org/. Specific information about the *Through Deaf Eyes* film project is at http://www.florentinefilms.org/inproduction/02_deaf.htm.

3. The other two texts used in her analysis and presentation are not included in this special issue. One of those, a collaborative presentation by Dr. Susan Burch and Dr. Hannah Joyner, was about the "interpreting" work of a historical biography of Junius Wilson, *Unspeakable: The Story of Junius Wilson*; Burch and Joyner's work with Junius Wilson was recently published by University of North Carolina Press. Wilson was an incarcerated, institutionalized, and castrated deaf black man in North Carolina who was finally set free after sixty-eight years of institutionalization. (The New York Times ran a story on Junius Wilson and his "freedom" on February 6, 1994.) The other text Jessica Stewart worked with for her senior research presentation was from Eileen Katz, author of *Making Sense of It All: The Battle of Britain Through a Jewish Deaf Girl's Eyes*. As told to Celeste Cheyney, Katz's narrative recounts her early years as a Jewish girl in a deaf school in London during World War II. The Katz/Cheyney narrative is one of three collected in Deaf Women's Lives.

4. Since Lang began work on Davila's biography, Dr. Davila himself has come out of retirement to take up a position as Gallaudet University's 9th president, following on the protests over the appointment of Dr. Jane K. Fernandes to that position in May 2006.

5. For more information about Dr. Harry Lang and his publications, see his Web site at: http://www.rit.edu/~490www/Individuals/langh.html.

6. Susan Plann is a Professor of Romance Languages and Linguistics at UCLA. She held the Powrie V. Doctor Chair of Deaf Studies at Gallaudet University in 1994. She has published one book in Deaf Studies, *A Silent Minority: Deaf Education in Spain, 1550–1835* (University of California Press, 1997), that also intersects with her primary field of research and teaching, Romance languages, history, and linguistics. She has another book in these intersected areas newly published from Gallaudet University Press: *The Spanish National Deaf School: Portraits from the Nineteenth Century* (http://gupress.gallaudet.edu/bookpage/SNDSbookpage.html). Her academic bio is available at http://www.humnet.ucla.edu/spanport/faculty/Plann/.

7. Kim Nielson also participated in this panel but was unable to offer her text for the *Sign Language Studies* volume. Nielson has conducted a wide and impressive range of scholarship around Helen Keller, including two books: *The Radical*

Lives of Helen Keller (2004) and *Helen Keller: Selected Writings* (2005), both published by New York University Press.

8. Rachel Hartig is a Professor of French at Gallaudet University where she teaches and researches primarily in French Deaf Studies, the 19th-century French novel, and French drama. She has published *Struggling Under the Destructive Glance: Androgyny in the Novels of Guy de Maupassant* (1991). Her work on the exchange between Helen Keller and Yvonne Pitrois is part of a new book from Gallaudet University Press, *Crossing the Divide: Representations of Deafness in Biography.* Her faculty bio is at http://depts.gallaudet.edu/forlang/hartig.html.

9. "Blind Rage" has also been published in *Southwest Review* (83, no. 1 [1998]: 53–61) and is part of Kleege's most recent publication, *Blind Rage: Letters to Helen Keller* (Gallaudet University Press, 2006).

10. Georgina Kleege is an Assistant Professor of Creative Writing and Disability Studies in the Department of English at Berkeley. Her research and teaching interests include creative nonfiction, Disability Studies, and disability autobiography. She has published a novel, *Home for the Summer* (1989) and a collection of essays, *Sight Unseen* (1999) and has a collection of these epistolary essays to Helen Keller from Gallaudet University Press (*Blind Rage: Letters to Helen Keller).* She has published many essays in literary journals such as *The Southwest Review, Raritan,* and *The Yale Review* and in academic journals such as *Social Research* and *The Journal of Visual Culture.* She served as one of the initial members of the Modern Language Association's Committee on Disability Issues and also organized a key exhibit at the Berkeley Museum of Art, "Blind at the Museum."

11. Christopher Jon Heuer is an Associate Professor of English at Gallaudet University. He is a doctoral candidate in Adult Literacy and Educational Counseling at George Mason University. He has published poetry and stories in *The Tactile Mind Quarterly* and *The Deaf-Way II Anthology.* His book of poems, *All Your Parts Intact: Poems* is from the Tactile Mind Press (see http://www.thetactilemind.com/books/aypi.html). His new book, *Bug: Deaf Identity and Internal Revolution,* has been recently published by Gallaudet University Press (http://gupress.gallaudet.edu/bookpage/BUGbookpage.html).
A biographical sketch of Heuer is available at http://clerccenter.gallaudet.edu/WORLDAROUNDYOU/Fall2003/Heuer.pdf.

12. Maggie Lee Sayre was born deaf near Paducah, Kentucky, in 1920 and lived most of her life on a river houseboat; her family made a living through fishing on rivers in Kentucky and Tennessee. A collection of her photographs, accompanied by descriptive captions from Sayre, *Deaf Maggie Lee Sayre: Photographs of a River Life,* was edited by Tom Rankin and published by the University Press of Mississippi in 1995. The first camera Sayre used was given to her sister in 1930 by the Kodak Company; that year, in celebration of its 50th anniversary, Kodak donated free cameras to children who were 12. A blurb from the Center for the

Study of Southern Culture at the University of Mississippi claims her photography as a form of "oral autobiography" and "a means of communicating with the
hearing world":

> The camera seemed to empower Maggie, for making portraits of her fam-
> ily members and visitors to the houseboat was her means of dialog. When
> she mounted her pictures in albums, adding text and dates, she created a
> pictoral narrative analogous with oral autobiography. It is the documen-
> tary record of a river life and of a photographer who used her camera as a
> means of communicating with the hearing world. Sayre's portraits detail-
> ing life on the river include portraits of her family and friends, of fish,
> and of everyday life on the houseboat home. (The Center for the Study
> of Southern Culture, http://www.olemiss.edu/depts/south/register/95/
> summer/09maggie.html)

13. Harmon's analysis of her students' "textual strategies [as] postcolonial
writers" parallels, quite provocatively, the critical-autobiographical—and collaborative—work of Chandre Talpade Mohanty and Biddy Martin in "What's Home
Got to Do With It?" (Mohanty & Martin 2003).

14. Kristin Harmon is an Associate Professor in the English Department at
Gallaudet University. She specializes in ethnography and folklore studies, as well
as creative writing, literary theory, Deaf Studies, and ASL poetry. She worked, as
a researcher, on the Smithsonian's "History Through Deaf Eyes" exhibition. She
has published essays in two book collections, *Signing the Body Poetic: Essays on
American Sign Language Literature*, ed. H.-D. Bauman, J. Nelson, and H. Rose
(2006) and *Women and Deafness: Double Visions*, ed. B. J. Brueggemann and S.
Burch (2006),and in several literary and academic journals, such as *Midlands,
Southern Folklore*, and *Disability Studies Quarterly*.

15. Tonya Stremlau is Professor of English at Gallaudet University. She is active in the Deaf Academics network and the editor of *The Deaf Way II Anthology*,
featuring literature by deaf and hard-of-hearing writers from around the world.
Information on the anthology can be found at http://gupress.gallaudet.edu/book-
page/DW2Abookpage.html.

16. Gina Oliva is a Professor of Physical Education and Recreation at Gallaudet University. Her book *Alone in the Mainstream: A Deaf Woman Remembers
Public School* has been widely cited and reviewed to date. (See, for example,
http://deafness.about.com/od/historicprogress/fr/alonemainstream.htm; http://
gupress.gallaudet.edu/reviews/AITMrevw2.html.)

17. All three authors in the *Deaf Women's Lives* volume gave presentations and
readings from their memoirs at this Gallaudet University Press Institute event,
"Narrating Deaf Lives: Biography, Autobiography, and Documentary," November
3–5, 2004. The other two authors who appear in the *Deaf Women's Lives* volume

with Bainy Cyrus are not excerpted here: Eileen Katz's as-told-to narrative (with Celeste Cheyney), *Making Sense of It All*, and part of Frances M. Parsons's travel narratives, *I Dared*.

18. Further information about the *Deaf Women's Lives* books is available at http://gupress.gallaudet.edu/bookpage/DWLbookpage.html.

19. R. H. (Bob) Miller is a Professor Emeritus at the University of Louisville, where he served for more than a decade as Chair of the Department of English. His memoir, *Deaf Hearing Boy: A Memoir*, has been widely reviewed, and Professor Miller has given many successful readings from it. See http://gupress.gallaudet.edu/reviews/DHBrevw3.html.

20. Madan Vasishta's story, *Deaf in Delhi: A Memoir*, is featured at http://gupress.gallaudet.edu/bookpage/DIDbookpage.html. He retired from the New Mexico School for the Deaf as Superintendent after twenty-five years as an administrator and teacher there. He chaired the Conference of Educational Administrators of Schools & Programs for the Deaf (CEASD) residential-living committee and has made presentations on a variety of issues internationally. He was also been involved in the Center for Abuse Prevention and Education-Deaf/Hard of Hearing at the University of North Carolina-Greensboro.

21. Emmanuelle Laborit's filmography is available through http://www.imdb.com/name/nm0479608/. Reviews, a sample chapter, and further information about her book, *Cry of the Gull*, can be accessed at http://gupress.gallaudet.edu/0726.html. Further biographical information is at http://perso.wanadoo.fr/mondalire/laborit.htm.

22. The Australian Paul Jacobs, author of a recent book published in the series *Neither-Nor: A Young Australian's Experience with Deafness*, did not attend the "Narrating Deaf Lives" conference in November 2004. In fact, his book, published in 2007, was just being reviewed as a new manuscript at the time of the conference. His anxious "between" experience in both (and yet neither) the deaf and the hearing worlds would, however, have added considerably to the program. (See http://gupress.gallaudet.edu/bookpage/NNbookpage.html.)

CHAPTER 5

1. This essay is based on a lecture given at the Columbus, Ohio, Museum of Art on February 17, 2005. The lecture was in conjunction with an exhibition of the Allen Sisters' photography at the Columbus Art Museum, and it was sponsored in part by the Ohio Humanities Council and the Collaborative Public Humanities Institute at The Ohio State University, directed by Dr. Christian Zacher. Dr. Zacher, Kristina Torres, and Bobbi Bedinghaus were integral in making the lecture successful (and accessible to deaf and hearing audiences alike); I wish to acknowledge, and thank them for, their collaboration and support. In addition, three colleagues were particularly important in helping me sketch more carefully

some of the historical context for the Allen Sisters and their photography—Susan Burch, Susan S. Williams, and Suzanne Flynt.

2. Much of my autobiographical information about the Allen Sisters comes from a thorough and remarkable book about them and their photography: Suzanne L. Flynt, *The Allen Sisters: Pictorial Photographers 1885–1920*, Deerfield, MA: Pocumtuck Valley Memorial Association (with the University Press of New England), 2002.

3. With Jane Addams, Ellen Gates Starr in 1889 founded the Hull House settlement in Chicago, where she also lived for nearly thirty years. She is known for her significant social reform efforts aimed at improving child labor laws and the working wages and conditions for immigrant factory workers, as well as her strong support of, and belief in, the value of arts and crafts for communities and individuals alike.

4. Throughout their photographic careers, the sisters often took portrait images of each other.

5. The sisters' biographer, Suzanne Flynt, notes that the Allen Sisters' neighbors were said to have had to direct "lost" visitors and portrait-seekers to the home of Mary and Frances Allen. On this matter, I speculate that it is quite possible that the visitors may well have first shown up at the correct address. But, given the fact that the sisters were, of course, deaf and may well have been in the darkroom, elsewhere in the house, or busy with a sitting, it is quite possible they did not hear the first knocks of their visitors. And, when they did not answer the initial knocking, their visitors likely wandered off to another nearby house—a house where someone actually did answer the door—and inquired about the correct address of the sisters.

6. The concept of their photography as "sketching" follows a tradition within the history of photography, beginning with William Henry Fox Talbot's work, "The Pencil of Nature." I wish to thank my colleague, Susan Williams, for sketching out this tradition for me. In her study of mid- to late-19th-century female authorship, Williams discusses the association that women often made between their writing talent and their ability to observe, capture detail, and create realistic "sketches."

7. For further reading in this era and the impact of oralism and A. G. Bell on the deaf community, see Baynton; Van Cleve and Crouch; Van Cleve, Ed.; Winefield.

CHAPTER 6

1. I owe the idea for the form of this essay to my good friend and colleague Georgina Kleege and to another academic-artist acquaintance, Joseph Grigely. Kleege's bold epistolary (auto)biography, *Blind Rage: Letters to Helen Keller*, inspired my attempt to write, as well, to Mabel Hubbard Bell (whom Helen

Keller knew, of course). My additional use of images with the letters (which then become postcards of a fashion) borrows as well from Joseph Grigely's essay "Postcards to Sophie Calle," a piece written "in the spring of 1991, as a response to Sophie Calle's exhibition, *Les Aveugles*, at Luhring Augustine Gallery in New York." Calle's exhibit is a collection of photographic images she made in response to meeting "people who were born blind. Who had never seen. I asked them what their image of beauty was" (Grigely 31). Grigely is an artist whose "White Noise" and "Conversations With the Hearing" collections have appeared in such places as the Musée d'Art Moderne de la Ville de Paris, the MIT List Center for the Visual Arts, the Center for Contemporary Art in Kitakyushu, Japan, and the Whitney Museum's Contemporary Series for emerging and midcareer artists; he is "deaf since the age of ten" and, according to an ArtForum interview with him,

> has long relied on writing as a surrogate for speech, inviting his inter-locutors to jot down their questions on cocktail napkins, hotel stationery, gallery announcements—whatever they find at hand. In 1994, Grigely be-gan employing these once discarded notes to create a series of witty, wry installations and mixed-media assemblages that explore the potential—as well as the limits—of human communication (http://artforum.com/index.php?pn=interview&id=1532)

In "borrowing" a form from Kleege and Grigely, I also then attempt to enter into a conversation with them, as well as with their own subjects, Helen Keller and Sophie Calle. In this conversation I, like Kleege and Grigely, also take up the representation of disability and disabled people in modern art and culture and the power of writing as not just an alternative for, but as another way of, "speaking."

I also owe a considerable debt to another close colleague and friend, Susan Burch, for her physical and spiritual support in doing some of the original research on Mabel and for her consistent, nurturing enthusiasm for my work. Susan's shadow is everywhere present in this essay, as well.

Finally, I have worked to describe what is on the front of the postcards in the letter on their imagined backside. I have done so largely so that the essay will be accessible to any readers who are blind or vision impaired.

CHAPTER 7

1. The description of the "Disability Studies and the Legacies of Eugenics" institute from its Web site is as follows:

> The topic of the 2004 seminar, "Disability Studies and the Legacies of Eugenics," sought to understand the contemporary situation of disabled people in Germany today through an assessment of the historical facts

surrounding the killing of more than 240,000 disabled people during World War II. To assess this legacy, the seminar contemplated the development of German Disability Studies and its critique of practices in modern day disability arenas such as education, medicine, rehabilitation, genetics, and bio-ethics. The program included visits to contemporary memorial sites, archives, and former T-4 locations. In addition to seminar sessions, public lectures by contemporary scholars in German disability studies were offered as featured events, and open to the public, as a part of the Einstein Forum lecture series. (http://www.uic.edu/depts/idhd/DSGermany/home/home.htm)

2. Key sources to read (alphabetically) for more information about the T-4 program are: Horst Biesold, *Crying Hands: Eugenics and Deaf People in Nazi Germany*; Michael Burleigh and Wolfgang Wipperman, *The Racial State: Germany, 1933–1945*; Suzanne E. Evans, *Forgotten Crimes: The Holocaust and People with Disabilities*; Henry Friedlander, "Holocaust Studies and the Deaf Community," in Ryan & Schuchman; Henry Friedlander, *The Origins of Nazi Genocide: From Euthanasia to the Final Solution*; Hugh G. Gallagher, *By Trust Betrayed: Patients, Physicians, and the License to Kill in the Third Reich*; Patricia Heberer, "Targeting the 'Unfit' in Radical Public Health Strategies in Nazi Germany," in Ryan & Schuchman; Robert J. Lifton, *The Nazi Doctors: Medical Killing and the Psychology of Genocide*; Benno Müller-Hill, *Murderous Science: Elimination by Scientific Selection of Jews, Gypsies and Others; Germany 1933–1945*; Robert N. Proctor, "Eugenics in Hitler's Germany," in Ryan & Schuchman; Robert Proctor, *Racial Hygiene: Medicine under the Nazis*; Artzekammer Berlin exhibit, *The Value of the Human Being: Medicine in Germany, 1918–1945*; Donna F. Ryan and John S. Schuchman, eds., *Deaf People in Hitler's Europe*; "T-4: Was Life Unworthy of Living?" The Shoah Education Project, http://www.shoaheducation.com/t4.html; U.S. Holocaust Memorial Museum, "Victims of the Nazi Era, 1939–1945," http://www.fcit.usf.edu/holocaust/people/USHMMHAN.HTM; Paul Weindling, *Health, Race and German Politics between National Unification and Nazism 1870–1945*.

3. The 1933 "Law for the Prevention of Genetically Diseased Offspring" (Gr. *Gesetz zur Verhütung erbkranken Nachwuchses*) or "Sterilization Law" was enacted on July 14, 1933; it allowed the compulsory sterilization of any citizen who in the opinion of a "Genetic Health Court" (Gr. *Erbgesundheitsgericht*) suffered from a list of alleged genetic disorders: "(1) Any person suffering from a hereditary disease may be rendered incapable of procreation by means of a surgical operation (sterilization), if the experience of medical science shows that it is highly probably that his descendants would suffer from some serious physical or mental hereditary defect. (2) For the purposes of this law, any person will be considered as hereditarily diseased who is suffering from any one of the following diseases:– (1) Congenital Mental Deficiency, (2) Schizophrenia, (3) Manic-Depressive

Insanity, (4) Hereditary Epilepsy, (5) Hereditary Chorea (Huntington's), (6) Hereditary Blindness, (7) Hereditary Deafness, (8) Any severe hereditary deformity. (9) Any person suffering from severe alcoholism may be also rendered incapable of procreation." The law applied to anyone in the general population, which made its scope significantly larger than the compulsory sterilization laws in the United States, which generally applied only to people in psychiatric hospitals or prisons.

4. I describe each image here not only as an analytical move that points out some of the rhetoric at work in the poster but also as a matter of access for blind and vision-impaired readers who could not otherwise "read" the image itself.

5. See, for example, Jewish World's "Society Today" essay by Daniel Eisenberg, M.D., "The Death of Terri Schiavo: An Epilogue" (http://www.aish.com/societyWork/society/The_Death_of_Terri_Schiavo_An_Epilogue.asp); William Federer's essay "The Court Ordered Death of Terri Schiavo" at www.townhall.com and "Restoring Our Heritage," http://www.restoringourheritage.com/federer_schiavoarticle.htm; Diane Alden's "Futile Care: The Terri Schiavo Case" for NewsMax.com (http://www.newsmax.com/archives/articles/2003/10/16/223430.shtml); and dozens of blog posts from late March and early April 2005.

6. Phenytoin was marketed in the 1960s as "Dilantin"; this drug appeared, for example, in the 1962 novel *One Flew Over the Cuckoo's Nest* by Ken Kesey, both as an anticonvulsant and as a mechanism to control inmate behavior. See http:www.mentalhealth.com/drug/p30-dos.html.

Works Cited

BOOKS AND JOURNAL ARTICLES

Aly, Götz, Peter Chroust, & Christian Pross. 1994. *Cleansing the fatherland: Nazi medicine and racial hygiene*. Trans. Belinda Cooper. Baltimore: Johns Hopkins University Press.

Aristotle. 1991. On rhetoric: A theory of civic discourse. Trans. George A. Kennedy. New York: Oxford University Press.

Artzekammer Berlin. 1991. *The Value of the Human Being: Medicine in Germany 1918–1945*. Berlin.

Bahan, Ben. 1992. American sign language literature: Inside the story. In *Deaf studies, what's up?* ed. Jackie Mann, 153–166. Washington, DC: College for Continuing Education, Gallaudet University.

———. 2006. Face-to-face tradition in the American deaf community: Dynamics of the teller, the tale, and the audience. In *Signing the body poetic: Essays on American sign language literature*, ed. H.-Dirksen Bauman, Jennifer L. Nelson, & Heidi M. Rose, 21–50. Berkeley: University of California Press.

Baldwin, James. 1985. *The price of the ticket: Collected nonfiction, 1948–1985*. New York: St. Martin's Press.

Baldwin, Stephen C. 1993. *Pictures in the air: The story of the national theatre of the deaf*. Washington, DC: Gallaudet University Press.

Bangs, Donald R. 1989. Deaf theatre in America: Practices and principles. Ph.D. diss., University of California, Berkeley.

Barthes, Roland. 2001. The death of the author (1968). In *Modern literary theory: A reader*, ed. Philip Rice & Patricia Waugh, 185–188. New York: Oxford University Press.

Batson, Trenton. 1987. Poetry in American sign language. In *Encyclopedia of deafness and deaf people*, ed. John Van Cleve, 222–224. New York: McGraw-Hill.

Batson, Trent, & Eugene Bergman, eds. 1973/1997. *Angels and outcasts: An anthology of deaf characters in literature*. Washington, DC: Gallaudet University Press.

Bauman, H.-Dirksen. 1997. Towards a poetics of vision, space, and the body. In *The disability studies reader*, ed. Lennard J. Davis, 315–131. Oxford: Routledge.

———. 2003. Redesigning literature: The cinematic poetics of American sign language poetry. *Sign Language Studies*, 4.1: 34–47.

———. 2006. Getting out of line: Toward a visual and cinematic poetics of ASL. In *Signing the body poetic: Essays on American sign language literature,* ed. H.-Dirksen Bauman, Jennifer L. Nelson, & Heidi M. Rose, 95–117. Berkeley: University of California Press.

Bauman, H.-Dirksen, Jennifer L. Nelson, & Heidi M. Rose, eds. 2006. *Signing the body poetic: Essays on American sign language literature.* Berkeley: University California Press.

Bauman, Zygmunt. 1989. *Modernity and the Holocaust.* Ithaca: Cornell University Press.

Baur, Erwin, Eugen Fischer, & Fritz Lenz. 1931. *Human heredity.* Trans. Eden Paul & Cedar Paul. New York: Macmillan.

Baynton, Douglas C. 1996. *Forbidden signs: American culture and the campaign against sign language.* Chicago: University of Chicago Press.

Bechter, Frank. 2008. The deaf convert culture, and its lessons for deaf theory. In *Open your eyes: Deaf Studies talking,* ed. H.-Dirksen L. Bauman, 60–82. Minneapolis: University of Minnesota Press.

Biesold, Horst. 2002. *Crying hands: Eugenics and deaf people in Nazi Germany.* Trans. William Sayers. Washington, DC: Gallaudet University Press.

Bishundayal, Ann J. 1995. *Mabel Hubbard Bell: A biography.* Atlanta: Protea.

Bonner, Stanley F. 1977. *Education in ancient Rome: From the elder Cato to the younger Pliny.* London: Methuen.

Bragg, Lois. 1991. ASL literature's cultural milieu: Audience expectations and participation. Paper presented at the ASL Literature Conference, National Technical Institute for the Deaf, October.

Breivik, Jan-Kåre. 2005. *Deaf identities in the making: Local lives, transnational connections.* Washington, DC: Gallaudet University Press.

Bruce, Robert. 1973. *Bell: Alexander Graham Bell and the conquest of solitude.* Boston: Little, Brown.

Brueggemann, Brenda Jo. 1999. *Lend me your ear: Rhetorical constructions of deafness.* Washington, DC: Gallaudet University Press.

———. 2004. *Literacy and deaf people: Cultural and contextual perspectives.* Washington, DC: Gallaudet University Press.

———. 2005. Delivering disability, willing speech. In *Bodies in commotion: disability & performance,* ed. Carrie Sandahl & Philip Auslander, 17–29. Ann Arbor: University of Michigan Press.

Brueggemann, Brenda Jo, & Susan Burch, eds. 2006. *Women and deafness: Double visions.* Washington, DC: Gallaudet University Press.

Buchanan, Robert. 2001. *Illusions of equality: Deaf Americans in school and factory, 1850–1950.* Washington, DC: Gallaudet University Press.

Bulwer, John. 1975. *Chirologia; or, The natural language of the hand.* New York: AMS Press.

Burch, Susan. 1997. Deaf poets' society: Subverting the hearing paradigm. *Literature and Medicine,* 16.1: 121–134.

———. 2002. *Signs of resistance: American deaf cultural history, 1900 to World War II.* New York: New York University Press.

Burch, Susan, & Hannah Joyner. 2008. *Unspeakable: The story of Junius Wilson.* Chapel Hill: University of North Carolina Press.

Burleigh, Michael. 2000. *The Third Reich: A new history.* New York: Hill & Wang.

Burleigh, Michael, & Wolfgang Wipperman. 1991. *The racial state: Germany, 1933–1945.* New York: Cambridge University Press.

Burton, Gideon. *Silva rhetoricae* (The Forest of Rhetoric). http://rhetoric.byu.edu/.

Chorost, Michael. 2005. *Rebuilt: How becoming part computer made me more human.* Boston: Houghton Mifflin.

Cixous, Hélène. 1990. The laugh of the Medusa. Trans. Keith Cohen & Paula Cohen. In *The rhetorical tradition: Readings from classical times to the present,* ed. Patricia Bizzell & Bruce Herzberg, 1232–1245. Boston: Bedford St. Martin's Press.

Colker, Ruth. 2005. *The disability pendulum: The first decade of the Americans With Disabilities Act.* New York: New York University Press.

Cooper, Sheryl B. 1997. Academic status of sign language programs in institutions of higher education in the United States. Ph.D. diss., Towson University.

Corbett, Edward P. J. 1969. The rhetoric of the open hand and the rhetoric of the closed fist. *College Composition and Communication,* 20.5: 288–296.

Curtis, Verna Posever. 2001. Frances Benjamin Johnston in 1900: Staking the sisterhood's claim in American photography. In *Ambassadors of progress: American women photographers in Paris, 1900–1901,* ed. Bronwyn A. E. Griffith, 24–37. Giverny, France: Musée d'Art Américain.

Cyrus, Bainy. 2007. All eyes. *Sign Language Studies,* 7.2: 220–224.

Cyrus, Bainy, Eileen Katz, Celeste Cheyney, & Frances M. Parsons. 2005. *Deaf women's lives: Three self-portraits.* Washington, DC: Gallaudet University Press.

Davidson, Michael. 1997. *Ghostlier demarcations: Modern poetry and the material word.* Berkeley: University of California Press.

———. 2002. Hearing things: The scandal of speech in deaf performance. In *Disability studies: Enabling the humanities,* ed. Sharon L. Snyder, Brenda Jo Brueggemann, & Rosemarie Garland-Thomson, 67–87. New York: Modern Language Association Press.

Davis, Lennard. 1995. Deafness as insight: The deafened moment as critical modality. College English, 57:8: 881.

———. 2007. Deafness and the riddle of identity. *Chronicle of Higher Education,* 12 (January): B6.

Deaf man, 96, freed after 68 years in the hospital. 1994. *New York Times,* February 6, 1:27.

Dembo, L. S. 1969. Interview with George Oppen. *Contemporary Literature,* 10.2: 159–177.

Derrida, Jacques. 1982. Signature, event, context. In *Margins of philosophy*. Trans. Alan Bass, 307–330. Chicago: University of Chicago Press.

Ede, Lisa, & Andrea Lunsford. 1984. Audience addressed/audience invoked: The role of audience in composition theory and pedagogy *College Composition and Communication*, 35.2: 155–171.

Edwards, Viv, & Thomas J. Sienkewicz. 1991. *Oral cultures past and present: Rappin' and Homer*. Cambridge, MA: Blackwell.

Eliot, George. 1984. *Daniel Deronda*. Ed. Graham Handley. New York: Oxford University Press.

Evans, Suzanne E. 2004. *Forgotten crimes: The Holocaust and people with disabilities*. Chicago: Ivan R. Dee.

Flynt, Suzanne L. 2002. *The Allen sisters: Pictorial photographers, 1885–1920*. Foreword by Naomi Rosenblum. Deerfield, MA: Pocumtuck Valley Memorial Association & University Press of New England.

Freud, Sigmund. 1926. Inhibitions, symptoms and anxiety. In *The standard edition of the complete psychological works of Sigmund Freud*, ed. James Strachey, 20. London: Hogarth Press.

Friedlander, Henry. 1995. *The origins of Nazi genocide: From euthanasia to the final solution*. Chapel Hill: University of North Carolina Press.

———. 2002. *Holocaust studies and the deaf community. In Deaf people in Hitler's Europe*, ed. Donna F. Ryan & John S. Schuchman, 15–31. Washington, DC: Gallaudet University Press.

Frishberg, Nancy. 1998. Signers of tales: The case for literature status of an unwritten language. *Sign Language Studies*, 159: 149–170.

Gallagher, Hugh. 1990. *By trust betrayed: Patients, physicians and the license to kill in the Third Reich*. New York: Henry Holt.

Glass, Bentley. 1981. A hidden chapter of German eugenics between the two world wars. *Proceedings of the American Philosophical Society*, 125.5: 357–367.

Grier, Katherine C. 1997. *Culture and comfort: Parlor making and middle-class identity, 1850–1930*. Washington, DC: Smithsonian Institution Press.

Grigely, Joseph. 2000. Postcards to Sophie Calle. In *Points of contact: Disability, art, and culture*, ed. Susan Crutchfield & Marcy Epstein, 31–58. Ann Arbor: University of Michigan Press.

Grunberger, Richard. 1971. *A social history of the Third Reich*. London: Penguin.

Gullestad, Marianne. 1996. *Everyday life philosophers: Modernity, morality, and autobiography in Norway*. Oslo, Norway: Scandinavian University Press.

Haraway, Donna. 1991. *Simians, cyborgs and women: The reinvention of nature*. New York: Routledge.

Harmon, Kristen C. 2006. 'If there are Greek epics, there should be deaf epics': How protest became poetry. In *Signing the body poetic: Essays on American sign language literature*, ed. H.-Dirksen Bauman, Jennifer L. Nelson, & Heidi M. Rose, 169–194. Berkeley: University of California Press.

———. 2006. Slain in the spirit. In *Women and deafness: Double visions*, ed. Brenda Brueggemann & Susan Burch, 205–225. Washington, DC: Gallaudet University Press.

———. 2007. Writing deaf: Textualizing deaf literature. *Sign Language Studies*, 7.2: 200–207.

Hartig, Rachel. 1991. *Struggling under the destructive glance: Androgyny in the novels of Guy de Maupassant*. New York: Peter Lang.

———. 2007. Crossing the divide: Helen Keller and Yvonne Pitrois dialogue on diversity. *Sign Language Studies*, 7.2: 177–185.

———. 2007. *Crossing the divide: Representations of deafness in biography*. Washington, DC: Gallaudet University Press.

Heberer, Patricia. 2002. Targeting the "unfit" and radical public health strategies in Nazi Germany. In *Deaf people in Hitler's Europe, 1933–1945*, ed. Donna F. Ryan & John S. Schuchnan, 49–72. Washington,DC: Gallaudet University Press.

Heuer, Christopher Jon. 2003. On the bottom. *The Tactile Mind Quarterly*, 7: 32–49.

———. 2005. *All your parts intact: Poems*. Minneapolis: Tactile Mind Press.

———. 2007. *BUG: Deaf identity and internal revolution*. Washington, DC: Gallaudet University Press.

———. 2007. Deafness as conflict and conflict component. *Sign Language Studies*, 7.2: 195–199.

Hott, Lawrence. 2007. Creating the *History Through Deaf Eyes* documentary. *Sign Language Studies*, 7.2: 135–140.

Jacobs, Paul. 2007. *Neither-nor: A young Australian's experience with deafness*. Washington, DC: Gallaudet University Press.

Jepson, Jill, ed. 1992. *No walls of stone: An anthology of literature by deaf and hard of hearing writers*. Washington, DC: Gallaudet University Press.

Kelleher, Jane. 1986. Literature of deaf Iowans: Linguistic form and social function. Ph.D. diss., University of Iowa.

Kisor, Henry. 1990. *What's that pig outdoors? A memoir of deafness*. New York: Hill & Wang.

Kleege, Georgina. 189. *Home for the summer*. Sausalito: Post-Apollo Press.

———. 1999. *Sight unseen*. New Haven: Yale University Press.

———. 2006. *Blind rage: Letters to Helen Keller*. Washington, DC: Gallaudet University Press.

———. 2007. Blind rage: An open letter to Helen Keller. *Sign Language Studies*, 7.2: 186–194.

Klima, Edward, & Ursula Bellugi. 1975. Wit and poetry in American sign language. *Sign Language Studies*, 8: 203–224.

Krentz, Christopher. 2006. The camera as printing press: How film has influenced ASL literature. In *Signing the body poetic: Essays on American sign language literature*, ed. H.-Dirksen Bauman, Jennifer L. Nelson, & Heidi M. Rose, 51–70. Berkeley: University of California Press.

———. 2007. *Writing deafness: The hearing line in nineteenth-century American literature.* Chapel Hill: University of North Carolina Press.

Krentz, Christopher, ed. 2000. *A mighty change: An anthology of deaf American writing, 1816–1864.* Washington, DC: Gallaudet University Press.

Laborit, Emmanuelle. 1998. *Cry of the gull.* Trans. Constantina Mitchell & Paul Raymond Côté. Washington, DC: Gallaudet University Press.

———. 2007. Writing my life. *Sign Language Studies*, 7.2: 242–252.

Lane, Harlan. 2007. Nancy Rowe and George Curtis: Deaf lives in Maine 150 years ago. *Sign Language Studies*, 7.2: 152–166.

Lang, Harry G. 1994. *Silence of the spheres: The deaf experience in the history of science.* Westport, CT: Bergin & Garvey Press.

Lang, Harry G., & Bonnie Meath-Lang. 1995. *Deaf persons in the arts and sciences: A biographical dictionary.* Westport, CT: Bergin & Garvey Press.

———. 2000. *A phone of our own: The deaf insurrection against Ma Bell.* Washington, DC: Gallaudet University Press.

———. 2004. *Edmund Booth, deaf pioneer.* Washington, DC: Gallaudet University Press.

———. 2007. Reflections on biographical research and writing. *Sign Language Studies*, 7.2: 141–151.

———. 2007. *Teaching from the heart and soul: The Robert F. Panara story.* Washington, DC: Gallaudet University Press.

Lentz, Ella Mae. 1987. Sign poetry and storytelling. In *Encyclopedia of deafness and deaf people*, 124–126. New York: McGraw-Hill.

Lifton, Robert Jay. 1986/2000. *The Nazi doctors: Medical killing and the psychology of genocide.* New York: Basic Books.

Maxwell, Madeline M. 1990. Visual-centered narratives of the Deaf. *Linguistics and education* 2.3: 213–229.

McKee, Rachel L. 2001. *People of the eye: Stories from the deaf world.* Wellington, New Zealand: Bridget Williams Books.

Miller, R. H. 2004. *Deaf hearing boy: A memoir.* Washington, DC: Gallaudet University Press.

———. 2007. *Deaf Hearing Boy*: An overview. *Sign Language Studies*, 7.2: 225–232.

Mohanty, Chandra Talpade, & Biddy Martin. 2003. What's home got to do with it? In *Feminism without borders: Decolonizing theory, practicing solidarity*, ed. Chandra Talpade Mohanty, 85–105. Durham: Duke University Press.

Monaghan, Leila, Constanze Schmaling, Karen Nakamura, & Graham H. Turner, eds. 2003. *Many ways to be deaf: International variation in deaf communities.* Washington DC: Gallaudet University Press.

Mow, Shanny. 1987. Theater, Community. In *Encyclopedia of deafness and deaf people*, ed. John Van Cleve, 288–289. New York: McGraw-Hill.

Müller-Hill, Benno. 1998. *Murderous science: Elimination by scientific selection of Jews, gypsies, and others, Germany 193–1945.* Trans. George R. Fraser. Oxford. Oxford University Press.

Nelson, Jennifer L. 2002. Bulwer's speaking hands: Deafness and rhetoric. In *Disability studies: Enabling the humanities,* ed. Sharon L. Snyder, Brenda Jo Brueggemann, & Rosemarie Garland-Thomson, 211–221. New York: Modern Language Association Press.

Newkirk, Thomas. 1997. *The performance of self in student writing.* Portsmouth, NH: Boynton/Cook.

Nielsen, Kim E. 2004. *The radical lives of Helen Keller.* New York: New York University Press.

———. 2005. *Helen Keller: Selected writings.* New York: New York University Press.

Noakes, J., & G. Pridham, eds. 1988. *Nazism 1919–1945: A history in documents and eyewitness accounts.* Vol. II: *Foreign policy, war and racial extermination.* New York: Schocken Books.

Novak, Peter. 2003. Shakespeare in the fourth dimension: *Twelfth Night* and American sign language. In *Remaking Shakespeare: Performance Across media, genres and cultures,* ed. Pascale Aebischer, Edward J. Esche, & Nigel Wheale, 18–38. New York: Palgrave Macmillan.

Oliva, Gina. 2004. *Alone in the mainstream: A deaf woman remembers public school.* Washington, DC: Gallaudet University Press.

———. 2007. A selection from *Alone in the Mainstream: A Deaf Woman Remembers Public School. Sign Language Studies,* 7.2: 212–219.

Ong, Walter J. 1982. *Orality and literacy: The technologizing of the word.* New York: Methuen.

Padden, Carol, & Tom Humphries. 1988. *Deaf in America: Voices from a culture.* Cambridge, MA: Harvard University Press.

———. 2005. *Inside deaf culture.* Cambridge, MA: Harvard University Press.

Peters, Cynthia. 2000. *Deaf American literature: From carnival to the canon.* Washington, DC: Gallaudet University Press.

———. 2001. ASL literature: Some traditional and non-traditional characteristics. In *Deaf world: A historical reader and primary sourcebook,* ed. Lois Bragg. New York: New York University Press.

Pitrois, Yvonne. 1922. *Une nuit rayonnante: Helen Keller.* Neuchâtel: A. Delapraz.

Plann, Susan. 1997. *A silent minority: Deaf education in Spain, 1550–1835.* Los Angeles: University of California Press.

———. 2007. Deaf lives: Nineteenth-century Spanish deaf girls and women. *Sign Language Studies,* 7.2: 167–176.

———. 2007. *The Spanish National Deaf School: Portraits from the nineteenth century.* Washington, DC: Gallaudet University Press.

Proctor, Robert N. 1988. *Racial hygiene: Medicine Under the Nazis.* Cambridge, MA: Harvard University Press.

———. 2002. "Eugenics in Hitler's Germany." In *Deaf people in Hitler's Europe,* ed. Donna F. Ryan & John S. Schuchman, 15–31. Washington, DC: Gallaudet University Press.

Ree, Jonathan. 1999. *I see a voice: Deafness, language, and the senses—a philosophical history.* New York: Metropolitan Books.

Rivers, Mary V., & Dvora Shurman. 2008. *Deaf lives in contrast: Two women's stories.* Washington, DC: Gallaudet University Press.

Rose, Heidi M. 1992. A critical methodology for analyzing American sign language literature. Ph.D diss., University of Arizona.

Rosenblatt, Louise. 1968. A way of happening. *Educational Record.* Washington, DC: American Council on Education.

Rutherford, Susan. 1987. A study of American deaf folklore. Ph.D. diss., University of California, Berkeley.

Ryan, Donna, & John S. Schuchman. 2002. *Deaf people in Hitler's Europe.* Washington DC: Gallaudet University Press.

Ryan, Stephen. 1993. Let's tell an ASL story. In *Deaf studies III: Bridging cultures in the 21st century,* ed. Jackie Mann, 145–150. College for Continuing Education, Gallaudet University.

Sayre, Maggie Lee. 1995. *'Deaf Maggie Lee Sayre': Photographs of a river life.* Ed. Tom Rankin. Jackson: University Press of Mississippi.

Sebastian, Simone. 2007. Campus for deaf, blind opposed; alumni fear social, safety issues if state schools share space. *Columbus Dispatch,* March 19, 01B.

See Hear. 2005. The deaf Holocaust: Deaf people and Nazi Germany. BBC broadcast. March 24.

Shaw, George Bernard. 1903/1981. *Man and Superman: A Comedy and Philosophy.* Baltimore: Penguin.

Siebers, Tobin. 2000. My withered limb. In *Points of contact: Disability, art, and culture,* ed. Susan Crutchfield & Marcy Epstein, 21–30. Ann Arbor: University of Michigan Press.

Smith-Rosenberg, Carroll. 1975. The female world of love and ritual: Relations between women in nineteenth-century America. *Signs,* 1.1: 1–29.

Stokoe, William C, Jr., Dorothy C. Casterline, & Carl G. Croneberg. 1965. *A dictionary of American sign language on linguistic principles.* Washington, DC: Gallaudet College Press.

Stremlau, Tonya M., Ed. 2002. The deaf way II anthology: A literary collection by deaf and hard of hearing writers. Washington, DC: Gallaudet University Press.

———. 2007. Narrating deaf lives: "Is it true?" Fiction and autobiography. *Sign Language Studies,* 7.2: 208–211.

Supalla, Ted. 1982. Structure and acquisition of verbs of motion and location in American sign language. Ph.D. diss., University of California, San Diego.

Swiller, Josh. 2007. *The unheard: A memoir of deafness and Africa.* New York: Henry Holt.

Talbot, William Henry Fox. 1969; rprt., 1844–1846 ed. *The pencil of nature*. New York. De Capo Press.

Thompson, Elizabeth. 2008. *Day by day: The chronicles of a hard of hearing reporter*. Washington, DC: Gallaudet University Press.

Valli, Clayton. 1993. Poetics of American sign language poetry. Ph.D. diss., Union Institute.

Van Cleve, John Vickrey, ed. 1993. *Deaf history unveiled: Interpretations from the new scholarship*. Washington DC: Gallaudet University Press.

Van Cleve, John Vickrey, & Barry Crouch. 1989. *A place of their own: Creating the deaf community in America*. Washington, DC: Gallaudet University Press.

Vasishta, Madan. 2006. *Deaf in Delhi: A memoir*. Washington, DC: Gallaudet University Press.

———. 2007. Selections from *Deaf in Delhi: A Memoir*. *Sign Language Studies*, 7.2: 233–241.

Weindling, Paul. 1989. *Health, race and German politics between national unification and Nazism, 1870–1945*. Cambridge: Cambridge University Press.

Welles, Elizabeth B. 2004. "Foreign language enrollments in United States institutions of higher education, Fall 2002." *ADFL Bulletin*, 35.2–3 (Winter–Spring): 7–26. http://www.adfl.org/resources/enrollments.pdf

Weyrather, Irmgard. 1993. *Mutterkreuz und muttertag. Der kult um die "deutsche mutter" im nationalsozialismus*. Frankfurt/Main: Fischer Taschenbuch Verlag.

Williams, Susan S. 2006. *Reclaiming authorship: Literary women in America, 1850–1900*. Philadelphia: University of Pennsylvania Press.

Winefield, Richard. 1987. *Never the twain shall meet: Bell, Gallaudet, and the communications debate*. Washington, DC: Gallaudet University Press.

Winzer, Margret. 1993. *The History of Special Education: From Isolation to Integration*. Washington, DC: Gallaudet University Press.

Wittgenstein, Ludwig. 2001. *Tractatus logico-philosophicus*. Trans. D. F. Pears & B. F. McGuinness. New York: Routledge.

Woodward, James. 1982. *How you gonna get to Heaven if you can't talk with Jesus: On depathologizing deafness*. Silver Spring, MD: T. J. Publishers.

Woolf, Virginia. 1986. Hours in a library. In *Granite and rainbow: Essays, by Virginia Woolf*. New York: Harcourt, Brace, Jovanovitch.

Wright, David. 1969. *Deafness: An autobiography*. New York: Stein & Day.

WEB SITES AND ELECTRONIC RESOURCES

American Sign Language Poetry. 2004. Slope. http://slope.org/asl/.

American Sign Language Teachers Association (ASLTA). http://www.aslta.org/index.html.

Cook, Ian. 2005. The Holocaust and disabled people: FAQ—frequently asked questions. Ouch! March 24. http://www.bbc.co.uk/ouch/closeup/holocaust/faq.shtml.

Cook, Peter. Professional Web site (including Flying Words Project). http://web. mac.com/peterscook1/iWeb/Site/Welcome.html.

Deerfield, Massachusetts, Memorial Hall Museum Web site. http://www.americancenturies.mass.edu/home.html.

Eugenics Archive. "Image Archive on the American Eugenics Movement." Cold Spring Harbor Laboratory. http://www. eugenicsarchive.org.

Gallaudet University Press institute hosts landmark conference. 2006. Inside Gallaudet, March 17. http://news.gallaudet.edu/?id=8345.

Genocide under the Nazis. 2005. BBC History. March 24. http://bbc.co.uk/history/war/genocide/.

Hearing Undergraduate Student. Gallaudet University Admissions. http://admissions.gallaudet.edu/admprocedures/HUG.htm

Image archive on the American eugenics movement. Dolan DNA Learning Center, Cold Spring Harbor Laboratory, New York. http://www.eugenicsarchive.org/

Kuusisto, Stephen. 2007. In our own backyard, no less. *Planet of the Blind* blog. March 20. http://kuusisto.typepad.com/planet_of_the_blind/2007/03/in_our_own_back.html

Nazi persecution of the mentally and physically disabled. The Jewish Virtual Library. http://www.jewishvirtuallibrary.org/jsource/Holocaust/disabled.html.

Novak, Peter. 2000. Shakespeare's *Twelfth Night*: An American sign language translation. Yale University. http://www.yale.edu/asl12night/index.html

———. 2007. The ASL Shakespeare project. http://www.aslshakespeare.com/.

NSF taps Gallaudet for science of learning center. 2007. *Inside Gallaudet,* January 12. http://news.gallaudet.edu/newsreleases/?ID=10049

Ohio State University, American Sign Language Program. http://asl.osu.edu.

Prosjekt Felles Framtid. 2005. Hadamar: Committed to Hadamar Hospital. On-line exhibition. The Center for Holocaust and Genocide Studies. http://www.chgs.umn.edu/Histories__Narratives__Documen/Hadamar/hadamar.html

Sundell, Margaret. Joseph Grigely's art of conversation. *ArtForum online*. http://artforum.com/index.php?pn=interview&id=1532

T-4 program: Was life unworthy of living? The Shoah Education Project. http://www.shoaheducation.com/t4.html.

The T-4 euthanasia program. http://www.mtsu.edu/~baustin/euthan.html.

The tactile mind: Literary quarterly for the signing community. http://www.thetactilemind.com/.

U.S. Holocaust Memorial Museum. Victims of the Nazi era, 1939–1945. http://www.fcit.usf.edu/holocaust/people/USHMMHAN.HTM

VIDEOS AND DVDS

Bahan, Ben, & Sam Supalla. 1992. *Bird of a different feather and for a decent living*. ASL Literature Series. San Diego, CA: Dawn Sign Press. VHS.

Flying Words Project. 2004. *The can't touch tours: Current work, 1990–2003*. Flying Words Project production. VHS.

———. 2004. *The year of walking dogs: Early   poems, 1984–1990*. Flying Words Project production. VHS.

Gallaudet University distance education program. 1997. *Telling tales in ASL: From literature to literacy*. Washington, DC: Gallaudet University. VHS.

Just Mindy and Theron: Music for the eyes. 2004. Just Mindy Productions, DVD.

Lentz, Ella Mae. 1995. *The treasure*. In Motion Press. VHS.

Luczak, Raymond, dir. 2006. *Manny ASL: Stories in American sign language (Manny Hernandez)*. DVD.

MacDougall, Cinnie. 1997. *Number signs for everyone: Numbering in American sign language*. San Diego: Dawn Sign Press. VHS.

Nathie: No hand-me-downs. 2005. Tactile Mind Press. VHS.

Novak, Peter. 2007. William Shakespeare's *Twelfth Night* performed in American sign language and English. Washington DC: Gallaudet University Press. DVD.

The preservation of American sign language: The complete historical collection. 1997. Burtonsville, MD: Sign Media. DVD.

Valli, Clayton. 1995. *ASL poetry: Selected works of Clayton Valli*. Dawn Sign Press. VHS/DVD.

Index

Page numbers in italics refer to illustrations on the page.

About the Author

BRENDA JO BRUEGGEMANN is Professor of English and Disability Studies at The Ohio State University, where she coordinates the Disability Studies program and serves as a Faculty Leader for the American Sign Language Program. She has authored, edited, or co-edited seven books to date, and she initiated the "Deaf Lives" series for Gallaudet University Press. She currently serves as co-editor of *Disability Studies Quarterly*.